Blockchain and IoT Integration

Blockchain and IoT Integration

Approaches and Applications

By Kavita Saini

CRC Press
Taylor & Francis Group
Boca Raton London New York

CRC Press is an imprint of the
Taylor & Francis Group, an **informa** business
AN AUERBACH BOOK

First edition published 2022
by CRC Press
6000 Broken Sound Parkway NW, Suite 300, Boca Raton, FL 33487-2742

and by CRC Press
2 Park Square, Milton Park, Abingdon, Oxon, OX14 4RN

CRC Press is an imprint of Taylor & Francis Group, LLC

ISBN: 978-0-367-55595-5 (hbk)
ISBN: 978-1-032-11486-6 (pbk)
ISBN: 978-1-003-09421-0 (ebk)

DOI: 10.1201/9781003094210

Typeset in Times LT Std
by KnowledgeWorks Global Ltd.

Contents

About the Editor vii
About the Contributors ix
List of Contributors xix

Chapter 1 Expounding the Blockchain Architecture 1

Pethuru Raj Chelliah and Kavita Saini

Chapter 2 Blockchain Technology for IoT-Based Healthcare Applications 27

Nilanjana Pradhan, Shraddha Sagar, Kiran Singh and Kavita Saini

Chapter 3 Blockchain to Secure IoT Data 43

M. Vivek Anand and S. Vijayalakshmi

Chapter 4 PR Wallet-Based Blockchain Access Protocol to Secure EHRs 65

Mehul Gupta

Chapter 5 Blockchain Securing Drug Supply Chain: Combating counterfeits 77

Kavita Saini, Kavita Kumari and Shraddha Sagar

Chapter 6 Blockchain to Secure Data in Internet of Things (IoT) 89

Pramod Mathew Jacob, Prasanna Mani, R.L. Hariharan and Jisha Mariyam John

Chapter 7 Blockchain IoT Concepts for Smart Grids, Smart Cities and Smart Homes 103

Shriyash Mohril, Mahipal Singh Sankhla, Swaroop S. Sonone and Rajeev Kumar

Chapter 8 SabPay: A Biometric-Based Blockchain-Enabled Payment System 123

Shubham Rawal, Yashvardhan Singh and Rakshit Singh

Chapter 9 Blockchain IoT Concepts for Smart Cities 131

Sakshi Jain, Shashank Chauhan and Ishan Adhikari Bairagi

Chapter 10 Role of IoT and Blockchain Technology for Enhanced Applications in Different Domains 145

Ruchi Agarwal and Kalpana Jha

Chapter 11 IoT for Smart Healthcare Monitoring System 163

Supriya Khaitan, Priyanka Shukla, Rashi Agarwal and Supriya Raheja

Index 183

About the Editor

Kavita Saini is presently working as an associate professor, School of Computing Science and Engineering, Galgotias University, Delhi NCR, India. She received her PhD degree from Banasthali Vidyapeeth, Banasthali. She has 17 years of teaching and research experience supervising Masters and PhD scholars in emerging technologies.

She has published more than 35 research papers in national and international journals and conferences. She has also published 116 authored books for UG and PG courses for a number of universities, including MD University, Rohtak, and Punjab Technical University, Jalandhar, with national publishers. Kavita Saini has also edited many books with international publishers, including IGI Global, CRC Press, IET Publisher Elsevier, and published 10 book chapters with international publishers.

Kavita Saini has also filed few patents. She has delivered technical talks on Blockchain: An Emerging Technology, Web to Deep Web and Other Emerging Areas and handled many special sessions in international conferences and special issues in international journals. Her research interests include Web-Based Instructional Systems (WBIS), Blockchain Technology, Industry 4.0 and Cloud and Edge Computing.

About the Contributors

Dr. Rashi Agarwal is professor, Department of Master of Computer Applications, Galgotia College of Engineering and Technology. Dr. Rashi did PhD (Computer Science) from Gautam Buddh Technical University, Lucknow in 2011. Her area of research is Fractal Geometry and its applications in computer science, in which she has been guiding M Tech and PhD students. She has published a number of research papers in international journals and conferences. Her publications focussed on the stability of fractals under different types of perturbations. She has 18 years of experience in teaching graduate and postgraduate students.

Dr. Ruchi Agarwal is a PhD (Technology) from Birla Institute of Technology (BIT), Mesra, Ranchi in the field of data analytics. She has more than 18 years of academic and industrial experience. Currently, she is working with JIMS Engineering Management Technical Campus, Greater Noida as head of the Department of Computer Applications. She has published various papers in international journals and conference proceedings. She is guiding PhD students in the area of Big Data Analytics. Her research interest areas are Big Data Analytics, Machine Learning, Data Mining and Customer Analytics.

M. Vivek Anand is a research scholar in the Department of CSE, Galgotias University, Greater Noida, Uttar Pradesh, India. He received an ME degree in Software Engineering from Anna University, Chennai, Tamil Nadu in 2013, and a BE degree in Computer Science from Anna University, Coimbatore, Tamil Nadu in 2011. He has more than six years of teaching experience. His research interests are the Internet of Things and Blockchain.

Ishan Adhikari Bairagi is from Saharanpur, Uttar Pradesh. He has done his schooling from Delhi Public School Yamuna Nagar and right now, he is pursuing B Tech in Computer Science with a specialization in Data Analytics at Galgotias University, Greater Noida. Data Sciences, Blockchain Technology and Statistics are his fields of interest.

Shashank Chauhan is from Greater Noida. He completed his schooling from Ryan International School, Greater Noida. Now, he is pursuing B Tech in Computer Science with a specialization in Internet of Things at Galgotias University, Greater Noida. He is very comfortable with programming languages including C, C++ and Python, and is now learning some advanced technologies like Machine Learning, Data Analytics, Web Development, Business Intelligence, Cloud Computing and Blockchain. IoT and Blockchain Technology are his main fields of interest.

Pethuru (Peter) Raj Chelliah is chief architect and vice president in the Site Reliability Engineering (SRE) division of Reliance Jio Platforms Ltd. Bangalore, India. He focuses on emerging technologies such as the Internet of Things (IoT), Artificial Intelligence (AI), Big and Fast Data Analytics, Blockchain, Digital Twins, Cloud-native Computing, Edge & Fog Clouds, Reliability Engineering, Microservices Architecture (MSA) and Event-driven Architecture (EDA). He has authored and edited many technology books. He holds a CSIR-sponsored PhD degree from Anna University, India.

Mehul Gupta is a former merit holder student from Vellore Institute of Technology, India. He holds a B Tech degree in Information Technology, and is currently associated as a Software Engineer with VISA Inc., the global payment technology giant. Apart from being skilled in mental arithmetic, his love and dedication in the field of programming are unparalleled. He holds several certifications, including cyber forensics from IITB and database developer from Oracle. He loves exploring new technologies and has dedicated this work to the caregivers, doctors and all the medical staff who have been helping us, especially during the COVID-19 crisis.

Mr. R.L. Hariharan has completed his Bachelor in Computer Science & Engineering from Kerala University and his Master in Networking from VIT. He is presently working as research scholar professor in the Department of Information Technology at National Institute of Technology, Suratkal, Karnataka. He has a teaching experience of more than three years and industrial experience of one year. His areas of interest include Machine Learning, Network Security and Cryptography and Data Science.

Mr. Pramod Mathew Jacob has completed his BTech in Computer Science & Engineering from Kerala University. He possesses MTech in Software Engineering from SRM Institute of Science and Technology, Chennai. Presently, he is working as an assistant professor at Providence College of Engineering, Chengannur, Kerala. He is also pursuing PhD at Vellore Institute of Technology (Deemed to be University), Vellore, India. He has a teaching experience of six years and research experience of three years. He has published ten papers in various international journals and conferences. His areas of interest include Software Engineering, Software Testing and Internet of Things.

Sakshi Jain is native to Delhi. She completed her schooling from Vikas Bharati Public School, Delhi (CBSE Board). Currently, she is pursuing B Tech in Computer Science with a specialization in Artificial Intelligence and Machine Learning at Galgotias University, Greater Noida. She studied Computer Science in her school days and learned many basic languages including C, C++, Java and Python. She is now learning advanced topics such as Android/ iOS Development, Web Development, Artificial Intelligence, Machine Learning, and especially Blockchain.

Ms. Kalpana Jha is an assistant professor, Department of Bachelor of Computer Application, Jims Engineering Management Technical Campus, Greater Noida, Uttar Pradesh, India. She is M Tech in Computer Science and BE in Information Technology from PDM College of Engineering affiliated to MD University, Rohtak. She has more than nine years of teaching experience. She has published several papers in national and international journals and conference proceedings.

Ms. Jisha Mariyam John has completed her Bachelor in Computer Science & Engineering from Cochin University and her Master in Computer Science from MG University, Kerala. She is currently working as assistant professor in the Department of Computer Science at Providence College of Engineering, Kerala. She has over five years of teaching experience. She has published her works in various national and international journals. Her areas of interest include Machine Learning, Discrete Mathematics, Data Science and Image Processing.

Supriya Khaitan is an assistant professor in the School of Computing Science and Engineering at Galgotias University, India. Supriya is B Tech in Computer Science and Engineering and M Tech in Information Technology. Her research interests include Network Security, Data Analysis and Machine Learning. She has more than 16 years of experience in teaching graduate and postgraduate students.

Dr. Rajeev Kumar was born on 1 July 1983 in Agra, UP, India. He has completed his BSc (ZBC) and MSc (Forensic Science) from Agra University, and completed his PhD (Forensic Toxicology) from SHUATS Prayagraj. He has been awarded the Young Academician Award & UGC-Junior Research Fellowship and Senior Research Fellowship and "Excellence in Reviewing" from International Journal for Innovative Research in Science & Technology (IJIRST). He had worked as senior scientific assistant (Chemistry) in Government Forensic Science Laboratory, Delhi for 18 months. Currently, he is working as an associate professor and division chair in the Department of Forensic Science, School of Basic & Applied Sciences, Galgotias University, Greater Noida. He has published more than 73 papers in peer review international Journals and published four book chapters. He is an active editorial board member of 28 international journals, associate editor in four international journals and Reviewer of 20 international journals. He has published many abstracts in international and national conferences, seminars and workshops, and has organized many conferences, seminars and workshops. He has been invited as guest speaker and session chair in many national and international conferences. He has completed 12 certified courses from Elsevier Research Academy. More than 40 students have completed their master's dissertation under his exemplary guidance, and currently, six research scholars are pursuing their PhD under his supervision.

Kavita Kumari has completed M Tech from School of Computing Science & Engineering, Galgotias University, Delhi NCR, India. Her research areas include Blockchain Technology and other emerging areas. She has published various research papers in national and international conferences and journals.

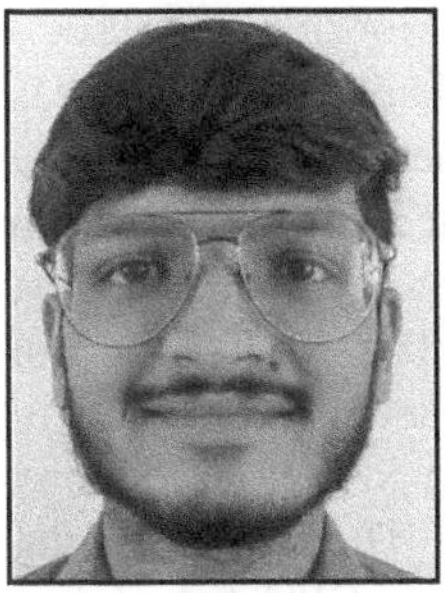

Mr. Shriyash Mohril was born on 12 February 1997 in Bhopal, India. He has completed B Tech in Electronics & Communication. Currently, he is working as process associate at Roboticswares Pvt. Ltd. Noida, UP. He has done trainings in BSNL, Huawei, project-based training program on "Home Automation and solar smart Energy Systems" from Skyfi Labs, and Industrial Training on Cisco Certified Network Associate (CCNA). He has published more than six research and review papers in peer review international journals. He has completed 28 certified online courses from various international universities. He has been participating and presenting his research work in various national and international conferences workshops and seminars.

Dr. Prasanna Mani has completed his MS in Computer Science and Engineering from Anna University. He received his doctorate in Software Engineering from Anna University. Presently, he is working as associate professor in Vellore Institute of Technology (Deemed to be University), Vellore, Tamil Nadu. He possesses a teaching experience of about 20 years from various reputed colleges and universities. He has published nearly 25 papers in various national and international journals. He is guiding research scholars in the area of Software Testing and is an eminent reviewer of various international journals. He has also authored a book for cracking interview questions of C programming. His areas of interest include Software Engineering, Software Testing and Internet of Things.

Nilanjana Pradhan has an extensive experience of 12 years as an assistant professor of Computer Science. She has previously worked in University of Petroleum and Energy Studies and Galgotias University, respectively, as an assistant professor (CSE). Currently, she is working as professor of Machine Learning in Pune Institute of Business Management, a reputed institute under the affiliation of Pune University. She has completed B Tech in Information Technology from University of Calcutta, West Bengal and M Tech in Information Technology from West Bengal University of Technology. Currently, she is pursuing PhD from Galgotias University, Greater Noida in Alzheimer disease prediction modeling using machine learning and deep learning concepts.

Dr. Supriya Raheja is currently working as associate professor in Amity University, Noida, India. She has over 13+ years of teaching experience at undergraduate and postgraduate levels. She completed her M Tech from GJU&ST, Hisar and PhD from Banasthali University, Rajasthan in the area of Vague Set Theory. For the last eight years, Dr. Supriya Raheja is actively involved in research related to areas of Operating System, Designing of CPU Schedulers Using Fuzzy Set Theory, Designing of CPU Schedulers Using Vague Set Theory and Designing of CPU Schedulers Using Intuitionistic Fuzzy Set theory. Her research articles are published in reputed international journals (SCI/SCIE/ESCI/SCOPUS), conferences and as book chapters (SCOPUS). Her areas of interest include Object Oriented Programming—C++, Python, Secure Coding & Vulnerabilities, Operating System and Cyber Security. She is the reviewer and assistant editor of various international journals. She has completed her certification in Software Security from University of Maryland.

Shubham Rawal, founder at SabPay Technologies and a B Tech Computer Science undergraduate at Galgotias University, India, is working in the field of Artificial Intelligence and Machine Learning.

He was recognized for his innovation by several international and national competitions and for his interests in Blockchain, Hybrid Application Development and Artificial Intelligence. He has been involved in Software Development since he was 15 years old, working with various clients across India.

Shraddha Sagar is an associate professor in School of Computing Science and Engineering, Galgotias University, NCR Delhi, India. She has completed a PhD in Computer Science from Banasthali University, Jaipur, India. Her main thrust research areas are Artificial Intelligence, Internet of Things, Machine learning and Big Data. She is a pioneer researcher in the areas of Artificial Intelligence, Internet of Things and Machine Learning, and has published more than 25 papers in various national/international journals. She has presented papers in national/international conferences, published book chapters in Taylor & Francis Group (CRC Press), Wiley, Springer, etc. She also edited a book for CRC Press and published three self-authored books in a publishing house.

Mr. Mahipal Singh Sankhla was born on 19 May 1994 in Udaipur, Rajasthan, India. He has completed B Sc (Hons.) Forensic Science, M Sc Forensic Science and Nano Diploma in Environmental Science. Currently, he is Pursuing PhD in Forensic Science from Galgotias University, Greater Noida, UP and also pursuing PG Diploma in Intellectual Property Rights from VMOU, Kota, Rajasthan and Diploma in Photography from UPRTOU. He has done training in Forensic Science Laboratory (FSL), Lucknow; CBI (CFSL), New Delhi; Codon Institute of Biotechnology, Noida; and Rajasthan State Mines & Minerals Limited (R&D Division), Udaipur. He was awarded "Junior Research Fellowship-JRF", DST-Funded Project at "Malaviya National Institute of Technology-MNIT", Jaipur, "Young Scientists Award" for Best Research Paper Presentation in the second National Conference on Forensic Science and Criminalistics and "Excellence in Reviewing Award" in International Journal for Innovative Research in Science & Technology (IJIRST) and Asian Journal of Advanced Research and Reports. He has published three book chapters in various national and international publishers, more than 62 research & review papers in peer review international journals and articles in various newspapers and websites. He has been serving as a managing editor in IMILRJ, editorial board member of 16 international journals and reviewer of 15 international journals. He has completed 12 certified courses from Elsevier Research Academy and certificate courses in Forensic Science and Criminal Justice from University of Leicester (UK), Forensic Anthropology from True Forensic Science Academy, USA and 35 courses from various different universities. He has been participating and presenting his research work in more than 58 national and international conferences and workshops or organized more than 30 national and international conferences, webinars, workshops & FDP. He has been serving as a managing editor for India's Frist Forensic Science Newsletter "Forensic Reporter".

Priyanka Shukla is assistant professor in School of Computing Science and Engineering at Galgotias University, India. Her research areas are Data Science and Natural Language Processing. She has completed her Master of Engineering in Computer Engineering and Bachelor of Engineering in Computer Science and Engineering.

Ms Kiran Singh is presently working as an assistant professor, Department of Computer Science and Engineering, Galgotias University. She received an MCA degree from Maharishi Dayanand University in 2008 and an M Tech degree in Computer Science and Engineering from Rajiv Gandhi Proudyogiki Vishwavidyalaya in 2015, Bhopal. She has overall experience of 11 years. Her research interests include Image Processing, Big Data and IOT. She has published papers in international journals and conferences.

Rakshit Singh is an undergraduate engineering student from Galgotias University, Greater Noida, India. He has been into software development for five years and has worked with many start-ups. He also created a module that let user pay in offline channels without the need of smartphone. He has been working as an independent freelancer and have served pan Indian clients & SMB's. He has also been recognised in innovation and startup competition, Rajasthan for creating truly contactless paying experience.

Yashvardhan Singh is an undergraduate engineering student from Galgotias University, Greater Noida, India. He has exceptional product management and strategy building skills and worked on various consulting projects as a marketing lead. Recently he got admitted into 100x.Vc Entrepreneurship Gurukul. He's been leading both national and international tech driven team and have been advising early-stage companies to build for scale.

Mr. Swaroop Sonone has completed his Bachelor in Forensic Science and is currently pursuing Master's degree in Forensic Science from Government Institute of Forensic Science, Aurangabad, Maharashtra. His broad areas of interest include Digital and Cyber Forensics, Forensic Psychology and Multimedia Forensics. He is currently working on Digital Transaction Security, Cybercrimes Vulnerabilities, Cyber Frauds, Mobile Forensics, Cyber Security, Digital Evidences and their legal aspects in Courtroom. He has been participating and presenting his work for more than five national and international conferences and workshops. He is an active member in Department of Forensic Science & Criminal Investigation, Legal Desire Media & Insights and has organized more than ten national and international conferences, webinars, workshops & faculty development programmes. He has delivered talks at Office of Commissioner of Police, District & Sessions Court about various fields of Forensic Science. He has given briefings about the instrumentations and their workings to the visitors at Government Institute of Forensic Science, Aurangabad.

Dr. S. Vijayalakshmi pursued a Bachelor of Science in the stream of Computer Science from Bharathidasan University, Tiruchirappalli, Tamil Nadu in 1995, Master of Computer Application in the same university in 1998, and Master of Philosophy in the same university in 2006. She received her Doctorate in 2014. She has been working as a professor, Galgotias University, Greater Noida, Uttar Pradesh, India. She has 20 years of teaching experience and ten years of research experience. She has published many papers in the area of Image Processing, especially in Medical Imaging.

Contributors

Rashi Agarwal
Galgotias College of Engineering & Technology
Greater Noida, India

Ruchi Agarwal
JIMS Engineering Management Technical Campus
Greater Noida, India

M. Vivek Anand
Galgotias University
Greater Noida, India

Ishan Adhikari Bairagi
Galgotias University
Greater Noida, India

Shashank Chauhan
Galgotias University
Greater Noida, India

Pethuru Raj Chelliah
Site Reliability Engineering (SRE) Division
Reliance Jio Infocomm. Ltd. (RJIL)
Mumbai, India

Mehul Gupta
School of Information Technology and Engineering
Vellore Institute of Technology
Vellore, India

R.L. Hariharan
Department of Information Technology, NIT Suratkal
Mangalore, India

Pramod Mathew Jacob
Department of CSE, Providence College of Engineering
Chengannur, India

Sakshi Jain
Galgotias University
Greater Noida, India

Kalpana Jha
JIMS Engineering Management Technical Campus
Greater Noida, India

Jisha Mariyam John
Department of CSE, Providence College of Engineering
Chengannur, India

Supriya Khaitan
School of Computing Science & Engineering
Galgotias University
Greater Noida, India

Rajeev Kumar
Department of Forensic Science
Galgotias University
Greater Noida, India

Kavita Kumari
School of Computing Science & Engineering
Galgotias University
Delhi NCR, India

Shriyash Mohril
Roboticwares Pvt. Ltd.
Noida, India

Nilanjana Pradhan
Pune Institute of Business Management
Pune, India

Prasanna Mani
School of Information Technology
Vellore Institute of Technology
Vellore, India

Supriya Raheja
Amity University
Noida, India

Shubham Rawal
Galgotias University
Delhi NCR, India

Shraddha Sagar
Galgotias University
Delhi NCR, India

Kavita Saini
School of Computing Science & Engineering
Galgotias University
Delhi NCR, India

Mahipal Singh Sankhla
Department of Forensic Science
Vivekananda Global University, Jaipur, India

Priyanka Shukla
School of Computing Science & Engineering
Galgotias University
Greater Noida, India

Kiran Singh
Galgotias University
Delhi NCR, India

Rakshit Singh
Galgotias University
Delhi NCR, India

Yashvardhan Singh
Galgotias University
Delhi NCR, India

Swaroop S. Sonone
Department of Digital and Cyber Forensics
Government Institute of Forensic Science
Aurangabad, India

S. Vijayalakshmi
Galgotias University
Greater Noida, India

1 Expounding the Blockchain Architecture

Pethuru Raj Chelliah and Kavita Saini

CONTENTS

Introduction ... 2
Key Elements of Blockchain ... 3
Transactions ... 3
Blocks ... 3
Different Network Models for Blockchain ... 5
Centralized Model ... 5
Decentralized Model ... 6
Distributed Model ... 6
Hashing ... 7
Merkle Tree ... 8
Public/Private Key Encryption and Authentication ... 9
Digital Signatures ... 9
Transparency ... 10
Consensus Algorithms ... 10
The Popular Consensus Algorithms ... 11
Proof of Work (PoW) ... 11
Proof of Stake (PoS) ... 12
Delegated Proof of Stake (DPoS) ... 13
Proof of Elapsed Time (PoET) ... 13
Practical Byzantine Fault Tolerance (PBFT) ... 13
Digital Ledger: Append-Only ... 13
Smart Contract ... 14
Decentralized Applications (DApps) ... 15
The Key Attributes of DApps ... 15
Integrated Blocks ... 16
Types of Blockchains ... 17
Public Blockchain ... 17
Consortium Blockchain ... 17
Private Blockchain ... 17
Database versus Blockchain ... 17
Blockchain Reference Architecture ... 18
Implementation ... 19
Integration ... 20
Artificial Intelligence (AI)-inspired Blockchain ... 20

DOI: 10.1201/9781003094210-1

Cloud Integration ... 20
IoT Integration ... 21
Distributed Ledger ... 21
Ledger Conduits ... 21
Security ... 21
Open-Source Blockchain Platforms ... 22
Ethereum ... 22
BigchainDB ... 23
HydraChain (HC) ... 23
Corda ... 24
Conclusion ... 24
References ... 24

INTRODUCTION

The Internet of Things (IoT), artificial intelligence (AI), and blockchain represent an unprecedented opportunity for all kinds of enterprising businesses and organizations. Every establishment capable of exploiting these cutting-edge technologies can easily achieve real digital transformation. Enterprises can radically and rapidly streamline and enhance their processes, create new powerful business models, and develop premium products and state-of-the-art services. The increasingly connected world is inching towards the projected smart era undoubtedly through the evolutionary and revolutionary technologies and tools [1].

Experts have agreed on this definition of blockchain. A blockchain system is a distributed, append-only digital ledger, shared and replicated among participants, uses advanced cryptography for security, collaborative consensus mechanism ensuring synchronization, smart contract for enforcing business logic, and with no central point of control and no central point of failure – thereby generating trust, immutability, and provenance to the transaction log.

Blockchain as a technology has gained enormous attention in the recent past. From revolutionizing the music, supply chain, real estate, logistics, and healthcare industries, blockchain has been hailed as the most promising and potential technology for the digital era. With the IoT paradigm deftly disrupting several industries, the security of the transactions of IoT devices is being increasingly ensured through the smart application of the core strengths of the blockchain technology. Furthermore, with the seamless and spontaneous synchronization with the latest advancements in the field of AI, blockchain is innately empowered to be a trendsetter for worldwide businesses [2, 3]. On the other hand, as AI derives its unique power from data, the integration with blockchain is going to be beneficial for AI in the long run as blockchain is a cryptographically secured distributed ledger that ensures data security. Let us digress a bit here and start with some basics, which will clear up some of the persisting and perplexing doubts about the blockchain concept [4].

A blockchain ledger is a time-stamped collection of immutable records hosted and maintained by a group of computers. Various cryptographic principles are used to secure and connect each block of data. This results in a chain. The blockchain network is a decentralized authority where the verified and validated information is stored in blocks and visible to everyone [5].

Each blockchain is a linked list of blocks which are made up of transactions. The block contains data and a hash pointer. This hash pointer contains the hash of the data as well as the address of the previous block. This way, a chain of blocks is created and stored [6]. Why this phenomenon is being termed as a paradigm shift? Here is a real-world example. When we book railway tickets through any mobile application or the Web, the credit or debit card company takes its commission for processing the transaction [7]. Now if we embrace the blockchain technology, we (passengers) can pay directly to the railway service company. The intermediary is fully taken out. Each booked ticket is a transaction and multiple transactions combine to form a block, which is continuously added to the ticket blockchain [1]. Just as every monetary transaction on the blockchain is a unique, tamper-proof, and independently verifiable record, so is the case with each of the booked tickets. Hence, the ticket blockchain is nothing but a record containing all transactions for that day or for that train. This path-breaking phenomenon is being replicated across industry verticals.

KEY ELEMENTS OF BLOCKCHAIN

Transactions

Transactions are the smallest building blocks of a blockchain system. Transactions generally consist of a recipient address, a sender address, and a value. For example, a bitcoin transaction moves the value of some bitcoins from one address to another. A transaction changes the state of the agreed-correct blockchain. A blockchain system is a shared, decentralized, and distributed state machine. This means that all nodes (users of the blockchain system) independently hold their own copy of the blockchain, and the current known "state" is calculated by processing each transaction as it appears in the blockchain. Transactions are bundled and delivered to each node in the form of a block. As new transactions are distributed throughout the network, they are independently verified and "processed" by each node [8].

Transactions contain one or more inputs and one or more outputs. An output specifies an amount and an address. An input always references a previous transaction's output. This continual pointer of inputs to previous transactions outputs allows for an uninterrupted, verifiable stream of value amongst addresses as vividly illustrated in Figure 1.1.

Also included in the input data structure is a **scriptSig**. This is a cryptographic signature that proves that the creator of this transaction is allowed to create it given its inputs. The **scriptSig** contains the address **in the referenced transaction's output** and an Elliptic Curve Digital **Signature** Algorithm (**ECDSA**) signature of this current transaction.

Blocks

Blocks are the data structures that bundle sets of transactions and be distributed to all nodes in the network. Blocks are created by miners. Blocks contain a block header, which is the metadata that helps verify the validity of a block [1]. Typical block metadata elements (Figure 1.2) include the following [2].

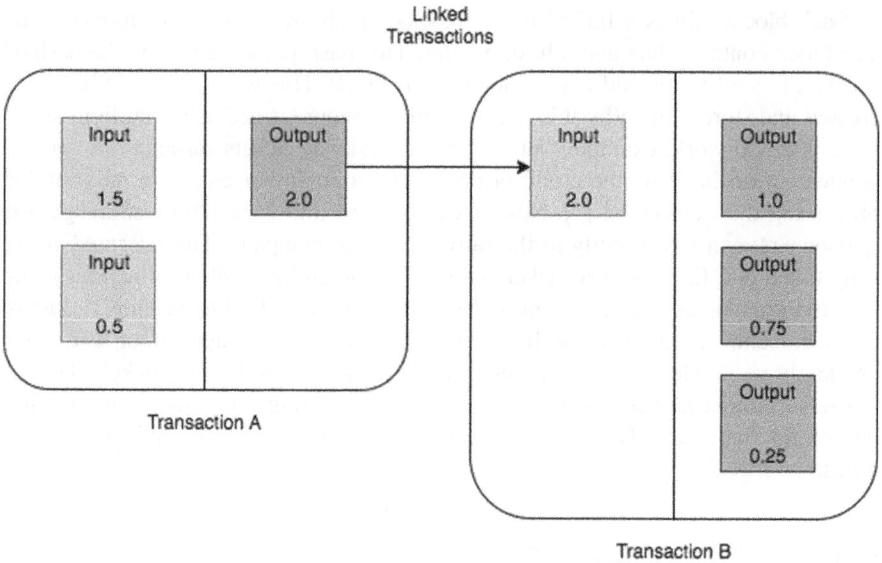

FIGURE 1.1 Concept of linked transactions in a blockchain.

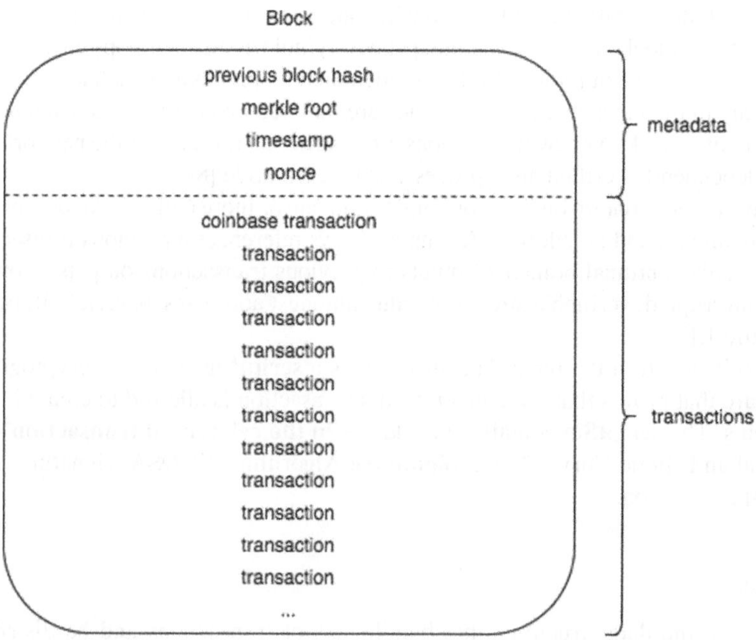

FIGURE 1.2 Elements of metadata in a block header.

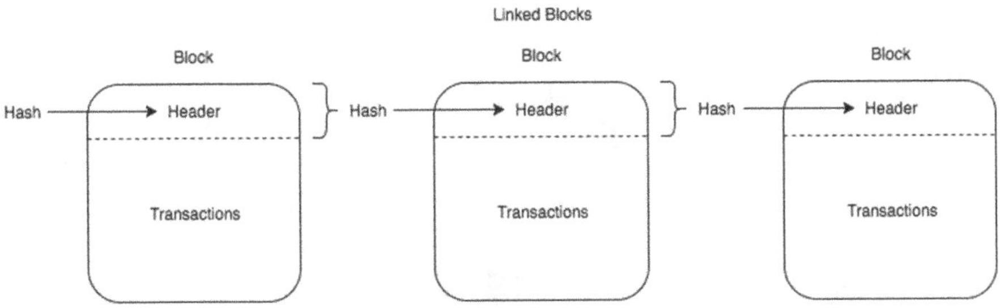

FIGURE 1.3 Typical structure of blockchain.

- version – the current version of the block structure
- previous block header hash – the reference this block's **parent block**
- Merkle root hash – a cryptographic hash of all of the transactions included in this block
- time – the time that this block was created
- nBits – the current **difficulty** that was used to create this block
- nonce ("number used once") – a random value that the creator of a block is allowed to manipulate however they so choose

These six fields constitute the block header. The rest of a block contains transactions that the miner has chosen to include in the block that they created. Users create transactions and submit them to the network, where they sit in a pool waiting to be included in a block [9]. Typical structure of a blockchain is shown in Figure 1.3.

It's important to realize that each miner (more generally, each user of a blockchain) is allowed to act however they want within this blockchain system. Consensus rules dictate that only valid changes to the blockchain will be accepted by everyone else [10]. This results in a system that economically guarantees that only valid blocks will be worked on, submitted to the network, and accepted by the greater community.

Different Network Models for Blockchain

A blockchain system is a digital transaction log or a ledger which can be implemented in three network models: centralized client-server model, decentralized client-server model, and peer-peer distributed model, as shown in Figure 1.4.

Centralized Model

A centralized client-server architecture is a model in which information is stored in central servers that can be requested and accessed by multiple users/clients [4, 5]. Web-scale applications such as Facebook, Google, and Amazon store the personal information, commercial transactions, comments, compliments, complaints, etc. of their users in large and centralized server machines [3]. Anyone with the Internet connectivity from any part of the world at any point of time can find, connect, and use the varied content and competencies of these web-scale and cloud-hosted applications.

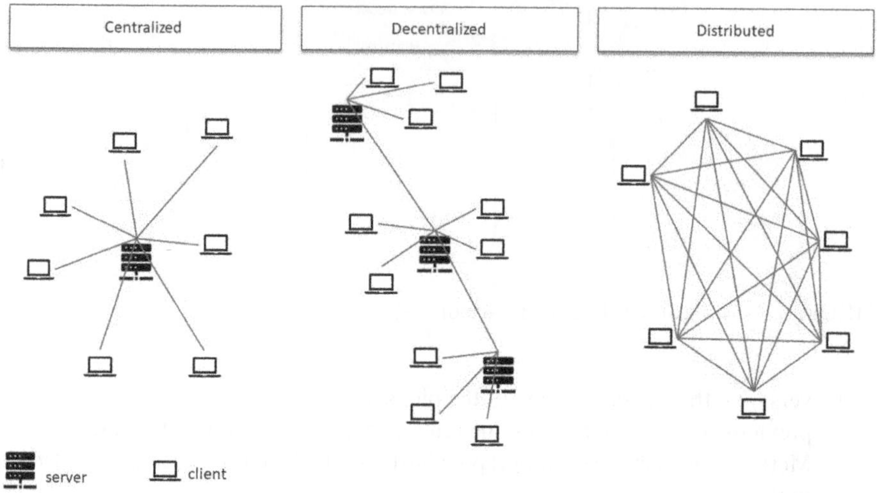

FIGURE 1.4 Different network models of blockchain implementation.

Decentralized Model

This network model has more than one central node or multiple intermediaries. This is a mostly client-server model with more servers to distribute load or address local needs. The prime benefit of using a decentralized model rather than a centralized database is that there is no single point of chokes and failures. Furthermore, with a decentralized ledger, there is not a single entity that owns all the data. That means nobody can monetize that data or use the data in a wrong way. With decentralization, the network participants have gained full control over their data and can decide what they want to do with it. The network participants can make money out of their data and make sense out of data. For example, data scientists and marketing people can buy and use the data to their advantage. By eliminating the intermediary, we are bound to lose the trust which we badly need to transact with others with all the clarity and alacrity [11]. In other words, instead of a single entity, we tend towards leveraging multiple entities to store transaction data. This transition is to automate a number of activities [6]. For example, instead of depending on banks and other financial organizations, we use online computers to stock data through blockchain software packages. The software also guarantees the trust that we need to transact across with confidence [12]. Through software programming, a number of manual banking activities get accelerated and automated to serve the varying purposes of the users. The security of data, which is in transit and at rest, is a challenge here too. Blockchain adroitly uses advanced cryptography methods to conceal the identities of network participants and the content of transactions [13].

Distributed Model

This model refers to peer-to-peer network which differs from this centralized model altogether. The main deviation is the absence of any intermediary between participating systems. Each participating node contributes as a client and a server [11]. This does not have any central server. Each node maintains its data and communicates with other nodes.

With blockchain, we could facilitate payments individually to each other without involving a third party (banks and financial organizations). We can do this today using cash, but to do this transaction online and to keep track of our transactions and maintain the ledgers ourselves, the concept of disintermediation (= no intermediary) is considered the way forward [6]. Such a peer-to-peer system should also provide security and ensure there are no disputes on the transactions made. Blockchains can keep records of the transactions with themselves, without any central authority or intermediary for validating or facilitating the process [7]. The much-maligned distributed architecture has some distinct advantages that are useful from a business process perspective.

- *Disintermediation* – With continuous advancements, many economic transactions that are facilitated by central intermediaries today, including governments, can be executed by software-only solutions. All these are done without any dependence on a central intermediary. The advantages include process simplification guaranteeing efficiency gains in time and cost.
- *System resiliency* – There is no single point of authority/control to be attacked to disrupt or take down the system and data gets synchronized with all nodes consistently. This leads to a greater system security and resiliency. An attacker needs to defunct all nodes to render the system unavailable.

With any type of network implementation, transactions can be entered into the ledger as they happen to keep track of them for reconciliation. With blockchain, the traditional double-entry accounting is now stored permanently and immutably on the blockchain through the use of cryptography.

Hashing

Hashing is a mathematical function that takes any length input (a character or phrase, a long sentence of words, or an entire book) and generates a seemingly random output with a fixed number of letters and numbers using a formula. For instance, if you create a hash of the line using the SHA 256 hashing function, "This is a hash function!", we will get 2c886077bbc252137f1d78d2915d96befe71bca1caf3ff9cc7b6dcb47b3c4248. How a hash function is produced for a given input is shown in Figure 1.5.

- **Message blocks** – the input message, of any length, is broken into 512-bit sections. Padding is added to the last section to make it 512 bits.
- **Initialization** – this is a vector of 256 bits; along with it, eight variables are used.
- **Bit-wise mixing algorithm** – the initialization bits are used with the message blocks in complex bit-wise operations, mixing, and rotations.
- **Temporary hash** – the intermittent values are created using bit-wise addition and reintroduced into the mixing algorithm and run for 64 iterations.

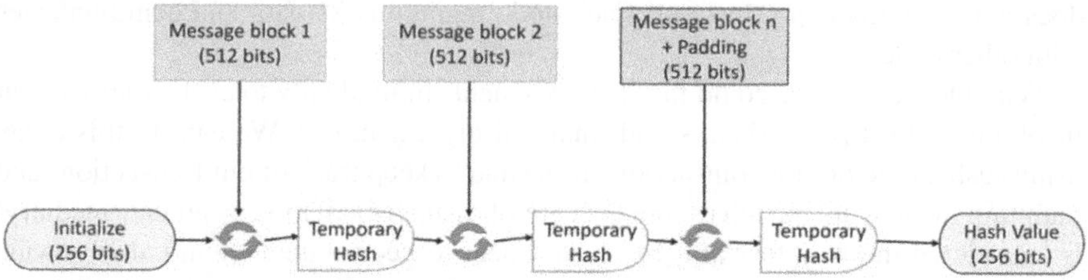

FIGURE 1.5 Generation of hash value for a given input.

- **Output hash** – once the iterations are over, the outputs are concatenated to produce the fixed-length 256-bit output, called the message digest.

Even for a small change in the input value, we will get a completely different output. The hashing function guarantees the following capabilities.

- The same input has to create the same output all the time.
- Two different inputs cannot produce the same output.
- It must be impossible to determine the input given the output.

Another noteworthy advantage is that it is easier to verify whether two files are identical. Instead of checking every character of files, create a hash for both the files and compare the hash value of each file [13]. The same hash value means the two files are exactly the same. As indicated earlier, even if there is a tiny deviation in one of the files, there is a difference in the hash value. For a real-world example, if we buy a digital book from Amazon.in, we can easily check whether the book purchased is the same as the original one. Hashing is primarily used in blockchain to create **digital signatures, which are** used to **integrate blocks of transactions sequentially** to form an immutable ledger.

Merkle Tree

Along with hashing, the produced hash pointers are then stored in a filing system called Merkle tree [13], shown in Figure 1.6. The specific property of this system is that hash pointers can be added. To describe with an example, let's assume

- One block has eight transactions, T(A) to T(H)
- Each transaction can be hashed individually to produce H(A) to H(H)
- The individual hashes can be added (H(A) + H(B) = H(AB))
- Furthermore, H(AB) + H(CD) = H(ABCD)
- Finally, H(ABCD) + H(EFGH) = H(ABCDEFGH)

There are several advantages being accrued out of this property. There are 10 nodes and 8 transactions. Let us say transactions T(A) to T(H) are on all of the 10 nodes. Now, for comparing if the data between the nodes matches perfectly, we need not compare each transaction data of the 10 nodes, instead just compare only the Merkle

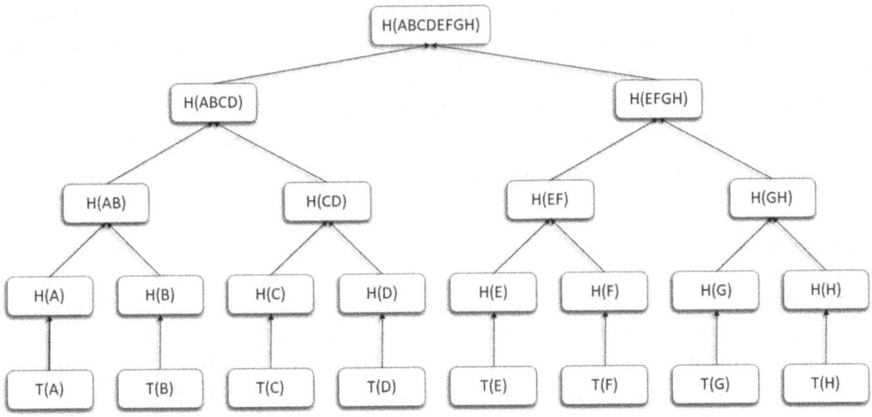

FIGURE 1.6 Storing hash values in a Merkle tree data structure.

root (H(ABCDEFGH)) of each node, If the Merkle roots are identical, the data must be identical [5]. This allows efficient verification and synchronization of data between numerous nodes and chains containing thousands or millions of transaction data. Thus, the successful implementation of distributed architecture is possible, without ever needing to transmit or read massive amounts of data that reside on those nodes. The Merkle tree structure also allows the source of the mismatch to be identified efficiently to the specific block and the transaction.

Public/Private Key Encryption and Authentication

This is a well-known security-enablement concept for long. There are symmetric and asymmetric encryptions. Symmetric encryption uses a single private key to encrypt as well as decrypt messages. One can produce the cipher text from the original text and the key. Similarly, one can recreate the original text using the cipher algorithm and the key as pictorially represented later. The drawback is that all participating parties have to have the private key to decrypt any incoming message. For that, in one or other ways, the private key has to be shared across. This is somewhat risky. In-person sharing is practically not possible. Sharing through emails is also not recommended.

This issue gets easily solved with asymmetric encryption. There are two keys: a public key and a private key. The two keys are mathematically linked so that any content getting encrypted using the public key can be decrypted using the private key. While this slows down the speed of transactions, it considerably increases data security. This facility is highly beneficial for blockchain protocols.

Digital Signatures

The process is as follows. First, the message sender hashes the message and then encrypts the message + the hash value obtained in the previous step. This combination serves as a digital signature, which is used to authenticate the identity

of the sender. This is also proving that no one has modified the message on its way. The receiver uses the public key to get the original file. He or she can compare the hash value of the received file with the hash value of the original file to make sure that the file is not touched by any one. Blockchain protocols combine these encryption methods to bring forth an incredible way to transmit information across any network in a secure fashion.

Transparency

Everyone's identity in a blockchain is masked by complex cryptographic functions and only represented by their public address. As a result, if we look at a person's transaction history in a blockchain, we won't find anything like "Bob sent USD 100". We will see something like 1MF1bhsFLkBzzz9vpFYEmvwT2TbyCt7NZJ sent USD 100. The identity of the person is kept hidden for security reasons, but his public address can be used to view all of his transactions. It is possible to view all of a user's transactions if we know his or her public address and type it into a web browser.

Consensus Algorithms

Consensus generally means an amicable agreement between two or more parties. Here is a motivational scenario. Army generals, each commanding a subset of the army, were stationed around a city. The generals communicated with each other through messengers. The goal of the generals was to formulate a plan to either attack the city together or not attack at all [6]. The generals knew that they would be successful in their offense only and only if all of the generals attacked the city together. As we all know, partial attack or partial retreat would result in heavy defeat [12].

Now, some of the generals or the messengers could be intercepted or corrupted such that they could, intentionally or not, pass the wrong message – e.g., retreat instead of attack or they do not pass a message at all. There was no other way for any of these generals to know what the other generals knew. This demands a counting strategy or a mathematical algorithm that would produce the correct message in spite of the known risk of faulty messages. The Byzantine Fault Tolerant (BFT) method is a prominent mathematical model to calculate the message correctly.

In the digital world, we can think of each general as a "node" or a computer in a cluster, and the messages communicated between these nodes are the binary messages of 1 or 0. There is no perfect knowledge around whether or which nodes are faulty. However, using this model, powerful algorithms can be designed to ensure system or the cluster as a whole could reach consensus with the mathematical certainty of the majority.

In the past, there are some very complex and computationally intensive algorithms that are used in the servers to guarantee fault-tolerance. These are termed as BFT algorithms. These algorithms are subsequently improved to ensure higher throughput. Miguel Castro and Barbara Liskov have introduced the hugely popular "Practical Byzantine Fault Tolerance" (PBFT) algorithm, which is very famous for providing higher performance in processing thousands of transactions per second.

Consensus ensures that within a distributed system, every node is in perfect synchronization or agreement for all information. Even with the presence of faulty nodes or bad actors, the algorithm ensures that the non-faulty majority prevails with the correct message. Consensus mechanisms ultimately help in generating agreement on a new transaction on blockchain before it is executed and recorded on the chain. Then, the transaction data becomes permanent and cannot be altered in any way. The data becomes the truth now. Thus, in a distributed environment adorned with multiple decision-makers, consensus algorithms play a very vital role.

Depending on the specific need of a network, a particular consensus mechanism may be preferred. The need for a private chain with five large institutions as participants, with verified identities, and executing large number of transactions daily is the high throughput rates.

Similarly, a public chain with thousands of anonymous participants, unverified identities, and executing fewer transactions will be the transaction security, that is, it is all about discouraging and preventing fraudulent transactions at the expense of throughput and energy consumption. In summary, as indicated earlier, there are multiple authorities to take decisions in a decentralized network. That means there are multiple decision-making parties. This, if unattended, may lead to chaos. This scenario induces and insists for unearthing workable decision-making mechanisms to force and facilitate participants to come to an agreement on each of the transactions. Therefore, consensus algorithms are recommended to support and sustain the blockchain idea.

The Popular Consensus Algorithms

Consensus algorithms [12] enable network participants to agree on a "single version of the truth". Network participants have to use consensus algorithms to confirm whether any incoming transaction is valid or not. Also, it has to be verified that a person transferring an asset actually owns that asset in the first place. The widely discussed double-spend problem is being solved through consensus algorithms. Here are some commonly used consensus algorithms.

Proof of Work (PoW)

This is the first and foremost consensus algorithm. This is the algorithm that requires network participants to validate transactions using a mathematical puzzle that is computationally difficult. As an incentive, the good node is rewarded. Any hacker attempting to break into the blockchain system would be thwarted by the computational complexity. Since making any improvements to the blockchain after agreement takes a significant amount of time and effort. Consider the scenario of a large number of bitcoin transactions that must be checked. The network's nodes (known as miners) will then compete to mine the block of transactions to obtain the incentives associated with it. They do this by combining a number of various inputs, including:

a. any of the block's transactions.
b. when the block was hashed, this is the timestamp.
c. the block's complexity.

d. the hash of the previous transaction block.
e. an extra number known as a "nonce".

Bitcoin miners must solve the problem of taking many of the hash inputs, as well as determining a single hash output. Only by guessing a nonce and hashing the inputs would you be able to do this. If those inputs fail to produce the desired result, the miner must guess a new nonce and rehash the inputs. The miner repeats this process until the correct production is obtained. It's a guess-and-check exercise in math. The nonce is a programmable vector repeatedly to produce the desired result. The winner of the reward is the first miner who correctly guesses the nonce. The transactions and nonce must then be checked by all other nodes on the network to ensure that they are valid. After that, the nodes move on to the next block to repeat the process.

This method requires a lot of computational power as this is a brute force guess and check. However, as Proof of Work (PoW) networks scale up, the power consumption goes up sharply. Furthermore, if mining operations are restricted to a few players, there is a possibility for centralization in the decentralized network. In summary, this is designed for trustless or public blockchains. The protocol requires participant nodes, also known as miners, to compete to solve a cryptographic puzzle, to win the right to add the next block to the chain and win a reward. PoW is vulnerable to the 51% attack. If fraudulent miners control 51% or more of the mining (computing) power of the network, they could theoretically manipulate data to their own advantage. The PoW consensus algorithm is very slow, and hence, the transaction throughput is on the lesser side.

Proof of Stake (PoS)

The primary benefit with this algorithm is less energy consumption. In addition, the expensive hardware required to validate a series of transactions is appreciably less. With this method, our fragile environment is safe. The sustainability goal can be met and the computing is all set to become green. Furthermore, this decentralizes and democratizes the network as there are lower barriers for nodes to serve as miners.

In a Proof of Stake (PoS) system, there is no mathematics puzzle for nodes to compete against one another to find the correct nonce fast. Instead, validating nodes (termed as "forgers") are selected in a random manner. The probability of being selected as forgers is based on a combination of things. The number of network tokens the forger owns and the amount of time he/she has owned those coins for are being taken into consideration to decide prospective forgers.

Then there's the issue of how to ensure that these forgers aren't validating fraudulent transactions. PoS protocols mitigate this risk by requiring forgers to deposit their stake in an escrow account. If a forger validates a fraudulent transaction, the coins in the escrow account will be forfeited, and he will be barred from participating in the forging process for a set period of time.

Another important thing to consider is the incentive system. A PoS scheme, unlike a PoW system, does not have block incentives. Instead, nodes are compensated for validating transactions with transaction fees. Transaction fees are a way for PoS networks to keep track of how many forgers they have. If a network wishes to promote more forgers, transaction fees can be increased, and vice versa. To summarize,

PoS systems select validating nodes based on their network ownership. Second, PoS systems use less electricity and compute power to verify transactions. Third, PoS systems can boost decentralization by lowering the barriers to contributing by validating nodes. In conclusion, this is the second-most common algorithm, which is intended for use in a public or untrustworthy setting. This solves the problem of PoW's high energy consumption by requiring transaction validators (equivalent to miners) to purchase and stake cryptocurrency to gain the right to validate transaction blocks on the network. Deferred proof of function, delegated proof of stake (DPoS), proof of authority, proof of weight, and other consensus algorithms exist.

Delegated Proof of Stake (DPoS)

This is similar to PoS, but very different since validators with "stake" can vote for a representative to whom they can delegate their right to validate the next block. The benefits over PoS are a better distribution of rewards. Fraudulent activity by one representative may result in not getting votes next time. This is a kind of discouragement for any malicious action.

Proof of Elapsed Time (PoET)

This can be used in both public and permissioned networks. It uses specialized hardware to keep random wait times between block creations. And then randomly selects the leader, who will propose the next block, like the lottery. This protocol has been adopted by Hyperledger Sawtooth. The main downside is that it needs specialized hardware from Intel.

Practical Byzantine Fault Tolerance (PBFT)

This is a popular algorithm for permissioned or private blockchains. We have discussed this previously. The primary drawback is that it cannot be used in public or trustless environments. This is being adopted due to its incredible efficiency and no energy concerns like PoW.

Digital Ledger: Append-Only

A ledger includes transactions generally involving two or more entities. Most of the digital ledgers can be changed or updated. That means, even past data can be changed. If we come across any missing or wrong data in past transactions, if identified through routine checks or periodic audits, correct data can be incorporated. Databases typically support four basic functions (C-Create, R-read, U-update, and D-delete). Because the digital databases allow those functions, by design, past data can be changed or deleted. The flip side of this convenience is a threat of trust and tampering with past data. This means that all data needs to be audited periodically.

On the other hand, blockchain has been developed to allow only two of these four operations

- Create (create or add new data)
- Read (read existing data)

Therefore, only new data can be added to the chain as transactions in new blocks, and, thereafter, data can be read anytime but cannot be edited any more. This has a profound implication in having secure systems. The software ensures the data is accurate. Data can only be added to the chain if it is agreed by all the parties through one or other consensus method. This is insisted for ensuring immutability, and hence, blockchain achieves the heightened security when compared with traditional databases. If one needs to "reverse" or "update" an already approved and recorded transaction, the only way made available is to create another transaction, run through the standard cycle of consensus, and then get added to the ledger. That is why blockchain is designated as an append-only ledger.

Blockchain ledger is a collection of transactions only and not a collection of assets. And asset ownership of an entity on the blockchain is always calculated by adding up all of the transactions the entity carried out since the beginning of the ledger. To carry out this requirement flawlessly, blockchain employs cryptography and data structure that allows very efficient aggregation of related data, even among thousands of transactions or blocks. Data is incrementally added to the chain while retaining past data unchanged. These together allow blockchain to provide a much-needed provenance feature.

Provenance generally relates to the place of origin or earliest known history of something. This is primarily beneficial in the supply chain domain. For proving the quality and authenticity along with the ownership of any artwork or antique, the provenance capability is being given thrust. The idea is to track all relevant pieces of information about an object or event through the history or its existence. For example, Walmart is tracking vegetables from the farm to its shelves. IBM is offering blockchain solution to track each of the 30,000 parts coming from 5,000 suppliers required to assemble every single car, using blockchain to enable tracking and monitoring quality and authenticity of each item in the supply chain.

Smart Contract

This can be incorporated on the blockchain to facilitate certain transactions to take place on the chain in an automated manner. Smart contracts provide logic to be incorporated in software programs to automate certain actions when some specified conditions get fulfilled. Recent blockchain platforms, including Ethereum, Hyperledger, natively support this next-generation capability of smart contracts by specifically allowing custom or user-defined programming scripts to be executed as a functionality. These custom scripts could be something very simple like "A can send less than 30 coins to B on any day". This script puts a limit on how many coins can be transferred on a given day for a given account. This script can be given to very complex programs with hundreds or thousands of lines of code. This functionality of adding programming scripts has opened up limitless opportunities for blockchains.

Therefore, blockchain guarantees trust, immutability, and provenance without the need for a third party or an intermediary or audits. The qualities and benefits of blockchain are being decisively understood across and every industry is keenly embracing this trendsetting digital technology to achieve real digital transformation. If properly implemented, blockchain can bring forth business process simplification, reduction in cost and time, better data management, and resiliency. Blockchain is inspiring fresh possibilities and opportunities for any enterprising business.

We have discussed various promising blockchain components in this chapter. Disintermediation is being pronounced as one of the important pointers. This feature leads to situations such as currency without the need of a government, stock exchange minus the exchange authority, and autonomous governments with rules defined within the chain. Large financial services providers such as banks, who also function as intermediaries themselves, are dependent on other intermediaries, such as other banks, government's entities, and international bodies. These large organizations are looking to lessen dependence on intermediaries through blockchain. The general expectation from disintermediation is process simplification, efficiency gain, and reduction in cost and time.

Decentralized Applications (DApps)

The first blockchain apps that will be genuinely consumer-facing are decentralized applications (DApps). As a result, they would be able to introduce blockchain technology to the general public rather than just early adopters. The back-end functionality of a DApp is provided by a distributed network of servers (rather than a centralized conventional server) to store information and process transactions. DApps are a modern form of software that is not owned by a central authority and, most significantly, cannot be shut down by someone or experience downtime. They are open-source programs that run transactions on a blockchain using smart contracts.

As the paradigm is steadily growing, a few of the leading characteristics of these applications are given below. Here we can recollect the underlying technology behind DApps. We are aware that blockchain is a ledger of transaction records arranged in "blocks" that are interlinked by cryptographic validation to form chains of blocks. Each block is linked to its previous block and successive block and because of this linkage, it is impossible to tamper with the data written into a block.

A specific blockchain involves digital storage of consensus between all the parties involved in the chain of transactions. Each transaction is being preserved perpetually and visible to everyone in the loop. The noteworthy point is that this ledger is distributed across multiple nodes. That means the ledger is not stored in a centralized location and not managed by a single entity.

The Key Attributes of DApps

All the changes being made on DApps have to be decided by the consensus of the majority of users. The code base of the DApp must be available for scrutiny. All operational records of a DApp must be stored on a public and decentralized ledger (blockchain) to ensure the control does not fall into a centralized authority. Validators within the blockchain invest work (human effort, computing power, and electricity) to verify transactions and add blocks to the chain.

The community around the DApps must agree on a cryptographic algorithm to demonstrate proof of value. For instance, both Bitcoin and Ethereum are currently using PoW, with the latter also conducting research on a hybrid PoW/PoS. If the earlier traits are considered, Bitcoin certainly is the first DApp to be developed and implemented.

Integrated Blocks

Another intriguing aspect of a blockchain protocol is this. Hashing is useful for sequentially combining multiple blocks of transactions to construct an "immutable ledger." It is critical to comprehend how this integration occurs. The genesis block is often referred to as the first block in a blockchain. Since it is hardcoded into the network and contains the blockchain's initial parameters, this first block stands out from the rest. When this block's transactions are authenticated, they are hashed to create a value that uniquely identifies the block. The transactions from the second block, as well as the hash value from the first block, are used as inputs to establish the second block's unique hash value when the second block is validated. The process is then repeated to create a block chain. Since hackers must break through all previous blocks in the chain to crack one block, blockchains are immutable. Any other node would immediately notice this, allowing required counteractions to be taken quickly.

Another significant advantage of connecting blocks in this way is that the hash of the most recent block includes any transaction that has occurred on the chain up to that stage. Miners will quickly come to an understanding on the "chain's current condition" by deciding on the most recent hash value. Every block, as shown in Figure 1.7, contains transaction data. T(A) to T(D), for example, their hashes are combined to generate the root Tx Root = H (ABCD). Furthermore, each block includes the previous block's hash (Prev hash) and thus is chained sequentially.

As inscribed earlier, these data structures or blockchains reside on multiple nodes synchronizing data between all the nodes consistently. The blockchain protocols are built in such a way that tampering with the data at one or two faulty or malicious nodes will not impact the data on remaining majority nodes; thereby, the system is immutable.

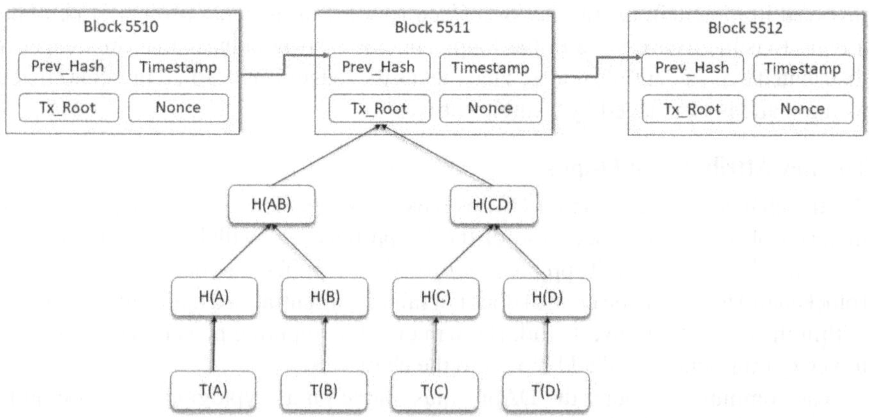

FIGURE 1.7 Structure of integrated, multiple blocks.

Types of Blockchains

Public Blockchain

The PoW consensus algorithm is used in public blockchain protocols. Without needing permission, anyone from anywhere in the world can connect to the Internet and participate in these blockchains. Anyone can download and run the code on their computer to help verify transactions. That is, he or she will participate in the blockchain network as a miner [3]. This also helps in determining the state of various blocks that are continuously added into the chain. Anyone can submit transactions via this network, and if they are found to be legitimate, the transactions will be added to the blockchain. Also, anyone can read the transactions on a public block explorer. The transactions are all clear, but they are all anonymous. That is to say, everyone can see the transactions but not the true identities of the users.

Consortium Blockchain

Consortium blockchains are often managed by a group. They don't let anyone participate in the transaction verification process [4]. These blockchains are more scalable, faster, and provide stronger transaction privacy. Currently, consortium blockchains are commonly used in the banking industry. Here, the consensus process is being accomplished through a preselected set of nodes. The ability to read the entire blockchain could be open to the public or restricted to a small group of people. These blockchains reduce data redundancies and transaction costs. EWF and R3 are the popular consortium blockchains.

Private Blockchain

Private blockchains contain different groups and participants who can easily verify various transactions internally. Like database management and auditing applications, for example, are often internal to a specific enterprise, write permissions are kept centralized within one organization, while read permissions can be available to the public or restricted to some extent. That means public readability may not be necessary at all, in certain cases [4].

Public audit permissions may be desired in certain cases. Private blockchains guarantee efficiency and security against fraud. Financial service providers embrace private blockchain for ensuring unbreakable and impenetrable security [3]. MONAX and Multichain are some of the popular private blockchain [14].

The differences between different blockchains are captured and conveyed in Figure 1.8.

Database versus Blockchain

In the conventional client-server architecture, the database server retains all the necessary information in a single place. That way, it is considerably easier to update the database as it is a centralized one. When it comes to blockchain, it is a distributed and peer-to-peer network, and hence, each participant within the network preserves, approves, and updates any new entries. Each member makes sure that all records and procedures are in order. Put simply, blockchain is a decentralized and distributed

Property	Public blockchain	Consortium blockchain	Private blockchain
Consensus determination	All miners	Selected set of nodes	One organization
Read permission	Public	Could be public or restricted	Could be public or restricted
Immutability	Nearly impossible to tamper	Could be tampered	Could be tampered
Efficiency	Low	High	High
Centralized	No	Partial	Yes
Consensus process	Permissionless	Permissioned	Permissioned

FIGURE 1.8 Comparison among different types of blockchain.

ledger, whether it be public or private. This makes it impossible to alter the data without the consent of each separate computer. For a block to go on the blockchain database, the following four things must happen:

1. A transaction needs to occur.
2. The transaction needs to receive verification.
3. The transaction goes into storage in a block. The dollar amount and both your digital signature and the sites (let's say your transaction was done on Amazon.in) are all in this block.
4. The block receives a hash value, which is obtained by applying a hash function and then the block is officially added to the chain.

The blockchain technology, a kind of digital ledger technology (DLT), allows for the distribution of digital information. This distributed ledger provides a sense of transparency, trust, and data protection. Blockchain guarantees three factors: decentralization, accountability, and security. As a result, the operational efficiency and the cost effectiveness can be achieved.

BLOCKCHAIN REFERENCE ARCHITECTURE

Let's look at the layers of the blockchain reference architecture in this section; implementation, smart contract, convergence, distributed ledger, and encryption are only a few examples. The exponential development of blockchain technology is actually fascinating. It all began with the emergence of the cryptocurrency. To build DApps and smart contracts, we have integrated and plug-in-play blockchain platforms. To develop complex real-world applications across business domains, blockchain is being combined with other IoT, AI, digital twins, and other new technologies. The reference architecture depicted in Figure 1.9 will serve as a foundation and facilitator for developing and deploying various applications of blockchain technology for the wide usage of industry-use cases.

It depicts a layered architecture that depicts the main components and services needed to develop blockchain applications for business applications. It could be used

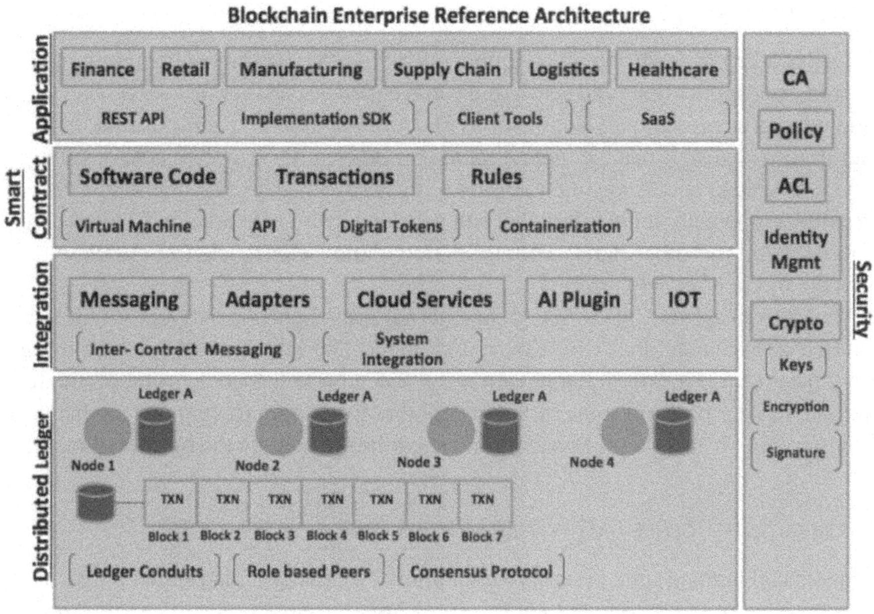

FIGURE 1.9 Blockchain reference architecture.

to build a single or multiple blockchain networks. This may affect several business units or even the entire company. Blockchain applications can be built using the reference architecture that are both permissioned (private) and permissionless (public).

Blockchain applications can be built using the reference architecture described earlier. The architecture is divided into important logical layers. The layers are Application, Smart Contract, Integration, Distributed Ledger, and Security. Let's take a closer look at each of these layers and the components that make them up.

Implementation

Any end-user functionality resides in the application layer. By initiating a transaction, the application usually kicks off the business workflow. A smart contract is used to perform the transactions by the nodes. It can be written in any programming language and run on a variety of operating systems. To connect with other network nodes, any blockchain framework implementation's command line interface (CLI) method or a language-specific software development kit may be used for the application.

We can see sophisticated and integrated resources for supporting the blockchain platform as recognition and comprehension of the differences in the blockchain paradigm grows. Different types of events that occur on the blockchain network can also be received and reacted to by the client application. The event could be as easy as sending a network status update to the application. It's also essential to have a dedicated app for monitoring the blockchain network.

Integration

We are heading towards integrated applications. As the distributed computing gains prominence, applications and services have to connect, collaborate, and collate to do integrated processing and visualization. Thus, integration and communication have acquired special significance in the digital era. In a similar way, blockchain network should be able to access any data outside of the network. The data could be a part of an external application or system that can provide significant value to the blockchain workflow. On the other hand, external systems must also be able to communicate with the blockchain network.

One proven approach is to set up an external event hub as a medium/middleware solution to exchange data with external systems. The interaction happens through event messages. An external application can listen on to a specific event on the hub and accordingly perform some task. On the other hand, a smart contract can listen to events coming from external systems and accordingly execute the business function.

Artificial Intelligence (AI)-inspired Blockchain

As indicated many a time before, blockchain is essentially a distributed ledger with a decentralized and automated approach towards a transaction settlement process. The settlement happens through consensus. Due to the collection and stocking of a large amount of transaction data, the role of AI is bound to grow. Machine learning (ML), which is a part of AI, can work on the data to bring in business optimization, process/workflow excellence, and prediction capability.

ML algorithms can also be used to detect useful anomalies/outliers. They also come handy in visualizing the ways and means of accelerating transaction process, reducing transaction cost, and increasing the revenue of for all parties across the blockchain network. In short, the combination power of AI and blockchain can be a real game changer for worldwide institutions, individuals, and innovators.

Cloud Integration

Now cloud environments are being positioned as the one-stop IT solution for various business needs. That is, cloud infrastructures are the highly optimized and organized IT infrastructure to host and run enterprise-class business workloads and a variety of IT services are being provided in an affordable, agile, and adaptive fashion through the distinct advancements in the cloud space. Blockchain is also being extended to be provided as a service leveraging competent cloud-based blockchain platforms and applications. Special components for enabling a number of application integration services such as routing, data and protocol translation, and message enrichment are hosted in cloud to deliver blockchain as a service (BaaS). This specialized component can act as a middleware, offering its capabilities to composed and provide "BaaS". The blockchain implementation can provide adapters to connect to the middleware component from within the blockchain network and outside of the network.

On the other hand, the blockchain middleware component can also be hosted in a secured "sandboxed" environment or inside a secured virtualized container.

Any external application can interact with the blockchain middleware using different adapters and upon obtaining valid certificates to access the blockchain network.

IoT Integration

With IoT devices proliferating fast, there is a new wave of integration between ground-level IoT devices and cloud-based blockchain application. Scores of IoT sensors and actuators can inject data into the blockchain network. The data can then be validated by the blockchain nodes. A standardized middleware can capture IoT data and do the required cleansing and modification. Furthermore, the nodes (miners and validators) in the blockchain network can then go about validating this data using a specific consensus algorithm using smart contracts.

Distributed Ledger

This distributed ledger is the most important ingredient in the blockchain architecture. It provides a decentralized and distributed database for stocking the transaction entries. These entries are recorded in the order of their occurrence and composed into hashed blocks. The database or the ledger is a chain of hashed blocks of transactions. As indicated earlier, each block refers to the previous block in the chain. The ledger is shared across the blockchain network. That means, every node has an identical copy of the ledger. By this arrangement, each node verifies the transactions independently.

When every node agrees and confirms the authenticity of the transaction, the ledger is said to be in consensus. The blockchain network uses different consensus algorithms to arrive at the consensus. We have written consensus algorithms in detail in this chapter.

Ledger Conduits

For a permissioned-based blockchain network, one can implement a pattern called ledger conduits. Conduits can be thought of as private channels in the blockchain network where two or more nodes perform transactions privately. The nodes must be members and authorized to use these conduits. Conduits are small networks inside a large network. Such a pattern further enforces security when implementing blockchain in an enterprise.

Security

Security is definitely one of the important components in the blockchain architecture. Based on the blockchain type (permissionless or permissioned), the required security and consensus methods are identified and applied. In a public blockchain, every node can participate in the network, while in the permissioned network, fully authenticated and authorized nodes can only participate in the blockchain network. Thus, permissioned network guarantees greater security. Precisely speaking, every entity in the blockchain network has to have an identity. In a permissionless network, entities are the users participating in the transaction. But for a permissioned network, the entities are restricted to organization, nodes, users, and anything that has a role to play in the blockchain network.

For any permissioned blockchain, Public Key Infrastructure (PKI) platform can be used where a trusted Certificate Authority (CA) can issue crypto credentials. The crypto credentials comprise certificates and keys. Private keys are for signing whereas public keys are for verification. This setup results in a trusted network where all the participants know who they are and their roots of trust. The parties involved in the blockchain network can have their own crypto credentials by setting up their own CA. This mandates the blockchain implementation to provide a plug-and-play service. That is, it has to have an abstraction to effectively manage, verify, and validate entities using different security mechanisms across the network. In summary, the blockchain security should be equipped with five effective measures: authentication, access control, integrity, confidentiality, and non-repudiation.

OPEN-SOURCE BLOCKCHAIN PLATFORMS

As we all know, blockchain is a decentralized and tamper-proof database, which is being termed as the trust protocol of the Internet. It helps in settling transactions between multiple anonymous entities over the Internet. There is no need for any centralized entity to settle any transaction twists and tweaks. The transactions in a blockchain are settled in a decentralized manner using a consensus mechanism. Throughout the entire process, transactions are secure only under the control of the users. Individuals, innovators, and institutions can leverage the power of the blockchain to manage and access their information securely. This ensures complete trust on the network. Nakamoto created the first cryptocurrency [5], the blockchain-based project called Bitcoin, which is the current leader, and Ethereum, Ripple, Bitcoin Cash, Litecoin, etc. are also emerging and evolving fast to cater to different needs.

Considering the needs for blockchain applications, platform providers came out with a few integrated platforms. DApps and smart contracts are being built on these platforms and run on cloud platforms. Cloud service providers, having understood the strategic significance of the blockchain technology for multiple business verticals, have incorporated additional blockchain-enablement services. BaaS (https://builtin.com/blockchain/blockchain-as-a-service-companies) is gaining mass adoption.

Ethereum

This is an open-source blockchain platform that aids in the execution of smart contracts and offers a variety of programming tools to create the smart contracts. It's a decentralized public blockchain network that makes it simple for developers to create and deploy a variety of next-generation DApps.

Ethereum is programmable, which means that developers can use it to build new kinds of applications. The IT industry can easily move from centralized to DApps, which are reliable and predictable. That is, once they are uploaded to the Ethereum blockchain platform, they will always run as programmed. They can control digital assets to create new kinds of financial applications.

The Ethereum community is the largest and most active blockchain community in the world. It includes core protocol developers, cryptosystem researchers, mining organizations, gamers, and application developers. Ethereum is maintained and improved over time by a diverse global community of contributors who work on everything from the core protocol to consumer applications. The advantages are as follows:

1. Any third party cannot update or make any changes to the data.
2. It is corruption- and tamper-proof, making censorship impossible.
3. Provides high security. Applications in Ethereum are well protected against any hacking attacks or fraudulent activities.
4. Zero downtime as applications never go down.

BigchainDB

BigchainDB is built using a federation of enterprise-ready DB nodes, like MongoDB instances, that store immutable information about assets in a synchronized manner.

BigchainDB is an open-source distributed ledger system for storing large amounts of data. As a result, its developers are able to deploy a range of blockchain applications. This is an excellent choice for running DApps in production. Based on the access permissions (public, permissioned, or private), the network of BigchainDB is accessed. In the case of a public BigchainDB, any of the participants can have access to the network or can deploy their own node and connect it to the database federation. A permissioned version can be managed by a consortium or any governing body, whereby each member of the consortium is responsible for managing his or her own node in the network.

With high throughput, low latency, powerful query functionality, decentralized control, immutable data storage, and built-in asset support, BigchainDB is like a database with the blockchain characteristics.

HydraChain (HC)

HydraChain is Ethereum-compatible and also provides the infrastructure for writing smart contracts in Python. This is an open-source Ethereum blockchain framework extension that helps in developing and deploying different permissioned distributed ledgers. It supports a wide range of tools, which helps in reducing development time and enhancing debugging capabilities. It also provides a high degree of customization, with various aspects of the device easily configurable to meet customer requirements. HC consensus is a byzantine fault-tolerant protocol to coordinate consensus on the order of transactions in blockchain systems. The byzantine fault-tolerant consensus protocol does not depend on the PoW consensus algorithm. Instead, it relies on a registered and accountable set of validators, which propose and validate the order of transactions.

New blocks are negotiated by the validators, and hence, a quorum by the validators which signs the block is required, before the block is added to the chain. Thus, there will be **no forks or reverts.** Once a block is committed, the state is final. The protocol allows for **sub second block times**.

HydraChain provides an excellent platform to develop smart contracts using the Python language. The noteworthy benefits are significantly reduced development times and better debugging capabilities. As the Ethereum virtual machine (EVM) is bypassed, native contract execution is faster. Native Contracts support the Application Binary Interface (ABI) and are interoperable with EVM-based contracts typically written in the Solidity or Serpent languages and can coexist on the same chain. The constraint that all the validators ought to run a node configured with the same set of native contracts is well manageable in private chain settings.

Many aspects of the system can be freely configured to fit custom needs. For example, transaction fees, gas limits, genesis allocation, and block time can easily be adjusted. Setting up a test network can be done with almost zero configuration. Dockerfile templates are available.

CORDA

This is an open-source blockchain platform for building and developing various permissioned distributed ledger systems. The source code is made available on GitHub under an Apache 2 licence. This was created by the R3 consortium, which comprises the largest banks and allows them to manage all the legal agreements between parties. It can be used by businesses including financial institutions to keep a shared ledger of all the transactions. The entire transaction history on the Corda ledger is completely encrypted and shared only with the required. This setup removes the need for all the involved parties to constantly keep a check on their books after they interact with each other. R3 Corda provides safe data storage and immutable records of data. Corda is also enabling to develop interoperable blockchain networks that can transact in strict privacy.

CONCLUSION

The blockchain phenomenon is rapidly and rewardingly adopted by businesses and service providers to automate some of the important processes, which could not be simplified and streamlined through the current technologies. Fresh possibilities and opportunities are being unearthed and accomplished through the smart application of the blockchain technology and tools. In this chapter, we have mainly focused on explaining various ingredients of any standardized blockchain system. Typically, blockchain is being composed out of multiple technologies and techniques. Therefore, this chapter is specially prepared and dedicated to demystify the confusing buzzwords towards empowering our esteemed readers with all the right and relevant details. Precisely speaking, this chapter delineates the blockchain architecture, which is to be continuously updated and upgraded to cater fast-evolving business needs.

REFERENCES

1. Saugata Dutta, Kavita Saini, "Statistical Assessment of Hybrid Blockchain for SME Sector", WSEAS Transactions on Systems and Control, Volume 16, 2021. E-ISSN: 2224-2856 2021, DOI: 10.37394/23203.2021.16.6

2. Zibin Zheng, Shaoan Xie, Hong-Ning Dai, Xiangping Chen, Huaimin Wang, "An Overview of Blockchain Technology: Architecture, Consensus, and Future Trends", In the Proc. of 6th IEEE International Congress on Big Data, pp. 557–564, 2017, 10.1109/BigDataCongress.2017.85.
3. Kavita Saini, P. R. Chelliah, D. K. Saini (Eds.). *Essential Enterprise Blockchain Concepts and Applications*. New York: Auerbach Publications, 2021.
4. Saugata Dutta, Kavita Saini, "Securing Data: A Study on Different Transform Domain Techniques", WSEAS Transactions on Systems and Control, Volume 16, 2021. DOI: 10.37394/23203.2021.16.8
5. S. Nakamoto, Bitcoin: A peer-to-peer electronic cash system, 2008. https://bitcoin.org/bitcoin.pdf.
6. Pethuru Raj, Kavita Saini, Chellammal Surianarayanan, *Blockchain Technology and Applications* (1st ed.). CRC Press. https://doi.org/10.1201/9781003081487
7. D. Akarca et al., "Blockchain secured electronic health records: Patient rights, privacy and cybersecurity." In 2019 10th International Conference on Dependable Systems, Services and Technologies (DESSERT), IEEE, 2019.
8. Y. Yorozu, M. Hirano, K. Oka, Y. Tagawa, "Electron spectroscopy studies on magneto-optical media and plastic substrate interface," IEEE Transl. J. Magn. Japan, vol. 2, pp. 740–741, August 1987 [Digests 9th Annual Conf. Magnetics Japan, p. 301, 1982].
9. Kavita Saini, "A Future's Dominant Technology Blockchain: Digital Transformation", in IEEE International Conference on Computing, Power and Communication Technologies 2018 (GUCON 2018) organized by Galgotias University, Greater Noida, 28–29 September, 2018.
10. M. G. Kim et al., "Sharing medical questionnaries based on blockchain." In 2018 IEEE International Conference on Bioinformatics and Biomedicine (BIBM), IEEE, 2018.
11. K. Christidis, M. Devetsikiotis, "Blockchains and Smart Contracts for the Internet of Things", IEEE Access, 4 (2016), 2292–2303.
12. Supriya Thakur Aras, Vrushali Kulkarni, "Blockchain and Its Applications – A Detailed Survey", International Journal of Computer Applications (0975–8887), 180, no. 3 (December 2017), 29–35.
13. Dongyoung Koo, Youngjoo Shin, Joobeom Yun, Junbeom Hur, "Improving Security and Reliability in Merkle Tree-Based Online Data Authentication with Leakage Resilience", Applied Science, 8 (2018), 2532; doi:10.3390/app8122532
14. N.-Y. Lee et al., "Modifiable public blockchains using truncated hashing and sidechains." IEEE Access, 7, 173571–173582.

2 Blockchain Technology for IoT-Based Healthcare Applications

Nilanjana Pradhan, Shraddha Sagar, Kiran Singh and Kavita Saini

CONTENTS

Introduction to Blockchain 27
Distributed Database 27
A Network of Nodes 28
Blockchain Generations 28
First Generations 28
Second Generation 29
Blockchain Characteristics 30
Internet of Things (IoT) 30
Blockchain and IoT Applications for Supply Chain 31
Blockchain Technology Innovations 31
Blockchain in Healthcare Application 34
Blockchain-Based Security Solution for Remote Patient-Monitoring System 34
Exchange and Access 39
Concept of Ontology-Based IoHT 40
Conclusion 41
References 41

INTRODUCTION TO BLOCKCHAIN

One of the utilizations of blockchain is bitcoin. The bitcoin is cryptographic money and is utilized to exchange digital assets on the web. Bitcoin utilizes cryptographic verification rather than outsider trust for two gatherings to execute exchanges over the web [13]. Every exchange is ensured through digital signature [1]. Working of blockchain technology is depicted in figure 2.1.

Distributed Database

There is no central server or system that retains blockchain information as shown in figure 2.2. More than millions of computers around the globe that are affiliated with the blockchain are transmitting the information. This framework allows the notarization of data as it is available on each node and can be verified publicly [17].

DOI: 10.1201/9781003094210-2

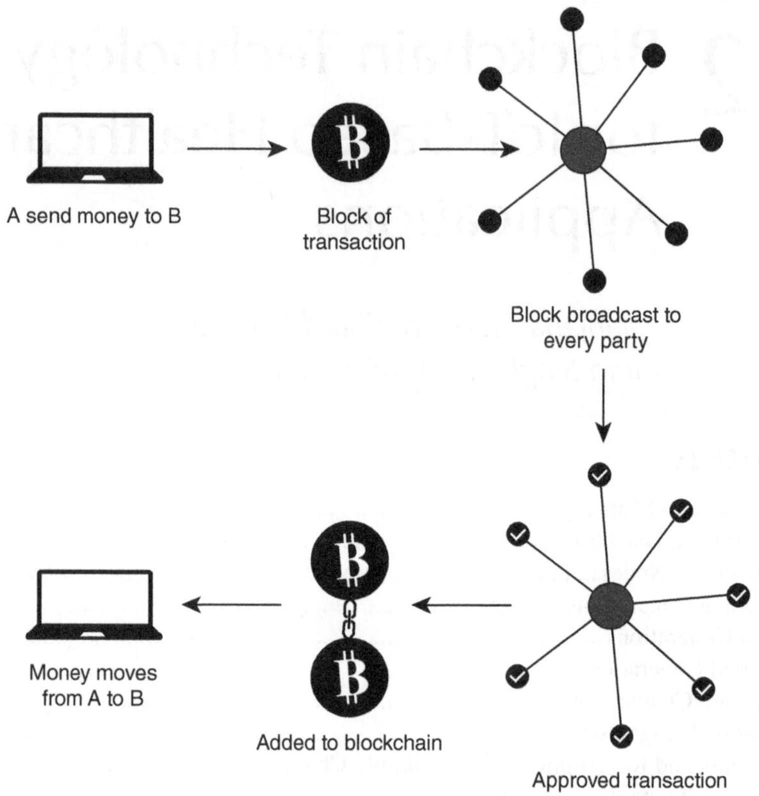

FIGURE 2.1 Working of blockchain technology.

A NETWORK OF NODES

A node is a PCconnected to the blockchain network. Node is synonymous with a client using blockchain. The client assists in approving the blockchain and propagates exchange. When a node is associated with the blockchain, a duplicate of the blockchain information is downloaded into the frame and the node is synchronized with the latest block of blockchain information. The node associated with the blockchain is called miners, which helps to carry out a transaction as an end result of a motivating force [19]. The blockchain network is depicted in figure 2.3.

BLOCKCHAIN GENERATIONS

First Generations

Blockchain was presented alongside bitcoin by Satoshi Nakamoto. The essential utilization of this original blockchain system was the electronic cash or digital currency utilizing bitcoin. The bitcoin organize utilized the blockchain innovation to record transactions that transfer bitcoin digital money [3].

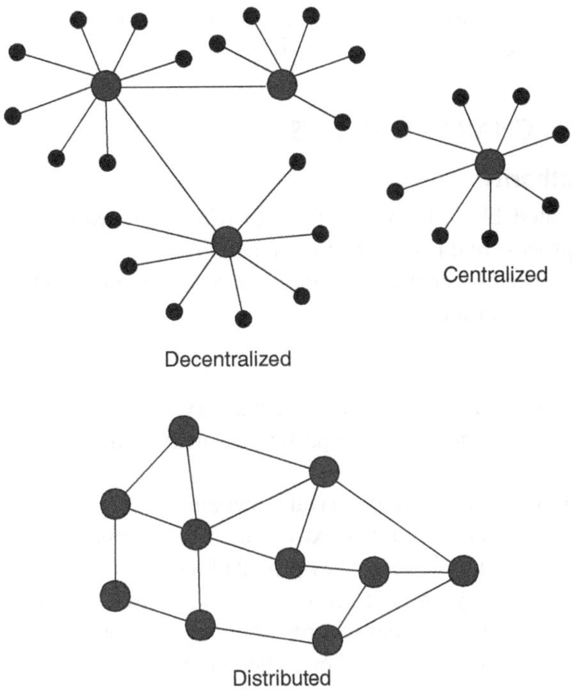

FIGURE 2.2 Decentralized, centralized and distributed database.

Second Generation

Ethereum is an open and programmable blockchain platform. Vitalik Buterin, in 2013, proposed the second-era blockchain network called Ethereum. In the Ethereum Whitepaper, Buterin suggested that rather than isolated blockchain networks for various kinds of cryptocurrencies, a single programmable blockchain system can be utilized to create various sorts of uses. Every application on this second-era blockchain

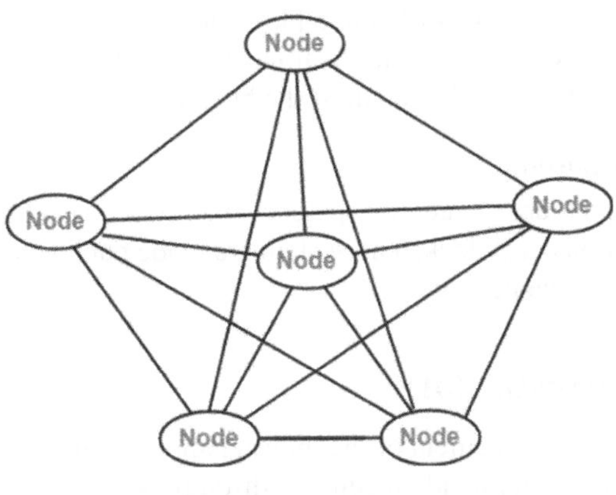

FIGURE 2.3 Blockchain network.

system appears as a "smart contract" [3]. The smart contract, executed in a high-level language, would be conveyed on the network.

BLOCKCHAIN CHARACTERISTICS

No Central Authority:

- An integrated blockchain is a fully distributed network with no central place to process and resolve transactions.
- Nonattendance by a central authority will result in lower exchange rates and faster settlement times.

Privacy:

- Although the transactions on a blockchain system are publicly announced to all the nodes, the executing parties' security is maintained by keeping their secret keys undisclosed.
- Each party has related public-private keypair.
- The address of the account is extracted from the public key. The private key is encoded with the secret key provided while the record is being made.
    - The private key and the secret record keys are necessary for sending transactions to different records. Although people usually can see the executing parties' public keys, there is no disclosure of the parties' actual identities [4].

Scalable and Available:

- Peers located far and large are holding an organizer of blockchain.
- The network remains accessible whilst the companions can join and leave the network.
- The very structure of the blockchain is duplicated over peers.

Immutable:

- Blockchain is a powerful and unchanging knowledge network that keeps track of the transactions on a trustless distributed system.
- Once a transaction is recorded in a block, it can't be changed or erased up to a long share of the computational intensity of the system and isn't constrained by peers who plot to adjust the blockchain.

Secure and Transparent:

- Blockchain provides greater transparency than centralized financial systems.
- The transactions in a blockchain system are made public and can be viewed by any node in the network.

INTERNET OF THINGS (IoT)

Today, the need for enhancement of the internet applications is strong. So Internet of Things (IoT) is a major advancement through which we can offer numerous useful web applications. Essentially, IoT is a network in which every single physical item is connected to the web by device gadgets or switches and trade details. IoT allows for remote monitoring of objects through existing network structures. IoT [5] is a generally excellent and insightful procedure that reduces human exertion as easily as physical gadgets are accessed. Equally, this strategy has an independent control highlight through which any gadget can control without human cooperation.

BLOCKCHAIN AND IoT APPLICATIONS FOR SUPPLY CHAIN

- **Supply Chain Tracking:** Blockchain and IoT [5] technologies can be used for supply chain tracking [4], e.g., food things can be tracked from their starting point to the consumer. Smart contracts can be used to maintain the tracking information of the food items. Thus, as the food items move from the farms to the shelves in the grocery stores, their time-stamped locations can be recorded within the smart contracts deployed on a blockchain platform.
- **Shipment Tracking:** Blockchain and IoT technologies can be used for tracking shipments. By using IoT technologies and RFID, NFC, or BLE tags, we can identify the location of the container as it moves from the source to destination. The time-stamped location information can be recorded within a smart contract and the access to this information can be provided to all the stakeholders. The benefit of this approach is that the shipment tracking can be automated and cryptographically [2] verifiable receipts of the shipment can be issued as the container is transferred from one party to another.
- **On-Demand Manufacturing:** Blockchain platforms for industrial and manufacturing systems can enable a marketplace of manufacturing services where the machines will have their own blockchain accounts [2] and the users will be able to provision and transact with the machines directly to avail manufacturing services.
- **Smart Diagnostics and Machine Maintenance:** Blockchain platforms can be used for creating smart diagnostics and self-service applications for machines where the machines will be able to monitor their state, diagnose problems and autonomously place service, consumables replenishment or part replacement requests to the machine maintenance vendors. Blockchain platforms [2] can be used for developing traceability applications for manufactured products. Smart contracts between the consumers and manufacturers can keep production records [3].

BLOCKCHAIN TECHNOLOGY INNOVATIONS

The blockchain is an encrypted, distributed database that records information, as if it were a digital record of any exchanges, agreements that should be recorded autonomously. One of blockchain's key highlights is that this digital record is available over several hundred thousand computers and will undoubtedly be kept in a lonely spot. Blockchain network has just begun to disrupt the money-related administration section, and it is this invention that facilitates advanced cash bitcoin transaction. With blockchain technology in the financial division, members can legally connect and render web-based transactions without an outsider's impedance.

Such transaction through blockchain won't share any personal data about the members and makes an exchange record by encoding the distinguishing data. The most important factor of blockchain is that it significantly lessens data breach probabilities. Conversely, with the customary procedures in blockchain, there are different mutual duplicates of similar information base, which makes it trying to wage a data breach or cyberattack. With all the misrepresentation-safe highlights, the blockchain innovation holds the possibility to alter different business segments and make processes smarter, secure, straightforward and more effective contrasted with the conventional business processes.

In Figure 2.4, we explained the validation phases of block technology. The blockchain is a distributed database that does not need to be centrally bothered with an authorization, and there is no requirement for outsider verification. A blockchain contains many blocks, and each block contains past block hash, making a chain of blocks from the block of genesis to the current block [1].

The primary square in a blockchain is a genesis block. The genesis block is hardcoded into the program very often. It's a rare case, because it doesn't refer to a past block. There's only a single path to the genesis block for every block on the blockchain. Originating from the block of genesis, there may nevertheless be forks. Forks are formed when two blocks are separated only for a few moments. The most recent block in the longest legitimate chain is being constantly picked at the point when that happens. The longest legitimate chain is determined depending on that chain's consolidated trouble, not the amount of blocks.

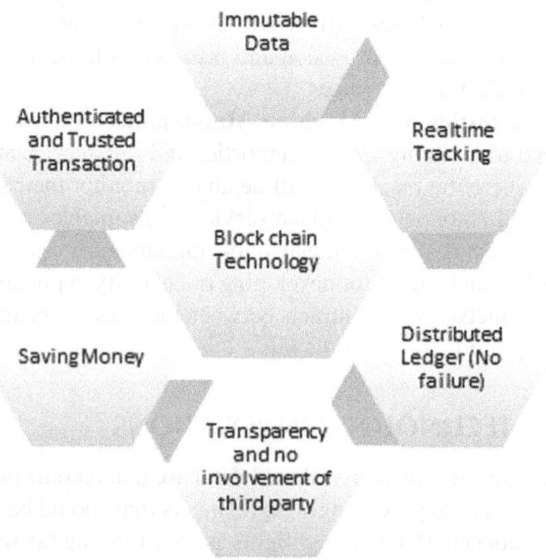

FIGURE 2.4 Blockchain technology validation.

The blocks in shorter chains are viewed as invalid chains and are regularly called orphan block.

There are a lot of transactions in blocks. A transaction is an exchange of values between different entities that are communicated to the network and collected in the blocks. All the exchanges can be seen in the blockchain. The transactions are mined by the purported pool miners or solo miners into a block. The technique of the pool miner is a mining approach, in which various gadgets called miners contribute to a block transaction. Pool miners or solo miners are organizations that have records of trade within the blockchain.

That procedure is called mining. Mining is deliberately intended to be resource intensive and troublesome.

Singular blocks must contain a proof of work (PoW) to be viewed as substantial in the blockchain. The PoW is confirmed by different miners each time they get a block. The basic role of mining is to permit the hubs in a framework to arrive at a protected, alter safe accord. Mining is likewise the methodology used to present new digital money (e.g., bitcoins) into the framework. The miners are paid an exchange charge just as a decided measure of recently made coins when they approve a block. This strategy effectively disseminates new coins in a decentralized way just as giving security to the framework. The framework naturally adjusts to the all-out mining intensity of the system keeping it steady to a particular measure of time (e.g., 10 min in bitcoin). The trouble focuses of the PoW is likewise balanced after each specific measure of blocks (e.g., 2016 blocks in bitcoin) in light of the system execution. A transaction sets aside effort to arrive at all the hubs in the system, and the postponement guarantees that all the exchanges are checked by all the hubs in the system, to forestall the purported double-spending issue. Double-spending is the aftereffect of utilizing some digital money more than once simultaneously [2].

Since it permits installment to be done with no bank or any middle person, blockchain can be utilized in different budgetary administrations, for example, digital resources, settlement, and online payment [3, 4]. Moreover, it can likewise be applied into different fields including digital contracts [5], public administrations [6], IoT [7], reputed frameworks [8] and security administrations [9]. Those fields favor blockchain in various manners. Most importantly, blockchain is unchanging. Transactions can't be altered once it is stuffed into the blockchain. Organizations that require high unwavering quality and trustworthiness can utilize blockchain to draw in clients. Also, blockchain is appropriated and can stay away from the single purpose of disappointment circumstance. With respect to digital agreements, the agreement could be executed by miners naturally once the agreement has been sent on the blockchain.

In spite of the fact that the blockchain technology has incredible potential for the development of things to come in internet frameworks, it is confronting various specialized difficulties. First, versatility is a tremendous concern. Bitcoin block size is constrained to 1 MB now while a square is mined about at regular intervals. In this way, the bitcoin system is confined to a pace of seven exchanges for every second, which is unequipped for managing high-recurrence exchanging. Be that as it may, larger blocks imply bigger extra room and more slow engendering in the system. This will prompt centralization bit by bit as less clients might want to keep up such an enormous blockchain. Along these lines, the trade-off between square size and security has been an intense test. Besides, it has been demonstrated that miners could accomplish bigger income through selfish mining techniques [10].

Miners conceal their mined block for more income in the near future. In that manner, branches could happen every now and again, which stops blockchain improvement. Thus, a few arrangements should be advanced to fix this issue. Additionally, it has been indicated that security spillage could likewise occur in blockchain; even clients just make exchanges with their public key and private key [11]. Besides, current consensus algorithms like PoW or proof of stake are confronting some significant issues. For instance, verification of work squanders a lot of power vitality while the notion that the rich get more extravagant could show up in the evidence of stake agreement process. A lot of research has been done in blockchain from different sources, for example, blogs, wikis, forum posts, codes, conference procedures and journal articles. Zhang et al. [12] made a specialized study about decentralized digital monetary forms including bitcoin.

BLOCKCHAIN IN HEALTHCARE APPLICATION

Blockchain in healthcare applications requires a strong security and protection component for elevated-level verification, interoperability and clinical records sharing to consent to the exacting legitimate prerequisites of the Health Insurance Portability and Accountability Act of 1996. Blockchain innovation in the medicinal services industry has gotten extensive exploration consideration as of late. This examination directs an audit to generously break down and map the exploration scene of current advances, essentially the utilization of blockchain in social insurance applications, into an intelligible scientific classification. Blockchain in medicinal services application is partitioned into three classifications. The main class that endeavored to create and plan human services applications coordinating blockchain, especially those on new engineering, framework structures, system, scheme, model, stage, approach, convention and calculation. The subsequent classification incorporates considers that endeavored to assess and investigate the appropriation of blockchain in the human services framework. At long last, the third class is identified with the combination of blockchain into social insurance applications. Moreover, this investigation gives recognized inspirations, open difficulties and suggestions on the utilization of blockchain in social insurance applications. In like manner, scientists and designers are given engaging chances to additionally create decentralized medicinal services applications through a far-reaching conversation of about the significance of blockchain and its joining into different human services applications.

BLOCKCHAIN-BASED SECURITY SOLUTION FOR REMOTE PATIENT-MONITORING SYSTEM

Most countries face a dramatic rise in the number of medical patients, and access to primary doctors or caregivers is becoming more difficult for patients. The growth of IoT and wearable devices in recent years has increased the quality of patient care through remote patient monitoring (RPM). This also allows the doctors to handle more patients. RPM provides monitoring and treatment for patients outside the

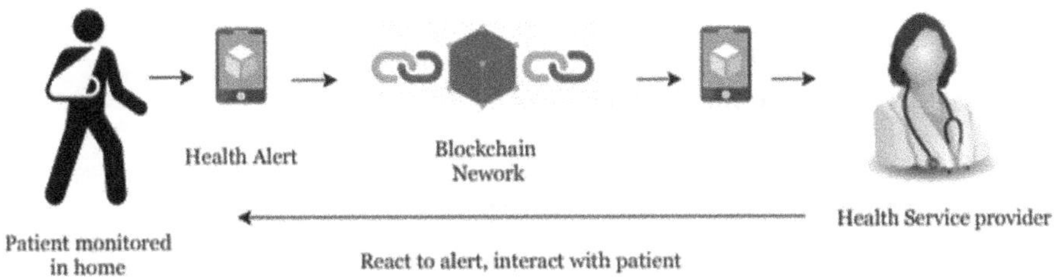

FIGURE 2.5 Remote patient monitoring.

traditional clinical setting (for example, at home). First, it allows for an inherent ease of service for patients. Patients can remain linked to healthcare providers as required. This also decreases medical costs and increases the quality of care. That's the key reason healthcare professionals are finding ways to bring RPM to the public.

A specially built monitoring tool for tracking and transmitting sensors, used to collect health data on smart contracts, may be the key component of an RPM network, a smartphone with internet access and an RPM framework (Figure 2.5). In RPM and in the current drive to build Smart Cities, wearable devices and IoT play an important part. Wearable apps gather health data from patients and send it to hospitals or medical facilities to enable health surveillance, diagnosis of diseases and care. By doing so, we see the creation of a big data situation through the review and transfer of all the patient data.

Sectors, such infrastructure, demand secure data sharing. Health data is highly private and sharing of data may raise the risk of exposure. Furthermore, the current system of data sharing uses a centralized architecture, which requires centralized trust.

One of the aspects of the IoT is the system of wearable gadgets, implanted with programming, hardware, sensors, actuators and network, which empowers the wearable gadget to associate and trade information (Figure 2.6). In a modern shrewd city, we won't just observe these wearable gadgets communicating medicinal services information, yet it is sensible to expect that wearable gadgets can share lot of information as we interconnect these gadgets. Consequently, the range of the thoughts introduced here in regards to wearable social insurance gadgets and utilizing blockchain innovation are further coming to than we show or can envision here. To deal with such patient information with different organizations, such foundation

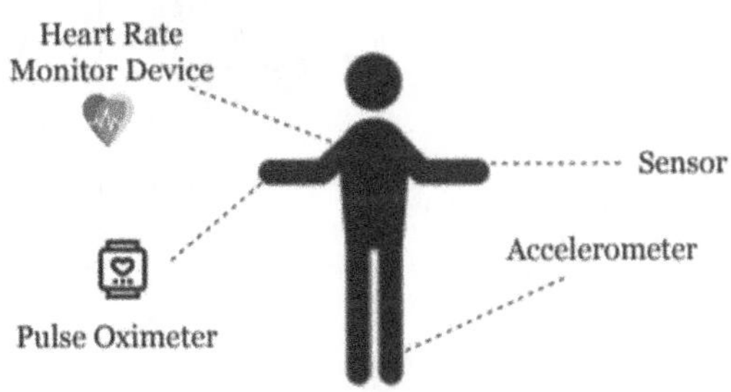

FIGURE 2.6 Wearable devices for the patient.

TABLE 2.1
Structure of the Blockchain

Field	Size
Magic number	4 bytes
Block size	4 bytes
Header: Next 80 bytes	
Version	4 bytes
Previous block hash	32 bytes
Merkle root	4 bytes
Difficulty target	4 bytes
None	4 bytes
Rest of Blockchain	
Transaction counter	Variable: 1–9 bytes
Transaction list	Depends on the transaction size: upto 1 MB

requests secure information sharing. Well-being information is profoundly private and sharing of information may raise the danger of introduction. Besides, the current arrangement of information sharing uses a brought-together engineering that requires incorporated trust.

The solution for data privacy and security could and should very well be blockchain technology. Blockchain technology provides the robustness against failure and data exposure. The blockchain is a shared data structure responsible for storing all transactional history. The blocks relate to each other in the form of a chain. The first block of the chain is known as genesis. Each block consists of a Block Header, Transaction Counter and Transaction. It acts as a decentralized architecture to record the data. The structure of blockchain is summarized in Table 2.1

Today the mHealth program is becoming increasingly famous all over the world. mHealth has many inevitable advantages as opposed to paper jobs. Many health programs can be used in the whole healthcare cycle. It is a Layered architecture of proposed mHealth system as shown in figure 2.7. The mHealth has been one of the ways

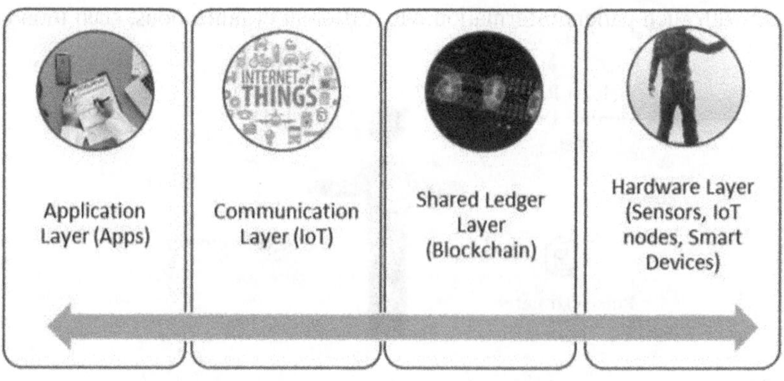

FIGURE 2.7 Layered architecture of proposed mHealth system.

that could be strengthened to provide both immediate medical assistance and healthcare facilities. mHealth allows early diagnosis of diseases and prompt medical treatment in emergency conditions resulting in providing proper treatment of the patients.

The use of sensors to track and relay patient vital signs is helpful in recognizing patients at risk. Blockchains are one of the latest technologies and one of the biggest developments in recent years that have taken the planet by storm. Blockchains are nothing more than a shared ledger that keeps transactions and event information running around the network. The most important feature in a blockchain is that once a bit of information is added to the shared database, no one can alter it, and the essence is completely protected. Any data stored on the ledger is basically fully secure. It is mandatory to make any modifications for all subsequent blocks after that one in the exchange for anyone to make the change to a block.

The IoT has become both a common and a new phenomenon providing internet connectivity using sensors for smart identity proof as well as management in such a complex communication situation. This evolving feature will allow for new interaction routes among disabled patients as well as care facilities that innovative network security interfaces with an independent living viewpoint. mHealth identified "wireless technology, health tools and advances in telecommunications for healthcare". Such a technological concept offers accessibility and usability for public health apps that are still connected.

The data has become a central structure obstruct for medicinal services. Computerization of well-being information has created incredible open doors as far as information transmission, persistent administration and investigation. The well-being data has been growing exponentially, with perpetual stages delivering data, including inside well-being associations. Data security is a developing test. Number of researchers are using blockchain innovation at the framework building layer, being appropriated naturally, going about as a distributed stage intended to associate the different substances, comparing to the numerous administrations or organizations that can store, create as well as alter mHealth data. End points in the framework synchronize with one another by following a lot of rules:

1. At whatever point a gadget creates another square, such a square would be sent to the system.
2. On the off chance that a hub participates in the system to another companion; at that point, the current square will be questioned.
3. At the point when a gadget finds a square with a higher order than the last recognized square, it either adds the square to its current blockchains or requests that another gadget gets the total blockchains.

Blockchains could be utilized to develop another system to improve mHealth administrations security. Blockchains must be utilized in a few circumstances: if there are a few members, further trust is required, there's a requirement for reliable checking activity and data needs to have been steady all through time span. The mHealth is experiencing a blast in data due to the universal wearables (for example, practice trackers), wellness tracking applications (for example, weight reduction observing) or ecological bolstered living stages. Framework for the complete healthcare system is displayed in figure 2.8.

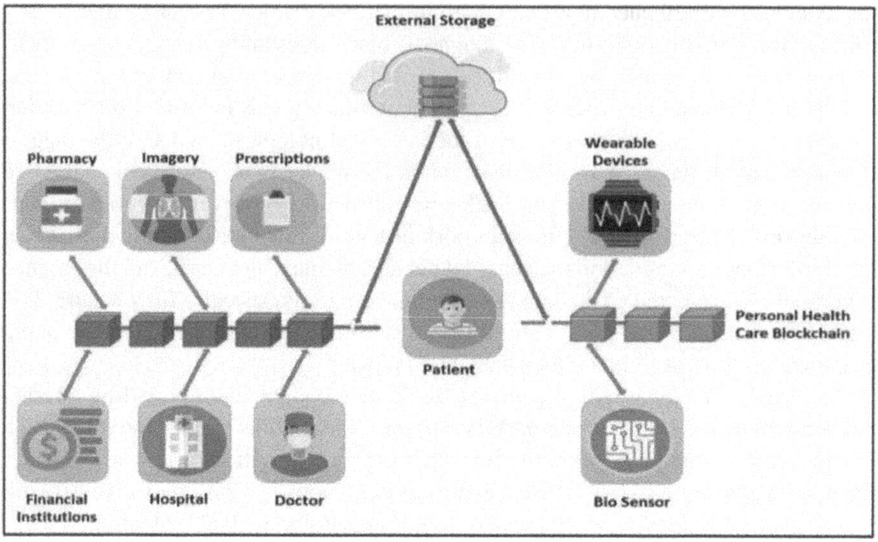

FIGURE 2.8 Framework for the complete healthcare system.

The amalgamation of the IoT, blockchain and machine learning for finding inconsistency in the conduct of the well-being information of the patient is the outside layer of the total system. The technique exhibited is fundamentally a framework that requests the utilization of the IoT module to block and get the information that is being created by the wearable gadgets worn by the patient. The Blockchain framework is ideally used for putting away what's more, keeping up the information of the patients as numerous exchanges and furthermore bolster get to control to the various partners separately. Besides, the Blockchain engineering is likewise utilized for supporting the clinical exploration by keeping up the pseudo-secrecy of the patient's recognizable proof and to give confirmed and confided in information to a more exact examination. The Machine Learning model is utilized essentially for the discovery of inconsistencies and to gauge certain situations that may emerge in the proper way of time by breaking down the information dependent on the boundaries that are passed on by the doctors for fundamental distinguishing proof of the conditions that are looked for by the patients.

The IoT module manages the way toward bringing and detecting the information from the wearable gadgets and the biosensors that are either worn by the patients or that are available in the earth in which patients are checked. In a more perspicuous manner, if a patient is experiencing some gentle treatment and catching up with some clinical tests, at that point a wearable sensor is a prime course of observing the information of every single second the patient is producing. The data that can be viewed as dependent on the wearable worn by the patient is heart rate, calorie release, breath strengthening and sleep stage monitoring. Additionally, if circulatory strain estimating sensors are utilized and furthermore on the off chance that pacemakers are embedded on the patient, at that point, such information can likewise be distantly detected utilizing the IoT application module. Presently, on the off chance that the patient is out of commission or is admitted to the emergency clinic, at that point, there is a monstrous necessity that the IoT sensors or the biosensors are to be put whereupon they can understand the natural conditions and take activities dependent on the circumstance.

Exchange and Access

Limitlessly dispersed and heterogeneous attributes attending with IoT assets and systems are referred to cause issues, for example, interoperability and item revelation. Along these lines, semantic information demonstrating is utilized to determine these issues, by improving tasks like separating, looking and information accumulation. Furthermore, they are credited with enhancing the information portrayals for IoT questions and give a rule to developing new IoT frameworks. In any case, the vast majority of these models can't give great deduction and proficient interoperability. Then, as illustrated prior, semantic web ontologies have kept on turning out to be significant instruments for taking care of the interoperability issues, particularly when a few frameworks that utilize different information portrayals and dialects collaborate with one another. Moreover, ontologies advance the data model, give semantic expansion, improve expressiveness to the data and address the referred to shortcomings of the information models [12, 16]. Subsequently, ontologies can likewise furnish a decent formalization language with intelligent derivation capacity to help data trade between various degrees of deliberation and between applications that are a significant objective of IoT frameworks.

As represented in Figure 2.9, cosmology-based models are appropriate for complex ideas and relationship articulation. Ontologies are answerable for making vows in form of psychological connections, which involves utilization of a jargon in manners predictable to various areas of uses [9, 14, 15]. In their commitment on the theme, Biryukov et al. [15], introduced center difficulties for building

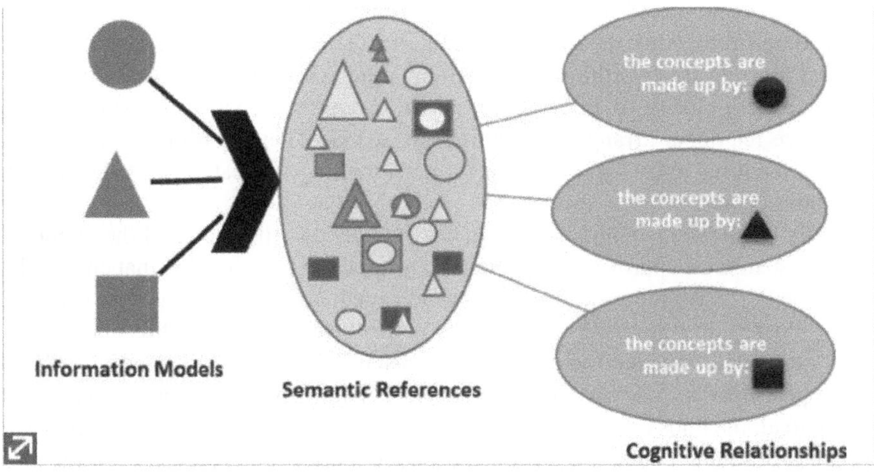

FIGURE 2.9 Concept of ontology IoHT.

applications that will oversee and deal with IoT assets (scale, profound heterogeneity, obscure geography, off base or fragmented information and one of the three IoT layers and contains three ontologies: gadget cosmology (for example, gadget depiction vault through physical layer), space metaphysics (which models information about physical ideas and their relations through data layer) and an estimation philosophy (which covers the data about assorted estimation models, including "credulous Bayesian learning, Kalman channel", conditions and administrations that determine and execute them). At long last, these ontologies are demonstrated to give interoperability and adaptability and to depict the ontologies all the more accurately.

CONCEPT OF ONTOLOGY-BASED IoHT

In a firmly related exertion, in Ref. [9], Foroglou proposed an IoT index framework (IoT-DS) that incorporates the semantic depiction, revelation and coordination of IoT things/objects. Tasks, for example, changing, including and expelling semantic realities and catching items and their connections to develop and accommodate philosophy are basic prerequisites for Semantic Data Platforms (SDP) [14]. Consequently, in that review, Semantic IoT Framework was based on SDP to encourage revelatory truth arranged way to deal with model where they are executed. Their proposed semantic IoT system comprises an occasion administrator, just as information preparing and scientific motors empower customers' appraisal of information to make changes when required.

There are additionally other philosophy considers concentrated on semantic information displaying, for example, in Refs. [20] and [21]. In Ref. [20], the creators used Semantic Information Broker (SIB) for applications on restricted registering situations and in that introduced a SIB structure for shrewd spaces dependent on the M3 engineering (for example, multi-gadget, multivendor and multi-area). This structure was promoted to help operator communication in savvy spaces by sharing and self-producing data and its semantics. This measured methodology was applied for high trustworthiness, extensibility and compactness. Essentially, utilizing semantic middleware, in Ref. [21], Cassar et al. presented a crossbreed semantic assistance relational arranger for outline IoT works. They coordinated probabilistic matchmaking with legitimate mark matchmaking to beat issues related with semantic synonymy.

At the point when another exchange is to be added to the chain, all the members in the system must approve it. They do this by applying a calculation that checks the exchange. Be that as it may, what is comprehended as "legitimate" is characterized by the blockchain framework and can vary between frameworks. In this manner, the ability to concur whether the exchange is substantial is chosen by a dominant part of the participants. A set of affirmed exchanges is then packaged into a square that is sent to all the hubs on the system. They, thus, approve the new square, where each progressive square contains a hash, which is a remarkable unique mark, of the past square.

CONCLUSION

The world in the present day has proceeded onward to the skirt where worldwide availability and synchronization is the essential thing that everybody is looking for. Likewise, the current situation of individuals around the globe has indicated an adjustment as far as the way of life and a bustling timetable along these lines; it has consistently been seen that individuals will in general disregard minor variations from the norm with respect to the well-being. The suggested system updates the concept of collecting knowledge far from the wearable devices and biosensors of the patient, if any, to provide them with comfortable and adequate assistance. With much thought to the accuracy, security and realness of the information produced from the patients, there has consistently been a prerequisite that the information must be constantly administered in an appropriate manner. Hence, to get to the executives and the capacity of the information to deal with the exchanges, we will study, in general propose, the idea of blockchain, which is a consortium of different partners, for example, hospital, doctors, pharmacy, pathology, imaging centers, medical research centers and insurance companies. In this manner, such frameworks can be considered a critical entire in inspiring the general public with precise and proficient human services.

REFERENCES

1. Bahga, A. and V.K. Madisetti. "Blockchain platform for industrial internet of things." *Journal of Software Engineering and Applications* 9 (2016): 533–546.
2. Bahga, A. and V. Madisetti. Internet of Things: A Hands-On Approach. Atlanta, GA: VPT/Create Space Inc., 2014.
3. The Blockchain Imperative: The Next Challenge for P&C Carriers, Cognizant white paper, November 2016. https://www.cognizant.com/whitepapers/the-blockchain-imperative-the-next-challenge-for-p-and-c-carriers-codex2360.pdf.
4. https://arxiv.org/ftp/arxiv/papers/1806/1806.03693.pdf.
5. www.edureka.co › blog › iot-tutorial.
6. Nakamoto, S. "Bitcoin: A peer-to-peer electronic cash system," 2008. [Online]. Available: http://bitcoin.org/bitcoin.pdf.
7. Jakobsson, M. and A. Juels. "Proofs of work and bread pudding protocols," in Secure Information Networks. Cham, Switzerland: Springer, 2015, pp. 258–272. [Online]. Available: https://link.springer.com/content/pdf/10.1007/978-0-387-35568-9_18.pdf.
8. Peters, G. W., E. Panayi, and A. Chapelle, "Trends in crypto-currencies and blockchain technologies: A monetary theory and regulation perspective," 2015. [Online]. Available: http://dx.doi.org/10.2139/ssrn. 2646618 563.
9. Foroglou, G. and A.-L. Tsilidou. "Further applications of the blockchain," 2015.
10. Kosba, A., A. Miller, E. Shi, Z. Wen, and C. Papamanthou. "Hawk: The blockchain model of cryptography and privacy-preserving smart contracts," in Proceedings of IEEE Symposium on Security and Privacy (SP), San Jose, CA, USA, 2016, pp. 839–858.
11. Akins, B. W., J. L. Chapman, and J. M. Gordon. "A whole new world: Income tax considerations of the bitcoin economy," 2013. [Online]. Available: https://ssrn.com/abstract=2394738.
12. Zhang, Y. and J. Wen. "An IoT electric business model based on the protocol of bitcoin," in Proceedings of 18th International Conference on Intelligence in Next Generation Networks (ICIN), Paris, France, 2015, pp. 184–191.

13. Sharples, M. and J. Domingue. “The blockchain and kudos: A distributed system for educational record, reputation and reward,” in Proceedings of 11th European Conference on Technology Enhanced Learning (EC-TEL 2015), Lyon, France, 2015, pp. 490–496.
14. Noyes, C. “Bitav: Fast anti-malware by distributed blockchain consensus and feedforward scanning,” arXiv preprint arXiv:1601.01405, 2016.
15. Biryukov, A., D. Khovratovich, and I. Pustogarov, “Deanonymisation of clients in bitcoin p2p network,” in Proceedings of the 2014 ACM SIGSAC Conference on Computer and Communications Security, New York, NY, USA, 2014, pp. 15–29.
16. Tschorsch, F. and B. Scheuermann, “Bitcoin and beyond: A technical survey on decentralized digital currencies.” *IEEE Communications Surveys Tutorials* 18.3 (2016): 2084–2123.
17. Hussien, Hassan Mansur, et al. “A systematic review for enabling of develop a blockchain technology in healthcare application: Taxonomy, substantially analysis, motivations, challenges, recommendations and future direction.” *Journal of medical systems* 43.10 (2019): 320.
18. Dwivedi, Ashutosh Dhar, et al. “A decentralized privacy-preserving healthcare blockchain for IoT.” *Sensors* 19.2 (2019): 326.
19. Alam, Tanweer. “mHealth Communication Framework using blockchain and IoT Technologies.” *International Journal of Scientific & Technology Research* 9.6 (2020).
20. Chakraborty, Sabyasachi, Satyabrata Aich, and Hee-Cheol Kim. “A secure healthcare system design framework using blockchain technology.” 2019 21st International Conference on Advanced Communication Technology (ICACT), IEEE, 2019.
21. Abou-Nassar, Eman M., et al. “DITrust chain: Towards blockchain-based trust models for sustainable healthcare IoT systems.” *IEEE Access* 8 (2020): 111223–111238.

3 Blockchain to Secure IoT Data

M. Vivek Anand and S. Vijayalakshmi

CONTENTS

Introduction..44
IoT Applications..45
Medical and Emergency..45
Smart City and Smart Home..46
Smart Supply Chain..46
IoT in Agriculture..46
Smart Metering..47
Other Applications..47
IoT Security Challenges..47
Increase in Number of IoT Devices..47
Infrequent Updates..47
Weak Default Passwords..47
Lack of Encryption..48
Inefficient Threat Detection Methods..48
The Rise of Botnets..48
Phishing Attacks..48
Small-Scale Attacks..48
User Privacy..49
IoT Financial-Related Breaches..49
Security Attacks..49
Physical Device Attacks..49
Software Attacks..49
Network Attacks..49
Encryption Attacks..50
Security Awareness on the Internet of Things..50
Blockchain..51
Bitcoin..52
Features of Blockchain..53
Decentralization..53
P2P Exchanges..53
Payment System..53
Distributed System..53
Micro Transaction..54
Data Transparency..54

DOI: 10.1201/9781003094210-3

Anonymity 54
Cryptography 54
Consensus 55
No Transaction Fees 55
Blockchain Working Principle 55
Miners 56
Hashing 56
Properties of Hashing 57
Merkle Tree 58
Genesis Block 58
Proof of Work vs Proof of Stake 59
Difference Between POW&POS 59
Blockchain and IoT Security 60
BIoT 61
Conclusion 62
References 63

INTRODUCTION

Internet of things (IoT) is a future-generation technology that can impact on its every application specifically for the entire business domain and can be taken as the connection of smart devices and objects through the Internet with well-defined infrastructure to produce more benefits. According to some predetermined estimates, the application of the IoT is extending for various applications, including security, services, logistics, smart cities, traffic congestion, emergency, healthcare, industrial sector, and waste management. IoT devices are not only connected to the Internet, but also each device is sharing the data between the devices in applications through the Internet. M2M is a machine-to-machine communication without human intervention. IoT devices can carry the information that is readily available before accessing the device.

The IoT is involving day-to-day applications and it's everywhere right now. IoT is steadily growing in its way and showing its potential in its applications. It can grow steadily in the market for a new invention of IoT devices. IoT technology is providing a good impact on the manufacturing and production of new IoT devices by maintaining the standards in productions by applying various topologies, and it has been around for some time; IoT is steadily growing with its popularity and it becomes one of the most ubiquitous technologies in our emerging world. Day by day, the connecting devices are increasing and electronics stores are getting filled with smart IoT devices as the way the technology is emerging in the world. Many of our needs will be streamlined by IoT technology in the future.

The IoT offers appropriate solutions for various applications, including the industrial sector, traffic congestion, security, emergency services, waste management, logistics, smart cities, and healthcare. The rise in the elderly population, the increasing cost of healthcare, and the occurrence of chronic diseases everywhere in the world straightaway demand the transformation of healthcare from a hospital-based system to a person-based environment by focusing on people syndrome management. A wide range of wearable and implantable devices has been developed to prolong the capabilities of IoT devices in the context of the human body and behaviour sensing. IoT healthcare system acted as a platform between local and public WIBSN (Wearable and Implanted Body Sensor Network) with specific needs. The practices of IoT in healthcare have widely increased across various specific areas like monitor patient care, maintain vital equipment, track equipment usage, and monitor medical assets.

The IoT is a network of connected devices with an embedded system allowing to sensing, reporting, and controlling remote devices. The idea of IoT affords a conceptual framework for connecting edge computing devices such as wearable sensors and smart devices for seamless interactions. Wearable IoT (WIoT) referred to as a technological infrastructure uses wearable health sensors to facilitate monitoring human factors such as wellness, health, behaviour, and other chronic data beneficial in enriching individuals' day-to-day quality of life. WIoT targets at connecting body-worn sensor devices to the medical domain such that physicians can supervise the health condition of their patients remotely. The sensor nodes are normally lightweight, easy to deploy and maintain, inexpensive, but the functionalities are limited by resources. However, smart wearable development poses challenges regarding less energy consumption and data security.

IoT APPLICATIONS

Medical and Emergency

The impact of IoT in the medical and emergency field is quite efficient. To monitor the patient health status, IoT is performing a major role to find the health status via any device with sensors accessing the temperature or the changes in the patient's body will inform the patient status to the hospital through the Internet. If the patient is requiring any medical emergency that can be given to the patient by monitoring at a remote place, a doctor can be aware of the patient's status and actions can be performed such as sending an ambulance and make ready for treatment tools and medicines. Devices available in patients' homes provide information about the history of their disease and necessary action can be taken for the same. The patient can have a smartwatch as a wearable device that indicating their status of the disease. The wearable device will find the heartbeat of the patient and automatically it will send the emergency call to the hospital to send the ambulance to the patient's living location. In this case, the patient can save their life and will get treatment very soon. The doctor will be ready for any treatment to be done for the patient by carrying the tools for the treatment. The doctor can minimize their time in monitoring the health status of the patient and they can check many patient statuses at the same time. Emergencies such as accidents are happening every day and saving the life of the human being is very essential while facing accidents. In such cases, IoT devices can trigger the emergency as an alarm to nearby devices or the nearby hospital by connecting any medium such as Bluetooth and WiFi. if there is any doctor or any medical person who can do the first aid to the patient.

Smart City and Smart Home

In a smart home, all the devices are connected with each other and communicating between them as per the user request and to reduce the human effort. The devices can be connected to the Internet in our home to communicate in-between to monitor the status of each device. Sensors can be used to detect the room temperature and adjust the temperature automatically for an air conditioner. The gas valve can be switched off through an IoT-connecting device from a remote place. The music system will play the music by finding the person who is standing near to our home and can calculate the blood pressure of the human by wearable devices. Electrical lights can be connected to the human temperature sensor and whenever we enter the room then it will blow the light that will help reduce the electricity wastages. The mobile phone can be connected to the fridge and we can see the things available in the fridge through the mobile phone.

In a smart city real, time problems will be resolved through the connected IoT devices in such a scenario of traffic. A device in a vehicle can detect the traffic of a place and that can pass the information to other devices which are inserted in other vehicles so that other device can change the root of the way and can reach the destination without any trouble. In other cases, the device available on the road will detect the traffic and it will pass the information to other vehicles to choose the different path to reach the destination.

Smart Supply Chain

The supply chain is a process from manufacturing to the delivery of the product. Current challenges in the supply chain are delivering the product safely to the customer by monitoring all the levels of the supply chain such as the supply of raw material, manufacturing, packaging, transporting, storing, delivering, and maintaining the goods. Every process in the supply chain is required to be monitored to complete the process on time. In such cases, IoT devices are performing a major role in monitoring every process, and communication between the devices is occurring to pass the data in each process. Transparency is assured in each phase of the supply chain with the help of the IoT devices.

IoT in Agriculture

The demand for food is raised due to the population increasing day by day. Farmers are turning to use new technology to increase production for the needs of the people. The government is also enhancing focus on technology to be used in the agricultural field to increase the production of food. IoT devices that are connected at the farm will detect every status of the crops and pass the information to the farmer to act upon the status of the crop. Farmers have good monitoring over the plant or crops and can take necessary action towards the growth of the plant. IoT devices are reducing the time for the farmers to keep on monitoring the same and give a better yield on investment. Different sensors can be used to sense the water usage for plant growth, soil moisture, and determine the amount of fertilizer the crop needs.

Smart Metering

IoT devices are residing in the home to find the reading in the energy meter and send the data to the electricity board to calculate the electricity bills. In this scenario, the human presence is not required to register the meter reading.

Other Applications

A device can be integrated with a vehicle to monitor the speed, fuel, and service date. In this scenario, IoT will provide information to the mechanic to be ready with their tools to service the vehicle at the right time. The IoT is collaborated with artificial intelligence in automatic car driver applications where the car is predicting everything to drive safely and reach the destination on time.

IoT SECURITY CHALLENGES

Increase in Number of IoT Devices

A few years before, security professionals focused on mobile devices, computers, and servers. But today, security professionals also have the responsibility to protect IoT devices due to the increase of IoT devices in the manufacturing industry. The increase in the devices estimated to reach 20 billion by 2020. Manufacturing of new IoT devices without vulnerability is essential than protecting from threats. The vulnerability is based on the topology, protocol, and medium, in which the data is transferred from IoT devices.

Infrequent Updates

The security of the IoT devices is assured by the security tools updated with modern security standards. If the systems are not updated to the modern security standards, it will lead to the misuse of data or tamper of data. Tampering of data in some crucial IoT applications will be a big problem to face the scenario. Cost for updating security tools is a burden for small-scale industries to ensure security.

Weak Default Passwords

The password which is appearing as a default in some devices is vulnerable to an attack. The attackers can get the credential by guessing the weak passwords. The passwords need to be changed at first but many of the users are not changing their default password. A brute-force attack can be able to find the default password by trying out all the possible combinations of inputs. Nowadays, the users have the direct authority to set the password for the devices without any default password to avoid the attacks from threats.

Lack of Encryption

Encryption is a process of changing the plain text into the ciphertext while transferring the data from the sender to the receiver. Plain text is the original message, and the ciphertext is a modified format of plain text. Ciphertext can be achieved by applying the encryption algorithm on the plain text. The plain text is changed into ciphertext at the sender side, and ciphertext is changed to plain text at the receiver side. It is very difficult to crack the original messages from the encrypted messages. Encryption provides the best way to protect data but some of the devices are not having processing capability. Inefficient algorithms can be easily hacked by the attackers in efficient systems.

Inefficient Threat Detection Methods

The enterprises are practicing various methods for detecting data threats such as monitoring user activity in log details, spotting common indicators, and other security protocols which are not able to detect the threats. Normal threat detection methods are not reliable for the variety of IoT devices with heterogeneous network connectivity, which makes the complexities for detecting the threats.

The Rise of Botnets

Botnets are increasing the way as the IoT is increasing in numbers. Many organizations are not capable to control the botnets to avoid the security breaches in their systems. Botnets can exist in the IoT systems, and that can control the systems remotely for unauthorized access. The enterprises may allow the botnets without any knowledge due to a lack of security solutions.

Phishing Attacks

Phishing is an attack used in IoT devices in which the hackers may send an unwanted signal to the devices that makes complications in the network. Even though phishing is a common security attack in the IoT environment, many firms fail to protect the network from phishing attacks.

Small-Scale Attacks

Most of the security professionals are focusing on larger attacks, but they are missed to see the small-scale problems. Small-scale attacks are emerging day by day and it is making a serious problem in IoT. Small-scale problems are not getting importance from security professionals but that is making a big impact on the security breaches.

User Privacy

The employees or the workers of the organization are using the IoT devices provided by their employers. The employer has to protect the data breaching from their workers or outside users. In this scenario, the worker may not be aware of the external users and their strategy of stealing the data. The employer has to take necessary action for the data breach, otherwise, it will make a severe problem in the network and private data will be compromised. The privacy of the data should be maintained with some security measures by the employers of the organization.

IoT Financial-Related Breaches

The possibility of stealing the user credential is when the IoT devices are involved in electronic payments. Even though IoT payment systems provide a fast and efficient way of transaction, but the vulnerability of IoT can lead to the breaching of confidential data for the financial applications. Not every organization is looking for a solution to the data breach. The users of IoT are also not aware of the vulnerability of the payment systems for their financial usage.

SECURITY ATTACKS

The privacy, security, authentication, and authorization are remaining foundational issues in IoT deployments. IoT is storing a large amount of data that must be collected, transferred, and delivered in a secure tunnel to all the users in the IoT environment. The attacks on IoT devices are in different forms such as tampering the data or revealing the confidential data in a common platform, denial of service attack. The following attacks are the common attacks that take place in the IoT environment.

Physical Device Attacks

The vulnerable physical devices can be attacked by the hacker for getting the credential with unauthorized access. Different methods can be used to get the credential such as key logger software running on the machine to read all the confidential passwords; confidential data of the user can be retrieved by applying phishing websites.

Software Attacks

The viruses and worms can be included in the network or device, which will employ malicious activities, causing a security breach. The viruses keep on replicating wherever they are residing and propagating to other parts of the system. Logic bombs can be included to destroy the data in IoT devices.

Network Attacks

The denial of service attacks to the IoT devices are attacks where the end devices are not able to communicate with the server, and they will remain idle if they do not get any commands from the servers. The wireless vulnerability exploits to make the device inability to contact other devices in the network connection.

Encryption Attacks

Password hacking with the brute-force password cracking method is not an easy task but the hackers are taking that in their hand for crucial application where they have a motive to crack the password. Man in the middle attack is also possible to steal the data in between the two IoT devices and masquerade the messages between the devices. There is no standard authority for connectivity requirements that is vulnerable to many types of threats to attack the devices and breach the security. Unsecured devices are the reason for an attack to happen in the IoT environment. Heterogeneous IoT networks with heterogeneous communication protocols will make the problem very severe.

SECURITY AWARENESS ON THE INTERNET OF THINGS

The attacks can happen if we did not have the security awareness on IoT. The vulnerability matrix should be defined for the IoT environment to prevent the devices from the attacks. IoT is depending on the client-server architecture, which may cause a problem to the IoT application if the server gets corrupted or down. IoT environment majorly depends on centralized servers and trusting a third party again is questionable for privacy and security. The central servers are requiring transaction fees to ensure the transaction in such financial applications. Instead of depending on a trusted third-party server for the IoT applications, distributed peer-to-peer (P2P) network is required.

In a few years, the physical world is going to be interconnected with smart devices. It is very difficult to manage IoT devices without essential security measures. Many of the security breaches happening day by day such as hackers can able to disable cars remotely, managed to control implanted cardiac devices, perform DDoS attacks. IoT is a large environment where the failure of the device to work without security will affect the entire network. The day-to-day activities performed by IoT, for example, smart home devices, have access to send the data between each device about our daily lives and routines. Most of the attacks are happening because of a lack of centralized control over these applications. A total of 60% of respondents are having a third-party risk management program, but only 29% actively monitor the risk of IoT devices used by third parties. Some organizations are actively monitoring for IoT device risks within their workplace and third-party IoT device risks.

Nowadays, various complex software running the systems have errors that make them very vulnerable and easy for the hackers to compromise the system. Security analysts identify and fix vulnerabilities before they lead to a problem. The security analyst teams find out about vulnerabilities that can cause malicious activity, perform program updates. The organization's software programs have to be updated periodically and can be downloaded and even installed automatically by their manufacturers. The action against the malware requires enormous investment.

Manual respondent to all the problems is not good for a security analyst. 24/7 support is needed for IoT applications that are involving in the real-world scenario. It requires cyberthreat intelligence to respond to the cyberattacks and their vulnerabilities.

IoT majorly relies on three architectural styles. First, the client-server architecture where the client requests to the server and server replies to the client's request. Second, the cloud architecture where the application itself running on the Internet and the data will be stored in a cloud server. Third, fog architecture where control and data plane are separated. Even though IoT is adapted to these architecture styles such as client-servers, cloud computing, and fog computing, the security of the data is breached by the intruders when it is connected to the Internet. The new architecture has to be proposed to secure the data in IoT. To secure the data of IoT, the suggestion from the researchers and scientists is to go for blockchain. Nowadays, IoT is not only the technology emerging, but blockchain is also giving a good impact on financial applications. Blockchain is successfully executed in cryptocurrencies such as bitcoins. Even though many problems occur at cryptocurrencies, but it is not impacting on the blockchain. The combination of blockchain and IoT would be the best solution to secure the data in the IoT environment. It is impossible to crack the security of the blockchain by hackers. Blockchain is maintaining security protocols in its implementation and nobody can breach the system. The robust encryption standards are available to protect the data in the blockchain. Tampering of data is impossible and there is no centralized server to rely on the service. A centralized system is not ensuring security because it is not maintaining the security standards on the services. The single point failure is not affecting the environment while we are using blockchain.

BLOCKCHAIN

Blockchain is a distributed, decentralized, P2P, shared, transparent ledger [1], in which the data is transparent to all and secure by its implementation procedures. The data which is stored in blockchain will be visible to all the nodes in the network. Blockchain technology is coined by a person called "Satoshi Nakamoto" and he published his concept in white paper "Peer to Peer Electronic Cash System". This paper published to avoid the problem of double-spending in digital money. Blockchain is first implemented in the application called bitcoin. P2P transaction is happening in blockchain network without any third party to verify the transaction. The special property of the blockchain is the data stored in the blockchain cannot tamper. In bitcoin, transactions are done between the peers without any third party, and every node is responsible for the transaction that is happened in blockchain because every transaction data is available to all the peers. The transaction cannot be reverted once it is done.

Tampering of data in the blockchain is highly impossible because it has to be approved by more than 50% of the network. Blockchain is cryptographically secure because it uses asymmetric cryptography where the public keys are used for sending and private keys for receiving. Blockchain is showing its security feature by its hashing technique. Hashing is a technique to produce a fixed length of output for a variable length of the input. SHA256 is a hashing algorithm where any form of input will be given a hash code of 256 alphanumeric values as an output. In bitcoin blockchain, each block consists of many transactions and each transaction details will be generated with hash code. All the hash value of each data is hashed as a root hash for a block. Root hash is the hash generated for a current block and it will be mapped with the previous block to make the chain as a blockchain. In a blockchain network, some of the peers will be called as a miner who verifies the data and wraps and adds into the blockchain network as a block. A block will consist of the current hash and the previous hash of the block. Tampering of data in a blockchain is impossible; it affects the hash of the block and it will affect the mapping of the previous hash, which will make an entire blockchain invalid in a single peer which tries to make changes in the data. The specialty of the hashing is that we cannot get the hash value for different inputs, and also it cannot be reverted. Blockchain can be used to protect the data from breaching and it is providing a safe environment to store the data. Blockchain which is successfully implemented in the first cryptocurrency is called bitcoins.

BITCOIN

The bitcoin blockchain is considered robust and secure because of the consensus method. In the consensus models, the participants do not require any authentication to join the network. The design of the bitcoin is open to all in the blockchain network and nobody can control it. Bitcoin provides a cryptographically secure environment over the network. Bitcoin is denoted in BTC. Since it is deployed, it attracted more people and it reaches 375,000 numbers of confirmed transactions per day in December 2017. It provides theft resistance, anonymity, no third-party influence, transparency, no taxes, and lower transaction fees. Bitcoin is the first cryptocurrency that is working with the blockchain network. The bitcoin blockchain is a distributed ledger that has all the transaction details. The cryptocurrency network is doing transactions without a third party, such as banks. Bitcoin was coined by Satoshi Nakamoto and he is the first man who entered into the blockchain network. A banking transaction bank will act as a trusted third party and it governs all the transactions over the network. The dependency of a trusted third party is essential for bank transactions. In the case of a bank robbery or a bank database hacking, it will lead to an uncontrollable situation. To avoid the third-party trust, cryptocurrencies came into the existence. Bitcoin is a cryptocurrency working on the concept of blockchain. The blockchain is a new era in which all transactions are treated as a chain of blocks and if the transaction has to be performed that will be added into the blockchain network. In blockchain, all transactions are stored in a public ledger and it is available to all the users.

In blockchain, the network nodes communicate without relying on a third party. Bitcoin transactions can be done through bitcoin wallets. Bitcoin wallets are available in the form of desktop wallets, web wallets, mobile wallets, hardware wallets, etc. Installation of bitcoin wallets will provide the service for transactions; in every transaction, the user can generate the public key as a transaction address. The public key can be distributed to the users in the blockchain network to send bitcoins to the corresponding public key. The private key is used for accessing their account to receive the bitcoins or send bitcoins. The private key provides anonymity over the network and the blockchain is having only the transaction address instead of a name.

FEATURES OF BLOCKCHAIN

Features of blockchain have to be reviewed thoroughly before implementing the blockchain into IoT environment.

DECENTRALIZATION

Blockchain is a decentralized network where every node is responsible for safeguarding its data. Transactions are not performed through architecture such as banks and agencies. Control of the network is divided into all the peers. Peers are distributed among the network where all the data are stored in a public ledger. Tampering of data is highly impossible because that to be approved by most of the nodes from the network. IoT also requires decentralization to avoid the maintenance and updates of the centralized servers.

P2P EXCHANGES

The network is formed by the P2P network where every node is having a connection with all nodes in the network. IoT also requires connectivity with each node and passing information through gateways.

PAYMENT SYSTEM

The transaction is performed without third-party assistance such as banks and agency. No transaction fees will be paid for the transaction. Transactions are carried out by the miners. Miners will collect all the transactions, verify the correctness of the transaction, and finally, some of the transactions are taken as a block and that will be inserted with the previous block if the cryptographic hash is found. Miners will find the matching cryptographic hash by using computational resources. The miners will get the reward as a bitcoin after adding the block into the transactions. Generally, more people are involving in mining, and they will share their amount after receiving the bitcoin as a reward. Miners will get the transaction to be carried by the users through the network as a broadcast message to all the miners. The miners who wish to take over their transaction will respond and do the transaction to get the reward.

DISTRIBUTED SYSTEM

Distributed system provides maintenance of common ledger and the works that are assigned to the network will be distributed among all nodes of the network.

Micro Transaction

In blockchain, every transaction will be noted in a common ledger to maintain traceability. IoT requires this feature of traceability to maintain the records properly to function.

Data Transparency

The data stored in the blockchain is visible to all nodes in a network. If any transaction added into blockchain ledger after finding the valid matching cryptographic hash, data will be visible to all the nodes. IoT requires transparency to monitor the activities that are happening in different places. Based on the updated data, the activities may be triggered in the network. Transparency is the main property of the distributed systems.

Anonymity

Anonymity is a feature of blockchain where the user can hide their identity and do a transaction in a network. The user of a blockchain network cannot have any identity and rather than public and private keys. IoT with blockchain will provide an environment that can hide the user identity and do data sharing without identity. The user can be identified through the public key and the user can create different transaction address for each transaction.

Cryptography

Cryptography is used with public and private keys. The public key in which the user wants to make a transaction, they can pick the transaction address from the wallet. The public key can be broadcasted by the receiver in the network to receive the transaction from the sender. The public key is like a mail id that should be available to the sender to initiate the transaction.

If the transaction is over then the user can give their public key to receive the transaction. Miners are verifying the transactions before adding into the blockchain and they will find the cryptographic hash to add the block into the previous block. If the hash value is matched with the previous block, it will be added to the previous block. If any miner is trying to validate the wrong hash value, the entire chain of the block becomes invalid. The above diagrams in Figure 3.1 and Figure 3.2 show the difference

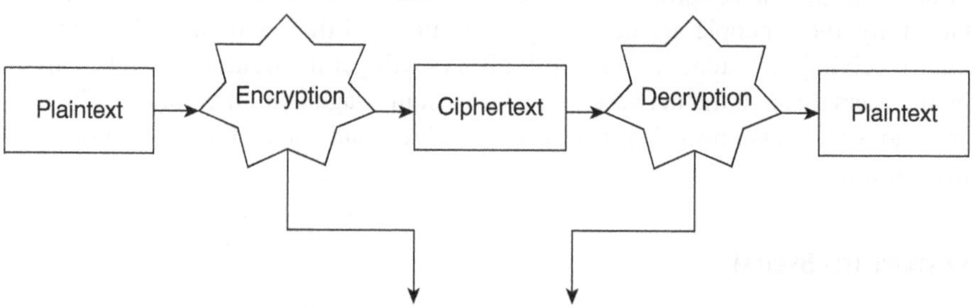

FIGURE 3.1 Symmetric key encryption.

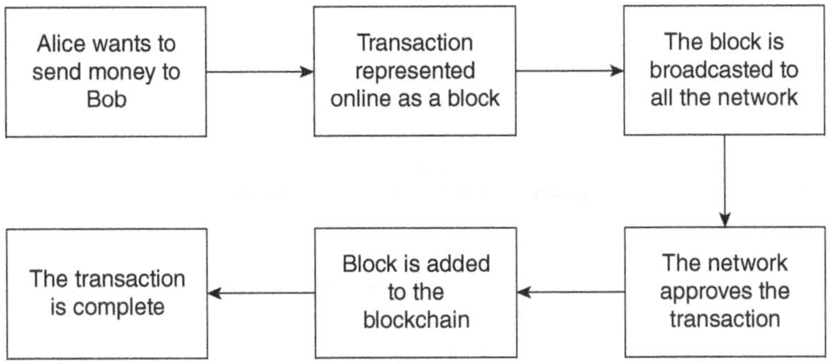

FIGURE 3.2 Asymmetric key encryption.

between the symmetric and asymmetric key cryptography. In symmetric key cryptography, a shared key is used for both the sender and receiver. The disadvantages of the symmetric key are, each time, a sender requires a different key for a transaction to a different receiver. In asymmetric key cryptography, public key is used to send and private key is used to receive the transaction by the receiver.

Consensus

The consensus is an agreement upon the valid transaction when the miners get the valid cryptographic hash. The miners of the network will try to validate the hash if it is found. The valid cryptographic hash is not acceptable if more than 50% of the miners are not agreeing on the transaction.

No Transaction Fees

In the blockchain, no transaction fees will be deducted because after verifying the transaction, the transaction block is added into the network, the miner will get the bitcoin as a reward. The reward for the miners will be automatically credited to the corresponding address of the miner who solved the cryptographic puzzle. Though the challenges that are raised while integrating blockchain and IoT, blockchain is inevitable nowadays in the IoT industry to make security in their applications. Finally, blockchain and the IoT will lead to a healthy environment in both industries and developers to service to the people with ensured security.

BLOCKCHAIN WORKING PRINCIPLE

The public key is taken as the transaction address and it is broadcasted in the network. The public key is an alphanumeric address that will be generated when we create a wallet. Public address can be changed for each transaction to maintain the anonymity over the network. The transaction in a blockchain is shown in Figure 3.3.

The hashing SHA256 algorithm is used for encryption and the transactions are verified by the miners. The public is used to send the data, whereas the private key is

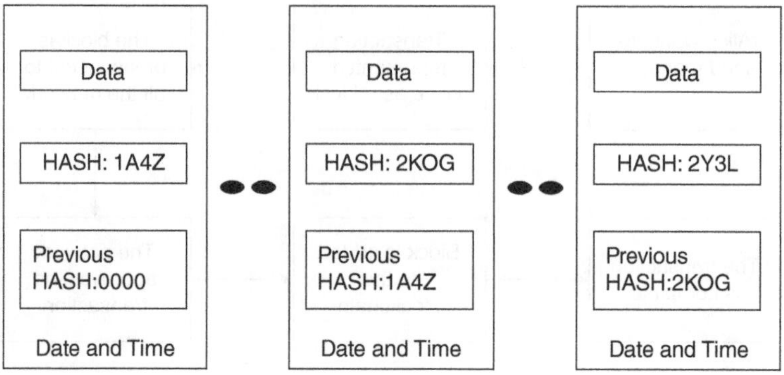

FIGURE 3.3 Transaction process in blockchain.

used to receive the data. The collection of transactions will be taken as a block and that will be verified by the miners in the network. If the transactions are valid, they will be added into the blockchain as a block. The transaction will be valid by the consensus approval from most of the peers.

Blockchain is not only used in cryptocurrencies such as bitcoin, but it can also be used in many applications that are not relying on the third party, relying on distributed, shared, and transparent environment to secure the data by its properties. Even though IoT is proceeding with different architecture such as client-server, cloud architecture, and fog architecture, the security of the data available in IoT is questionable [2]. The solution to this problem is to go for blockchain architecture for the IoT environment. Blockchain and IoT are belonging to two different eras but the benefit of these will be achieved when we combine these two domains. Adaptation of blockchain with the IoT is having some implementation changes such as scalability [3] but the result of the application would be very effective.

Miners

Bitcoin miners are involved in the process of the bitcoin transaction. Miners collect no transaction request from the network and make it as a block and this has to be added into the previous block with matching hash values. To solve the hash puzzle, large amount of power supply and nodes are required. Miners will automatically get the reward as bitcoin if the block is added into the existing block. The miner has to follow the rules of the blockchain network of the consensus protocol.

Hashing

Hashing is a process of changing the variable length of inputs into the fixed size of length output. The special property of hashing is that the output cannot be reverted. Two inputs cannot give the same output even if a small change occurs. A large set of data can be changed into a fixed-size length to maintain originality, for example, some of the software which can be downloaded from original websites will be converted to a fixed-size length of the output. If the same software is downloaded from fake websites, the hash code will not be the same as the original software due to malware embedded in the software from fake websites.

Example hash for fingerprint:

HASH:

7E0CE566ED2900D81508C7768A05A4A50CCBC3632E72EE8D32DE69636 B66336

Properties of Hashing

One Way Function

The input can be changed to a fixed-size length as a hash code. The hash code cannot be converted back to get the input.

Input → 3672854bsb238eb1992b....
??? ← 3672854bsb238eb1992b...

Pseudo Random

Even small changes in the input can also impact on the output hash.

1000 → 728wbw781289q16732hi...
1001 → fw326hsu02ja9dgh86233...

Collision Resistant

Different inputs cannot give the same hash code. If it is the same, the Algorithm is not a collision resistant. MD5 algorithm is recently found as collision algorithm where the two different inputs give the same output. SHA256 is used in blockchain with a collision resistant in its property.

Input → 3672854bsb238eb1992b....
??? → 3672854bsb238eb1992b...

Deterministic

The same input always gives the same hash code. It will not allow even small changes in the hash code.

1000 → 728wbw781289q16732hi...
1000 → 728wbw781289q16732hi...

The transaction details in the blockchain are taken as an input and the hash code will be generated for every transaction. The transaction details are such as sender-receiver, the amount for an exchange, and the public key of the receiver. Nonce is a value that is varied to create a unique hash address of the block, which should be less than the target hash value, block version number, and block header. The block

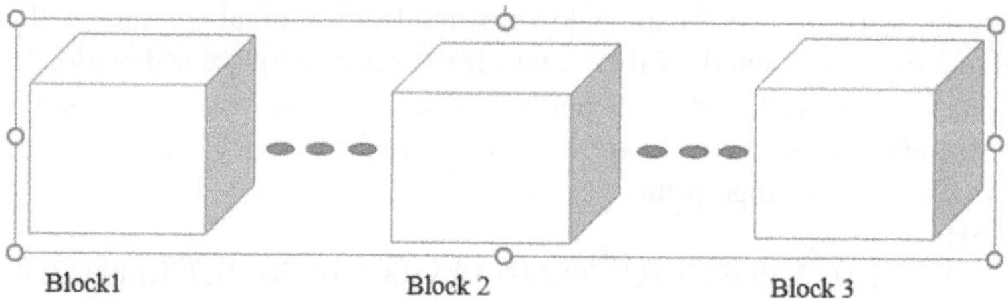

FIGURE 3.4 Blockchain link.

of multiple transactions is added into the blockchain and every block is maintaining hash code of their current hash value and the previous hash value. The previous hash is maintained for each block to make the chain for the blocks as a blockchain. Link of blockchain is shown in Figure 3.4.

Merkle Tree

The tree structure is formed in blockchain from every transaction hash code into the root hash called a Merkle tree. Figure 3.5 shows the Merkle tree structure of hashing. The transaction in each block has their hash value and the hash values of the transactions hashed to get the root hash as per the diagram depicted here [4].

Genesis Block

The first block is the genesis block in the blockchain network where the genesis block's previous hash value is considered as zero because it is not connected to any previous block. Genesis block is shown in Figure 3.6. In the bitcoin network, Satoshi Nakamoto created the first block as a genesis block, and after this block, each block is added as a block for 10 minutes.

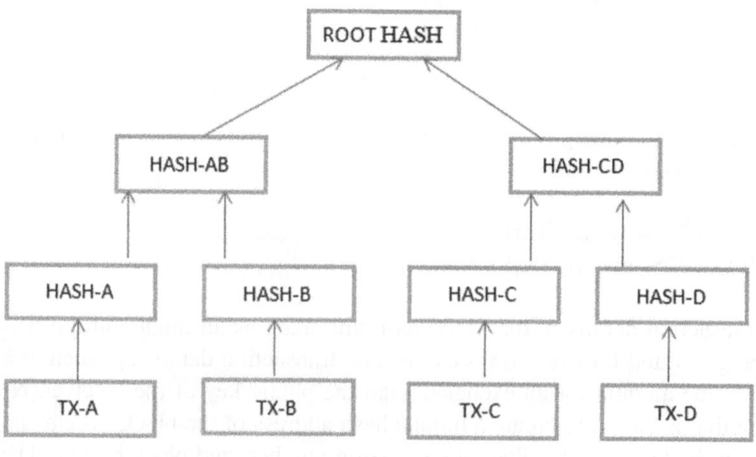

FIGURE 3.5 Merkle tree.

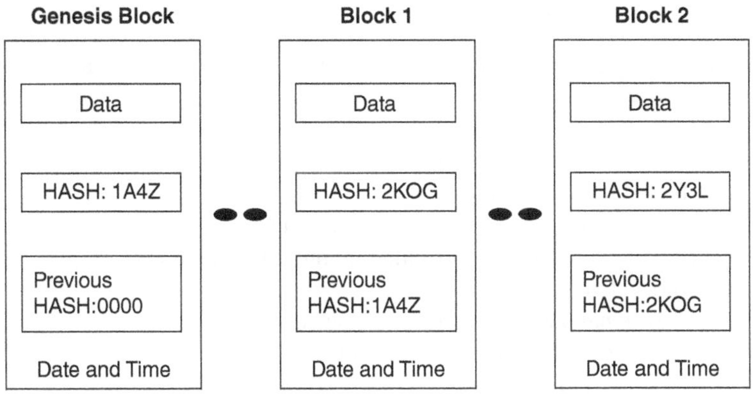

FIGURE 3.6 Genesis block.

Proof of Work vs Proof of Stake

Proof of work is the work to verify the transaction where the miners adding the block to the previous block. The competition from the miners is occurring as whose mined block is to be added into the blockchain. To compete with other miners, the cryptographic puzzle is distributed to all the miners as competition. The miners who solve the cryptographic puzzle will be adding the block into the blockchain with the consensus protocol. The miner who mines the block will get the reward as bitcoins in the bitcoin network. The miners have a large number of computational resources by spending more money on computational resources to solve the cryptographic puzzle. The miner who spent more energy in terms of the computational power will get the reward. This leads to genuine mining.

In the proof of stack, a miner having more stakes such as bitcoins in the network compared with other miners' accounts will be allowed to do the verification.

Difference Between POW&POS

Proof of work and proof of stack both are used to get the consensus among the network. Table 3.1 shows the difference of POW and POS.

TABLE 3.1
Difference Between POW&POS

Proof of Work	Proof of Stack
The first miner who solved the puzzle will add the block and get the reward. Focus given to solve the puzzle	This is using deterministic selection process. Focus on choosing the miners
Specialized equipment is required to optimize processing power	Standard servers are usually enough
Initial investment is needed for the hardware	Initial investment for a stake and make the reputation
High energy consumption	Standard energy consumption

BLOCKCHAIN AND IoT SECURITY

Convergence of blockchain to IoT requires some conditions to be satisfied for the real-time applications:

1. Are there the copies of the ledger?
   Yes – Blockchain is suitable
   No – Traditional database systems are sufficient
2. Are redundant copies are distributed in multiple computers?
   Yes – Blockchain is suitable
   No – Traditional database systems are sufficient
3. Whether all the IoT nodes trust each other?
   Yes – Blockchain is suitable
   No – Traditional database systems are sufficient
4. Would IoT entities require to trust a third party?
   Yes – Traditional database systems are sufficient with trusted third party
   No – Blockchain is suitable
5. Are the IoT devices to be deployed in permitted environment?
   Yes – Private blockchain
   No – Public blockchain
6. Is somebody has to control the blockchain?
   Yes – Permissioned blockchain
   No – Permission less blockchain

The IoT is making a relationship between the devices and also with a human to interact with a machine through the Internet. M2M communication that is a part of IoT environment connects the machine with another machine without human intervention. M2M machines are expected to be increasing dynamically from 780 million in 2016 to 3.3 billion in 2021. This shows the enhancement of IoT in different aspects concerning their applications. IoT can be applied in various applications such as wearables, emergency, smart home, smart agriculture, and supply chain management.... IoT is entirely changing the world through modern devices and data communications. IoT is making virtualization in the applications by applying the network function virtualization and minimizing the storage of data in client by applying software-defined networks where the control and data plane are separated in the network. Though IoT is providing good service in every aspect, the architecture of IoT is failed to provide security in the network. Although various architecture styles have been proposed for IoT such as client-server architecture, cloud-based architecture, and fog computing architecture, those are not enough to handle data breaching. IoT is not only involved in a sophisticated application, but it is also involved in the emergency application. The data breaches in emergency applications such as a remote patient health monitoring system where the patient's health condition is monitored through the wearable chip in the patient's body. The wearable chip will send the notification to the hospital when there is a change in the patient's body condition. According to the data, hospital management will call for the ambulance in a critical situation to save the life of the patient. In this case, IoT is serving a major portion to monitor a health condition through the sensor and giving the notification to the device that is embedded in the hospital. In this kind of scenario, if IoT is failing to perform the task due to data breaching, the patient's life would not be saved. A small organization cannot able to maintain the hardware and data storage in a private cloud. Security tools cannot be maintained by a small organization. In the case of the public cloud, the data may be misused by cloud service providers. Centralized server architecture is vulnerable to data breaching through the Internet. IoT devices will not perform the task without receiving commands and associated data from the centralized server. The entire system will fail if the server is hacked by an unauthorized person. This will lead to the misuse of data by hackers by tampering the data intentionally to spoil the system. Fog computing is rectifying some of the issues addressed in cloud computing such as latency and volume, which also work in the base of cloud servers. Although various security measures proposed for security in centralized servers are not enough to secure the system, the maintenance of the server is expensive by upgrading the security tools and techniques in the network. Since the centralized server architecture is not enough to handle data breaching, the important challenge in this regard is to propose the new architectural styles that are saving the data from an unauthorized person. In a decentralized architecture, the maintenance of the server is not required. In the way of looking for an architecture that is free from hacking and decentralized in nature, many suggestions are given by the expert to go for blockchain. The blockchain is providing the security to the application by anonymity and P2P distributed network. Blockchain that can be applied to IoT for making security in IoT applications will give a good impact on the applications in the world. Integrating the IoT and blockchain is securing IoT applications. An application such as supply chain management from marketing to the delivery of the product can be monitored by all the peers if the IoT is having the backbone infrastructure of the blockchain. Here smart contract can be applied to run the business [5]. IoT devices that are connected and data should be protected to perform a certain task without delay in several applications. The blockchain is not just applied in cryptocurrency. Blockchain-based IoT applications are evolving to ensuring the security in IoT applications [6]. Blockchain can be applied in IoT applications such as voting system, supply chain management, emergency applications, smart home, education, and academia [7]. Adapting the blockchain into the IoT application is a major challenge nowadays in the industry. Industries are looking for a smooth way for running applications that are free from hacking by embedding blockchain architecture into IoT applications [8]. Though the challenges are raised while merging blockchain and IoT, blockchain is inevitable nowadays in the IoT industry to make security in their applications. Finally, blockchain and IoT will lead to a healthy environment in both industry and developers to service to the people with ensuring security.

BIoT

The application of the blockchain with IoT (BIoT) is increasing the way the blockchain is adapted to IoT [9]. Even though many challenges are arising while merging BIoT, the number of applications of BIoT is increasing in our day-to-day life. Figure 3.7 shows the application of blockchain based Internet of things.

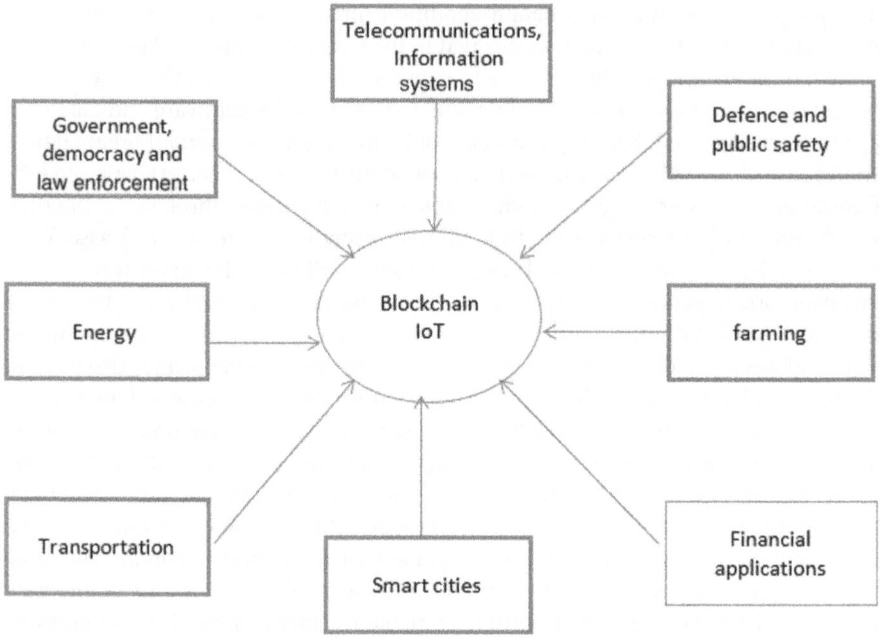

FIGURE 3.7 BIoT applications.

The above diagram shows the application of BIoT. Blockchain is going to change the IoT with assured security to serve the people.

CONCLUSION

Blockchain is a disruptive technology in IoT, which secures the IoT devices with the security measures. Blockchain is removing the vulnerability of the IoT devices and it is a backbone to secure the IoT network.

Scalability and storage-related problems are occurring while we connect IoT with blockchain, and for these reasons, various research is being carried out [10–12] to apply blockchain to IoT. Lightweight blockchain for IoT is a research going on to enhance security and to develop and expand the scope of IoT with the blockchain.

The data which is storing on the IoT is required to be minimized for a faster response; here are a few things that need to be considered. (1) Blockchain grows periodically, (2) many nodes intended to store large amounts of data, (3) waste of computational resources, and (4) increase of the energy consumption. In this case, the data stored in blockchain should be minimized. Emphasis on the scalability of the blockchain network is essential and data reduction on peers is also really important to save energy on peers and continue their work while working with blockchain.

Finally, IoT is involved in many of the sensitive applications, and IoT devices are collecting so much amount of information from the environment. In order to secure the data in IoT, blockchain is the eminent solution.

REFERENCES

1. S. Nakamoto. (2008). "Bitcoin: A Peer-to-Peer Electronic Cash System," Blockchain. info. 2013. http://bitcoin.org/bitcoin.pdf.
2. Tiago M. Fernández-Caramés and Paula Fraga-Lamas, "A review on the use of blockchain for the Internet of things," *IEEE Explore*, May 29, 2018.
3. S. Biswas, K. Shaif "A scalable blockchain framework for secure transactions in IoT," *IEEE Internet of Things Journal*, DOI 10.1109/JIOT.2018.2874095.
4. M. Vivek Anand and S. Vijayalakshmi, "Image validation with virtualization in blockchain based internet of things," *Journal of Computational and theoretical Nanoscience* vol. 17, pp. 2388–2395, May 2020.
5. K. Christidis and M. Devetsikiotis, "Blockchains and smart contracts for the Internet of Things," *IEEE Access*, vol. 4, pp. 2292–2303, 2016.
6. M. Conoscenti, A. Vetrò, and J. C. De Martin, "Blockchain for the Internet of Things: A systematic literature review," in *Proc. IEEE/ACS 13th Int. Conf. Comput. Syst. Appl. (AICCSA)*, Agadir, Morocco, Nov./Dec. 2016, pp. 1–6.
7. S. Huh, S. Cho, and S. Kim, "Managing IoT devices using blockchain platform," in *Proc. 19th Int. Conf. Adv. Commun. Technol. (ICACT)*, Bongpyeong, South Korea, Feb. 2017, pp. 464–467.
8. M. Samaniego and R. Deters, "Blockchain as a service for IoT," in *Proc. IEEE Int. Conf. Internet Things (iThings), IEEE Green Comput. Commun. (GreenCom), IEEE Cyber, Phys. Social Comput. (CPSCom), IEEE Smart Data (SmartData)*, Chengdu, China, Dec. 2016, pp. 433–436.
9. M. Samaniego and R. Deters, "Internet of smart things-IoST: Using blockchain and CLIPS to make things autonomous," in *Proc. IEEE Int. Conf. Cogn. Comput. (ICCC)*, Honolulu, HI, USA, Jun. 2017, pp. 9–16.
10. Ruinian Li, Tianyi Song, Bo Mei, Hong Li, Xiuzhen Cheng, and Limin Sun, "Blockchain for large-scale Internet of things data storage and protection", *IEEE Transactions on Services Computing*, DOI 10.1109/TSC.2018.2853167.
11. B. F. França. (Apr. 2015). Homomorphic Mini-Blockchain Scheme. Accessed: Apr. 10, 2018. [Online]. Available: http://cryptonite.info/les/HMBC.pdf.
12. J. D. Bruce. The Mini-Blockchain Scheme. Accessed: Apr. 10, 2018. [Online]. Available: https://www.weusecoins.com/assets/pdf/library/\The%20MiniBlockchain%20 Scheme.pdf.

4 PR Wallet-Based Blockchain Access Protocol to Secure EHRs

Mehul Gupta

CONTENTS

Introduction....65
What is Blockchain?....66
Blockchain and its Expansion in EHRs....66
Digitalizing Medical Records with Blockchain....66
Existing Research....67
Proposed System....67
Experimental Setup and Result Discussion....69
Limitations of the System....72
Conclusion....73
References....74

INTRODUCTION

The healthcare industry all around the world is emerging as one of the largest sectors, both in terms of the workforce involved and its contribution to the GDPs (Gross Domestic Products) of leading developing nations, according to the World Health Organization. With such tremendous growth, a massive amount of data is also generated in the form of patient's health records, clinical information, doctor's analysis, or data generated in the form of Internet of Things (IoT) (smartwatches or any health-monitoring applications). Hence, there arises an ever-growing concern for the security of this data [1, 2], which is highly sensitive to any patient. Since this huge data is normally centralized in nature, risks associated with its compromise may put the lives of many people at stake. Cyberattacks on these electronic health records (EHRs) are also common [3], with millions of records being compromised due to a small back door in the security of these systems. Studies estimated an amount of whopping $380 per medical record that was being compromised [4]. Blockchain, the technology that gained worldwide attention from developers after the launch of Bitcoin, has effectively addressed the issues related to data centralization, searching and sharing medical records across institutions, and helping the patient to control his/her medical records.

DOI: 10.1201/9781003094210-4

WHAT IS BLOCKCHAIN?

Blockchain, put simply, can be described as a technology, which can be used to store transactions and their metadata on nodes or blocks that are decentralized in nature. Depending on the configuration, a block can hold several transaction data. The blocks can contain the data about the transaction, details of participating parties, and most importantly, a unique hash of the previous block in the series. The first block, however, is an exception called the genesis block. The hash of a block is generated by algorithms like SHA-256, which changes even on slight modifications to block contents. Hence, each block is linked to the previous block, using this hash unique to each block. This characteristic makes the blockchain resistant to modification, and hence its immutability property.

Nodes are the building blocks of this decentralized ledger. A node can be any storage space that contains a copy of blockchain. In Ethereum, Geth is used to control any such node. As each node stores a copy of the blockchain, there is no single point of failure in the system as opposed to central servers. Blockchain, which was introduced as the underlying technology beneath Bitcoin, has revolutionized many sectors, including finance, automotive, and healthcare.

BLOCKCHAIN AND ITS EXPANSION IN EHRS

Blockchain can be explained, simply, as a chain of blocks tied together with the means of hash codes. As stated, each block in a blockchain apart from the genesis block consists of the hash of the previous block, and hence, even a slight modification to data shall render the complete chain invalid. Although blockchain has the potential to serve in many different applications in healthcare and medicine, its use is increasing at a limited pace due to some practical demerits. Patients, especially the old-age persons, or people suffering from chronic illness are prone to forget their secret keys and are unable to manage their medical records. Such persons need to be specially assisted in their health and medicines.

DIGITALIZING MEDICAL RECORDS WITH BLOCKCHAIN

The existing state of the art technologies is sweeping well into the healthcare sector to digitalize patient records (PRs) into EHRs with machine learning algorithms used to identify the contamination from medical images to NLP, which can help assist patient for common symptoms or develop medical notes using speech recognition. These technologies could perform much efficiently if these records can be digitalized. Now let us imagine a coronavirus patient going to the clinic with his physical copy of medical records. This contaminated physical copy of his record is often circulated to all the medical staff, including the physician and the chemist, which can further escalate the contamination numbers.

If this same medical record had been accessed through a digital medium, the detection, tracking, and observation of that patient would have been much easier. Blockchain shall help in not only digitalizing these records but also provide a safer decentralized medium for these accesses.

EXISTING RESEARCH

There have been many previous works on the use of blockchain in healthcare to secure EHRs. One such work is MedRec, a 2016 MIT Media Lab initiative to create a blockchain-based record management system of patient's EHRs [5]. Developed on Ethereum blockchain, MedRec not only allows patients to control how their medical data is shared but also allows them to keep their transactional history all at one place.

A similar EHR management system, namely, MedChain [6] was developed to improve the existing healthcare technologies. Developed on the Ethereum blockchain, the system uses that only the nodes with permissions shall access the personal blockchain. Several approaches and initiatives related to securing EHRs with blockchain are also being made, for instance, MedBlock [7], MIStore [8], Healthchain [9], and Ancile [10].

A number of researchers argued that using blockchain for securing the EHRs could pose several disadvantages, especially for elderly people or persons with some chronic illness due to which the patient is unable to interact or grant necessary permissions to the concerned institution [11, 12]. Cichosz et al. [13] presented an NEM blockchain solution for this problem, by introducing a multi-signature account for the patient. In the case of an emergency, the records can be accessed by authorizing permissions to the healthcare provider through a trusted party.

Hardware wallets have been a key asset in managing private keys in blockchain, but its integration in securing EHRs can add a new layer of security to it. D. Ivan [14] mentioned a similar use of security tokens in preserving patient medical records on blockchain. Md. Ashraf Uddin et al. [15] deals with patient monitoring with the help of the data generated through various wearable devices, smart sensors, or other IoT devices [16, 17]. It proposes a patient-centric agent that would manage the data streams and blockchain on which the distributed data be kept on.

Ms. R. Poorni et al. [18] discussed a digital certificate blockchain-based design to provide a more secure user authentication. It makes use of the immutability property of the blockchain, and hence, the serial numbers of the certificates are stored in the blockchain instead of the actual certificate. To avoid further forgery, the design incorporates the alpha-blending of unique imprints.

Leila Ismail et al. [19] proposed a lightweight blockchain that reduces the network overhead and the computational complexity as compared to the Bitcoin network. This architecture can be effective in healthcare as the medical records can invite high traffic simultaneously.

PROPOSED SYSTEM

The authorization system proposed is built over the Ethereum public blockchain. Ethereum enables DApps to run through a browser, without even the users have to mine a complete node of the blockchain. Smart contracts are an important feature of Ethereum, which, while eliminating the need for a third party, also ensures that the contracts are deployed with ease.

To address the issue of mishandling of crypto keys, we introduce a PR wallet. A PR wallet is particularly a password-protected peripheral device, which can be used to secure secret keys, and can be used for signing, authorization, etc. for transactions involved in managing EHRs. PR wallet shall contain the secret keys of the owner and can be used wherever authorization with private key is necessary.

This PR wallet can be password protected, or even biometric protected, using fingerprint scanner, or face unlock. Biometric enabled protection shall also guarantee access to medical data even when the patient is suffering from acute illness, or chronic diseases like Alzheimer's disease, where he is not able to share his credentials [12]. This shall eventually allow emergency access of essential services to the patient.

Since this PR wallet acts as a cold storage, the risk associated with its compromise as compared to other hot wallets is also very less. Moreover, if the device gets misplaced, the patient can just be issued another one, without him being punished for the loss of his medical records. This PR wallet can not only act as an authorization system to the blockchain DApp but can also be used to establish a role-based access control over the records. Using this, a similar multiparty authorization system can also be incorporated in the case of medical emergencies [20] to access patient's records.

Figure 4.1 explains the architecture of the application whenever the patient wishes to access his clinical records, through Metamask or either by any healthcare web/mobile DApp. The user is automatically logged in by fetching the private key from the wallet. The wallet can be used similarly for signing any record, or in the case of any authentication requirement. We shall further see the uses of this wallet for multiparty patient authentication. Figure 4.2 shows the feature provided by Metamask to connect a hardware wallet to it similar to PR wallet.

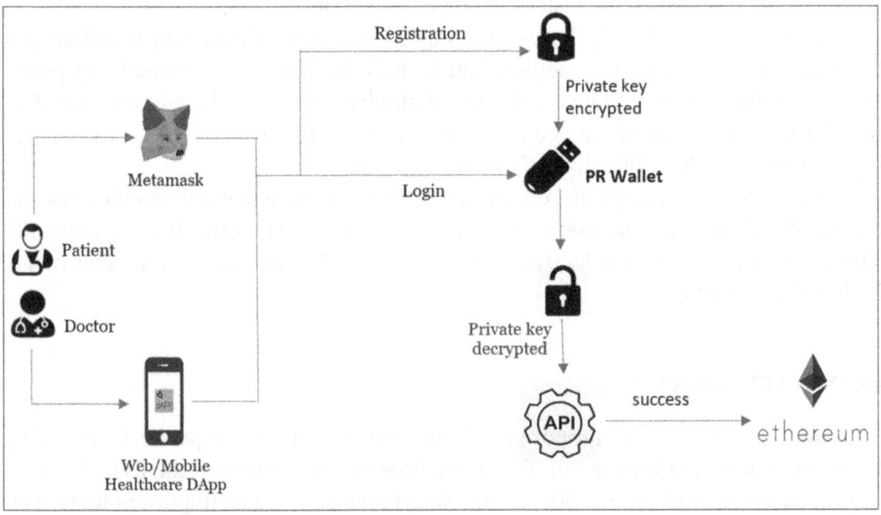

FIGURE 4.1 Protocol design of the proposed system.

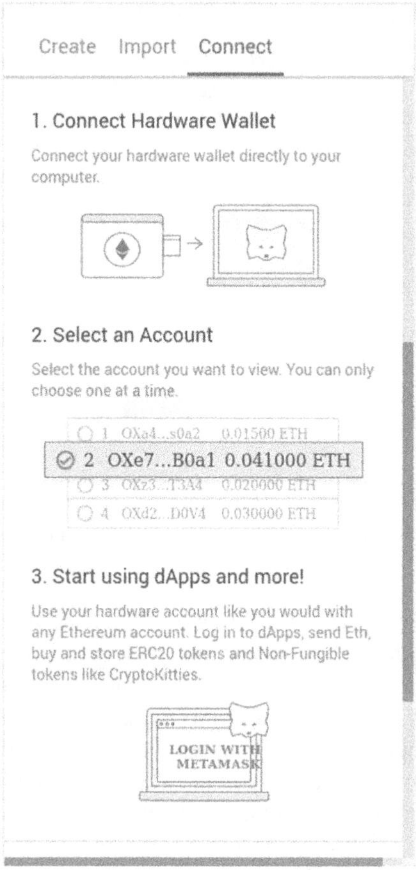

FIGURE 4.2 Connecting wallet through Metamask.

EXPERIMENTAL SETUP AND RESULT DISCUSSION

The application is developed using truffle and Ganache that are an easy alternative to develop local Ethereum blockchains. The app uses Nodejs to handle server-side Ajax calls. Figure 4.3 shows the patient registration module, which authenticates the user through Metamask after connecting the wallet to the blockchain. The application makes use of the smart contract to automate certain transactions, which gets deployed on the blockchain. The application provides facilities for easy management and sharing of EHRs, which are encrypted using AES-256 algorithm and stored in a separate address space.

Figure 4.3 depicts the scenario when the user tries to connect to the healthcare application for the first time. For the process, a smart contract is deployed on the blockchain after the patient enters his public Ethereum address, which is assigned to map a particular user. Public Ethereum address also restricts the use of legitimate user details, such as name, place, and DOB, thus maintaining the user's privacy as

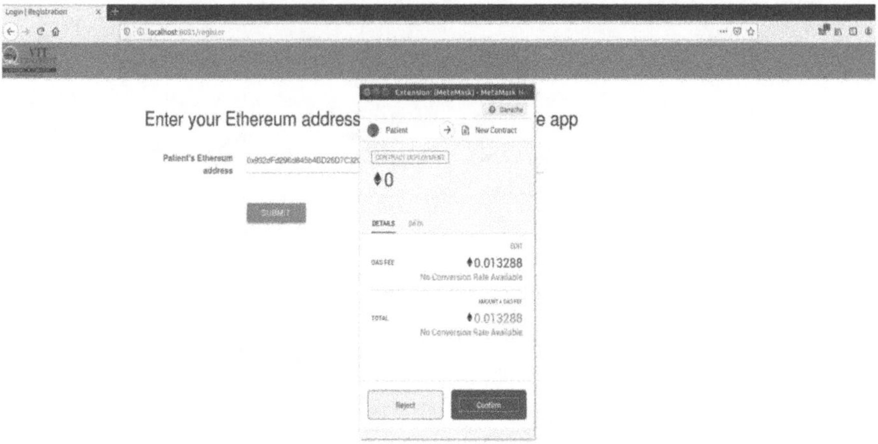

FIGURE 4.3 Patient registration on the DApp through smart contract.

well. Apart from deploying the smart contract, the user also requires to pay some processing fees, in the form of gas. The gas amount is paid in the form of Ethers, which is ultimately paid as a transaction processing fee to the miners. The regulating authorities, in this case, can determine the gas required for each transaction. The user also has the option to trade with another currency of his choice, in case he is not able or willing to transact with Ethers. The application automatically informs the patient, in the event of any errors, like insufficient funds, gas prices, or in the deployment.

Ethereum, the blockchain technology on which the app is built, disables any possibility of an external party that can control the blockchain and hence the data. This means that the app is evidently resistant to data leaks as opposed to other applications, probably based on central servers and the everyday glitches in their code. Moreover, the distributed architecture of Ethereum makes it protected from many cyberattacks, like DoS, DDoS, and SQL injection, which targets SQL databases explicitly. The authorized authorities are required to validate any transaction before being mined on the blockchain, which further eliminates any type of network fraud or corruption of any type.

An additional security feature has been incorporated into the application where the smart contract deployed can also function as multi-signature functionality. This means that the smart contract will be deployed only if some amount of permissioned authorities agrees to sign the contract. The feature can be used to eliminate certain corrupt members who are trying to validate fraudulent data. This can also be useful especially when a patient using a multiparty authentication feature cannot provide required permissions to the authority. In that case, other trusted parties can proceed with the process on behalf of the patient. Furthermore, the use of PR wallet acts as an alternative to grant access permissions and easy handling of the susceptible private key.

The application also deals with the issue of scalability, which can affect the transactions occurring per unit time on the blockchain and can thus reduce its computational capacity. The application consists of a storage pool, which contains the actual records encrypted through AES-256 algorithm using a randomly generated symmetric key, whereas the hybrid blockchain consists of the address of the storage, decryption key, hash of the previous block, and other metadata about the transaction, including the signature of the concerned authorities. The signature is required primarily for authentication and integrity, and at the same time, to avoid any replay attacks using nonce. When a record is accessed, the corresponding decryption key (symmetric key in this case) is fetched from the blockchain, the record is decrypted using this key, and the signature is matched and presented to the viewer.

For the purpose of testing and deploying the application, we have used Ganache. Ganache provides us with some virtual accounts with 100 Eth for testing and local development. When deployed on the Ethereum Mainnet, it provides a similar functionality, as exhibited by Ganache. Figure 4.4 shows some of the dummy transactions performed on the application by virtual accounts, with the transaction hashes and the contract address to which it was deployed. A column also displays the amount of gas required to deploy each transaction.

Reports estimated that around 41 million PRs were compromised in the United States in 2019, which amounts to about triple the numbers breached in 2018. This demonstrates how bad even a single attack can be, when we have not started calculating the cost of such breaches. Most of the breaches occurred as a result of systems being siloed and running on outdated technologies. The application solves the

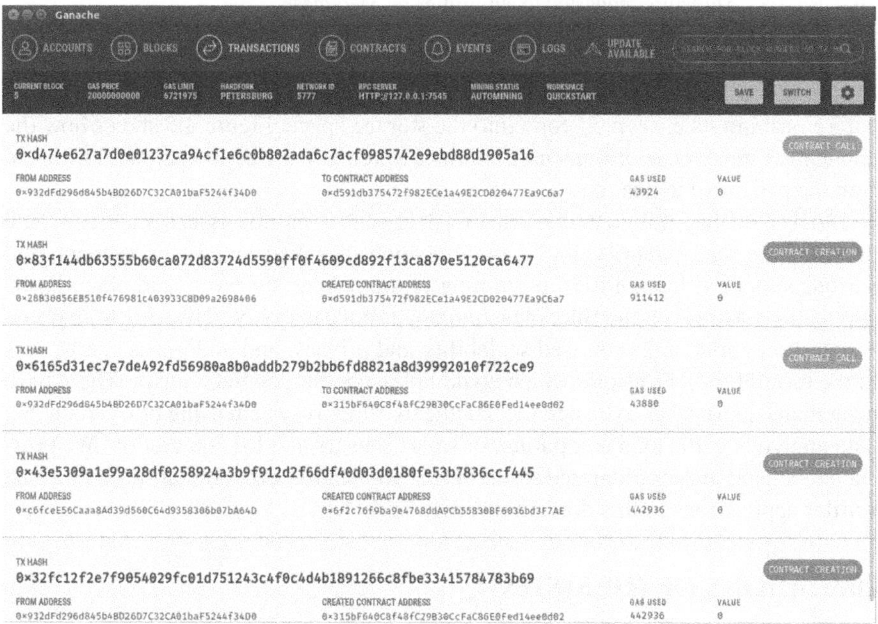

FIGURE 4.4 Transaction log of contracts deployed on blockchain.

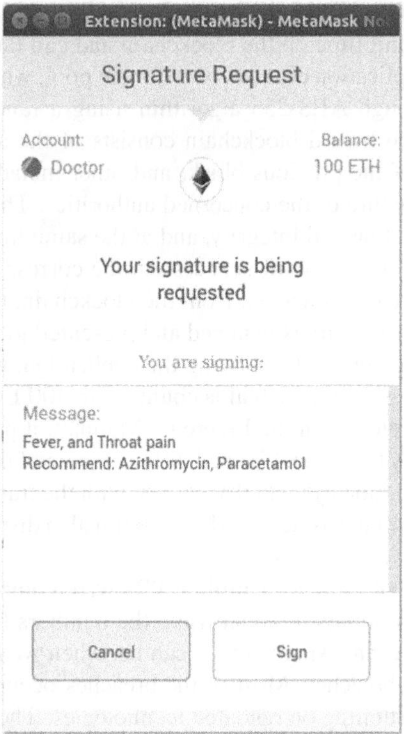

FIGURE 4.5 Signature requested to authorities by Metamask.

problem of traditional attacks on central servers and protects the secret key being compromised for malicious intents. The medical status of the patient is signed duly before pushing its encrypted copy into the storage space. Figure 4.5 shows how the application makes use of the smart contract to request the concerned authorities to sign the patient's medical note.

Blockchain has the characteristics to deal with common issues such as single node failure, data integrity, intercommunication in a distributed environment, and various system vulnerabilities, pertaining to many central servers and cloud-based applications. However, the Bitcoin technology is not capable of delivering high transaction throughput, and promised scalability and privacy, and undergoes energy loss in the form of miner's efforts which could not make it to the main chain. There have been many approaches to design the healthcare support system using blockchain, big data analytics with cloud computing, or smart sensors and IoT integration. We present a tabulated and summarized result of this application's functionalities with some similar applications in this domain through Table 4.1.

LIMITATIONS OF THE SYSTEM

The application is designed in such a way to address even the smallest issues pointed out by many researchers, including the question of security, scalability,

TABLE 4.1
Comparison of Different Applications for Healthcare Management [21]

	[22]	[23]	[24]	Our Proposed System
Blockchain-based	Y	Y	Y	Y
Smart contracts	N	Y	Y	Y
Scalability	Y	Y	N	Y
Integrity	Y	Y	Y	Y
Access control	N	Y	Y	Y
Multiparty authentication	N	N	N	Y
Integrated IoT support	N	N	N	N

and private key authorization by critical patients. However, there still remain some challenges that we need to address collectively. The health data in the EU is governed by the GDPR (General Data Protection Regulation), which allows the monitoring of all Personal Identifiable Information (PII) [25]. According to GDPR guidelines, patients must govern the data added to the blockchain, and hence, they have the right to update or modify this data. Also, they must have a right to wipe out this data. These two guidelines seem to conflict with the fundamental principles of blockchain. However, researchers have come up with some solutions as using modifiable blockchains [26]. The project is also capable of dealing with this cause to some extent as it uses a hybrid blockchain as mentioned earlier. Also, there are some uncertainties on the technology as it is new and hence not widely accepted. People are still not very reluctant to accept this, security and privacy being some of the major concerns.

Another prime concern is the extent to which the existing healthcare technologies are compatible with the modal. These technologies may find it difficult to interoperate with this decentralized web, which further questions its usefulness apart from the cost involved in its installment. Scalability still remains a paramount concern as the system shall be dealing with enormous volumes of data per second, as the Bitcoin network supports an upper bound of seven transactions per second. Although, as proposed in other research works [27], this application also attempts to fix this issue by implementing a separate storage space for the actual records, this issue can still be a bottleneck for the underlying technology.

CONCLUSION

As the tremendous data healthcare industry is generating, we must start thinking about ways to continually improve our data management techniques, but at the same, time not compromising on the security and privacy of this data at any cost relating to the sensitivity associated with it. The healthcare system thrives to move from a central authority-based system to a patient-driven modal. This shift comes with a series of challenges that are being addressed and blockchain effectively solves the underlying problems associated with this shift.

The proposed PR wallet acts as a medium to provide safe and simple access to the blockchain with hassle-free management of secret keys. It can also act as a medium for patients who hesitate to go digital with their records to move to EHRs. The device shall provide security and reliability with its cryptographical encryption algorithms that are not easier and feasible to break. The device shall prove successful in solving the patient's griefs of handling these keys and allows painless sharing and transfer of these records in the case of acute illness.

The application provides ways by which the patient can grant and revoke any record-specific permission to the authorities just with one tap. The use of Ethereum and smart contracts has made this automation very easier to implement. The latency in encryption and decryption of EHRs also affects the overall performance. For this purpose, we have used Cryptr, a Node.js module to encrypt strings via AES-256 algorithm in a quick and simple way. The application is also aimed at resolving the problems caused by direct transmissions of diseases in clinics, especially through hard copies of patients' medical records and the increased risk associated with further contaminations of chains of people, for a disease like Covid-19.

REFERENCES

1. Reddy, G. T., Sudheer, K., Rajesh, K., & Lakshmanna, K. (2014). Employing data mining on highly secured private clouds for implementing a security-asa-' framework. Journal of Theoretical and Applied Information Technology, 59(2), 317–326.
2. Iwendi, C., Jalil, Z., Javed, A. R., Reddy, T., Kaluri, R., Srivastava, G., & Jo, O. (2020). KeySplitWatermark: Zero watermarking algorithm for software protection against cyber-attacks. IEEE Access, 8, 72650–72660.
3. Numan, M., Subhan, F., Khan, W. Z., Hakak, S., Haider, S., Reddy, G. T., … & Alazab, M. (2020). A systematic review on clone node detection in static wireless sensor networks. IEEE Access, 8, 65450–65461.
4. Harshini, V. M., Danai, S., Usha, H. R., & Kounte, M. R. (2019, April). Health record management through blockchain technology. In 2019 3rd International Conference on Trends in Electronics and Informatics (ICOEI) (pp. 1411–1415), IEEE.
5. Azaria, A., Ekblaw, A., Vieira, T., & Lippman, A. (2016, August). Medrec: Using blockchain for medical data access and permission management. In 2016 2nd International Conference on Open and Big Data (OBD) (pp. 25–30), IEEE.
6. Daraghmi, E. Y., Daraghmi, Y. A., & Yuan, S. M. (2019). MedChain: A design of blockchain-based system for medical records access and permissions management. IEEE Access, 7, 164595–164613.
7. Fan, K., Wang, S., Ren, Y., Li, H., & Yang, Y. (2018). MedBlock: Efficient and secure medical data sharing via blockchain. Journal of Medical Systems, 42, 136.
8. Zhou, L., Wang, L., & Sun, Y. (2018). MIStore: A blockchain-based medical insurance storage system. Journal of Medical Systems, 42, 149.
9. Ahram, T., Sargolzaei, A., Sargolzaei, S., Daniels, J., & Amaba, B. (8–10 June 2017). Blockchain technology innovations. In Proceedings of the 2017 IEEE Technology & Engineering Management Conference (TEMSCON), Santa Clara, CA, USA (pp. 137–141).
10. Dagher, G. G., Mohler, J., Milojkovic, M., Marella, P. B., & Marella, B. (2018). Ancile: Privacy-preserving framework for access control and interoperability of electronic health records using blockchain technology. Sustainable Cities and Society, 39, 283–297.

11. Agbo, C. C., Mahmoud, Q. H., & Eklund, J. M. (2019, June). Blockchain technology in healthcare: A systematic review. In Healthcare (Vol. 7, No. 2, p. 56). Multidisciplinary Digital Publishing Institute.
12. Kassab, M., et al. (2019). Blockchain: A panacea for electronic health records?. In 2019 IEEE/ACM 1st International Workshop on Software Engineering for Healthcare (SEH), IEEE.
13. Cichosz, S. L., Stausholm, M. N., Kronborg, T., Vestergaard, P., & Hejlesen, O. (2019). How to use blockchain for diabetes health care data and access management: An operational concept. Journal of Diabetes Science and Technology, 13(2), 248–253.
14. Ivan, D. (2016, August). Moving toward a blockchain-based method for the secure storage of patient records. In ONC/NIST Use of Blockchain for Healthcare and Research Workshop. Gaithersburg, Maryland, United States: ONC/NIST (pp. 1–11).
15. Uddin, M. A., Stranieri, A., Gondal, I., & Balasubramanian, V. (2018). Continuous patient monitoring with a patient centric agent: A block architecture. IEEE Access, 6, 32700–32726.
16. R.M. Priya, S., Maddikunta, P. K. R., Parimala, M., Koppu, S., Reddy, T., Chowdhary, C. L., & Alazab, M. (2020). An effective feature engineering for DNN using hybrid PCA-GWO for intrusion detection in IoMT architecture. Computer Communications, 160, 139–149.
17. Bhattacharya, S., Kaluri, R., Singh, S., Alazab, M., & Tariq, U. (2020). A novel PCA-firefly based XGBoost classification model for intrusion detection in networks using GPU. Electronics, 9(2), 219.
18. Poorni, R., Lakshmanan, M., & Bhuvaneswari, S. (2019, July). DIGICERT: A secured digital certificate application using blockchain through smart contracts. In 2019 International Conference on Communication and Electronics Systems (ICCES) (pp. 215–219), IEEE.
19. Ismail, L., Materwala, H., & Zeadally, S. (2019). Lightweight blockchain for healthcare. IEEE Access, 7, 149935–149951.
20. Radhakrishnan, B. L., Joseph, A. S., & Sudhakar, S. (2019) Securing blockchain based electronic health record using multilevel authentication. In 2019 5th International Conference on Advanced Computing & Communication Systems (ICACCS), IEEE.
21. Shahnaz, A., Qamar, U., & Khalid, A. (2019). Using blockchain for electronic health records. IEEE Access, 7, 147782–147795, doi: 10.1109/ACCESS.2019.2946373.
22. Sahoo, M. S. & Baruah, P. K. (2018). HBasechainDB—A scalable blockchain framework on Hadoop ecosystem. In Asian Conference on Supercomputing Frontiers. Springer, Cham.
23. Zhang, P., et al. (2018). FHIRChain: Applying blockchain to securely and scalably share clinical data. Computational and Structural Biotechnology Journal, 16, 267–278.
24. Kim, M. G., et al. (2018). Sharing medical questionnaries based on blockchain. In 2018 IEEE International Conference on Bioinformatics and Biomedicine (BIBM), IEEE.
25. Akarca, D., et al. (2019). Blockchain secured electronic health records: Patient rights, privacy and cybersecurity. In 2019 10th International Conference on Dependable Systems, Services and Technologies (DESSERT), IEEE.
26. Lee, N.-Y., et al. (2019). Modifiable public blockchains using truncated hashing and sidechains. IEEE Access, 7, 173571–173582.
27. Cichosz, S. L., et al. (2019). How to use blockchain for diabetes health care data and access management: An operational concept. Journal of Diabetes Science and Technology, 13(2), 248–253.

5 Blockchain Securing Drug Supply Chain

Combating counterfeits

Kavita Saini, Kavita Kumari and Shraddha Sagar

CONTENTS

Introduction to Counterfeit Drugs Menace 77
Problems with Existing Drug Supply Chain 78
What is Blockchain Technology 80
  Peer-to-Peer (P2P) Network 80
  Distributed Ledger 80
  Consensus 81
  Smart Contracts 81
Inside a Blockchain 81
Features of Blockchain 82
  Low Expense 82
  Reliable 82
  Fast Exchange Settlement 82
  Transparent and Auditable 82
Types of Blockchain 83
Blockchain's Ability to Combat Counterfeit Drugs 83
Advantages of Using Blockchain in Pharma Supply Chain 84
Blockchain Applications in Drug Supply Chain 85
Conclusion 87
References 87

INTRODUCTION TO COUNTERFEIT DRUGS MENACE

The problem and complexity of counterfeit medications on the health of patients globally isn't a new trouble. In 2008, Berman referenced efforts to become aware of and decrease the occurrence and effect of counterfeit medications. Berman additionally mentioned that fees to society are impactful and include losses in employment, misplaced earnings and income tax sales, and prices related to elevated trade deficits. Although now not new, the counterfeit drug problem is turning increasingly more complex. Global estimates are that counterfeit drug use occurs at 10% of all prescription medicinal drugs used.

Counterfeiters don't care who is impacted by their crimes. Cancer patients, as an example, have been adversely impacted. In 2012, the United States Food and

DOI: 10.1201/9781003094210-5

Drug Administration (FDA) indicated 19 medicinal practices had bought counterfeit variations of Roche's most-selling cancer drug bevacizumab (Avastin) from a remote place supplier. Counterfeit medicines have severely impacted the life of patients.

The scourge of medicine counterfeiting is global in attainment and effect. French researchers have pointed to not only the most dangerous outcomes of counterfeit antibiotics that a man or woman suffers, but also the worldwide issues related to the usage of counterfeit medicinal drugs and the emergence of bacterial resistance with a global impact. After taking a look within the United Kingdom examining counterfeit medicines and use, Jackson and colleagues urged pharmacists to report suspected incidents to regulatory agencies and to provide advice to patients in all settings regarding counterfeit medicinal drugs and the purchase of such via the Internet.

The involvement of prepared crime is effortlessly obvious in counterfeiting. Dégardin and colleagues noted that counterfeiting is a severe worldwide issue, and the networks producing and distributing counterfeit medicines are elements of prepared crime. Medication counterfeiting is an extreme worldwide issue, comprising networks of manufacturer and distributors that are an indispensable a part of industrialized organized crime.

The FDA has been energetic in running to counteract the negativity of counterfeit use. The FDA-(pinnacle), a small transportable device invented by FDA scientists used to locate counterfeit medicines, is a new tool and a good way to permit for early identification of counterfeit medicinal drugs. The vast-scale use of this kind of tools will provide handy identification of counterfeit medicines early.

The Partnership for Safe Medication (www.Safemedicines.Org), an organization led by using President Marvin Shepherd, PhD, from the University of Texas, has been an outspoken and effective voice in efforts to pick out and combat counterfeit drug use and sale inside the United States. This business enterprise desires educational and expert guide to hold its effective mission.

Educational outreach from our schools, network corporations, the click (any and all. sorts of media), social networking alternatives, and pharmacy agencies is essential to provide resources and assets of records to the public at the significance of avoidance of the purchase and the use of counterfeit medications. All contributors of the academy need to play a proactive and necessary function. The effect of counterfeit medications is unknown; however, the approaches to lessen counterfeiting should be known and nicely endorsed to steer this principal nice of life deterrent now and within the destiny.

PROBLEMS WITH EXISTING DRUG SUPPLY CHAIN

Growing customer needs, adoption of new and upgraded business models (such as e-commerce), and increasing competition make the supply chains a highly complex system. Over the previous decade, web-based businesses and hand-held advanced gadgets had considerably changed the day-to-day lives of individuals, particularly in the manners in which they shop. There is an ever-expanding interest for tweaked items, a disentangled and proficient shopping experience, and straightforwardness about the worth and provenance of products. These requirements carry new chances to organizations, but create huge difficulties to current stock chains. These obsolete inventory anchors battle to improve request to the board, to give information perceivability to the whole stream, or to follow products from crude material to end customer—which are all massively intricate. Moreover, the old innovation of the present inventory network neglects to give sufficient hazard to the executives, to lessen costs, or to meet quickly changing business sector prerequisites.

Some major challenges in present drug supply chains are:

- ***Partner doubt***: Trust is a fundamental factor in store network and the executives, and a powerful inventory network must be arranged based on a strong establishment of it [1]. In any case, doubt among members is the single-most prominent impediment to improving inventory network systems [2]. Therefore, most partners in the system fundamentally depend on outsider go-betweens to fill in as specialists of trust and to check exchanges, which significantly increment operational cost and lessen process proficiency.
- ***Absence of detectability***: Over the most recent couple of years, discernibility has gotten urgent for supply chains to address, particularly as to client care and arranging and anticipating in business tasks. In any case, it is hard to convey an incorporated framework in an interconnected system, particularly where trust among members is constrained. Rather, there are a few discrete frameworks among included gatherings that comprise different databases that block item following all through the whole store network [3].
- ***Obsolete methods for information sharing***: In current inventory network systems, information are shared between numerous associations utilizing paper-based documentation. Frequently, significant reports, for example, bills of replenishing, letters of credit, solicitations, protection strategies, and different authentications, must go with their related products around the globe [4]. For instance, around 200 correspondences were required for Maersk, a worldwide vehicle and coordinations organization, to finish a solitary shipment of solidified products from Mombasa to Europe in 2014 [5]. These interchanges made a pile of archives around 25 centimeters in tallness [6]. Compelled by this obsolete and wasteful information sharing strategy, boats and planes are regularly postponed in ports when the desk work doesn't coordinate the conveyed merchandise [4].
- ***Constrained straightforwardness***: The expression "straightforwardness" in the inventory network alludes to the degree to which all partners possess a mutual comprehension of and access to exact and sufficient data about items [7, 8]. A straightforward store network improves trust among partners and ensures the honesty of items and related information. In any case, the discrete databases in current store network systems offer negligible straightforwardness, and the greater part of the helpful data in them is lost when items and information are moved starting with one partner then onto the next. Besides, there are issues with conflicting information sharing, depending on paper documentation, and lacking interoperability. These basic difficulties stay in spite of long stretches

of critical research speculation. The emergency of Chipotle Mexican Flame broil outlets [9] is a significant and miserable case of how the present inventory network framework is wasteful at, and conceivably unequipped for, offering straightforwardness all through the whole life cycle of items.

- ***Consistence challenges***: At present, organizations need to satisfy progressively severe administrative guidelines to give safe items and administrations to clients. As of late, the US Nourishment and Medication Organization and Government Exchange Commission embraced a few guidelines to build sanitation and offer full perceivability of nourishment streams in the production network. Be that as it may, under current production network forms, it is hard to acquire this data from an assortment of partners and to build up a database that agrees to new models.

WHAT IS BLOCKCHAIN TECHNOLOGY

Blockchain technology has recently gained a lot of traction. It gained a lot of attention after Satoshi Nakamoto, an individual or group of people who went by the pseudonym Satoshi Nakamoto, launched Bitcoin in 2009. Many people even mix up blockchain and bitcoin. However, bitcoin is only one example of a blockchain-based application. In addition to payment systems, blockchain can be used for a variety of other applications and use cases.

Hyperledger, Linux Foundation, has defined blockchain as a peer-to-peer (P2P) distributed ledger forged by consensus, as well as a smart contract system.

Now, since this description contains a number of unfamiliar words, let us begin by breaking it down into subparts and understanding each word separately.

Peer-to-Peer (P2P) Network

Tor and BitTorrent must be familiar to all as both of these are created by using a P2P network. P2P networking is a distributed application architecture that consists of computing devices that are connected to one another without the use of a central server.

The network's protection is dependent on a single organization in centralized networks. The security of the entire network is jeopardized if the single entity or central server is attacked. As a result, P2P networks are safer than centralized networks because there is no single point of failure.

Distributed Ledger

A ledger is a device that keeps track of all of a process's inputs and outputs. A distributed ledger, on the other hand, is a data structure that is shared between multiple computing devices. The system that distributes records across all clients is known as distributed ledger technology. Data model (current state of ledger), transaction language (which changes ledger state), and protocol are the three components of distributed ledger technology (DLT; used to form consensus). Blockchain is a form of distributed ledger technology. As a result, data is exchanged by all users, increasing accountability and reducing corruption.

Consensus

Consensus is a way of ensuring that all participants of a blockchain come to a consensus based on the current state of the blockchain [10]. Different blockchains use a variety of consensus mechanisms to arrive at a consensus. Bitcoin, for example, employs the proof-of-work algorithm, while Ethereum is transitioning from proof-of-work to proof-of-stake [11, 12].

Smart Contracts

Let's put smart contracts and blockchain aside for a moment and look at standard contracts in general. There are a few conditions that must be met or satisfied for a transaction (such as a money exchange) to take place. If you're trading a laptop with me, for example, a contract would state that I'm only obligated to pay you if the laptop works properly. Smart contracts, on the other hand, are pre-transaction conditions that must be met before a transaction can take place in a blockchain.

INSIDE A BLOCKCHAIN

A blockchain is nothing more than a series of interconnected blocks as shown in Figure 5.1. Four parts make up a block:

- The timestamp
- Previous hash
- Hash
- Data

A cryptographic hash of the previous block's data is included in every block. For adding the next block in the chain, the miners compute the nonce by decoding a

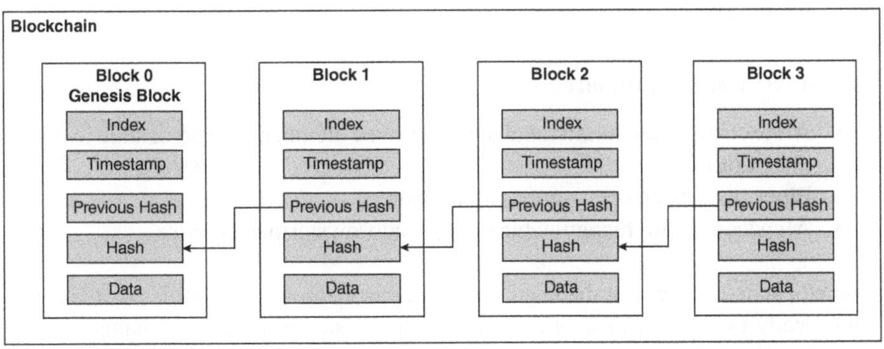

FIGURE 5.1 A block inside a blockchain.

cryptographic puzzle. Evidence of work is what it's called. Because of its cryptographic properties, the blockchain is believed to be immutable. However, this does not rule out the possibility of data manipulation. It means that manipulating the data is extremely difficult, and any alteration is easily detectable. A binary tree with hash pointers is known as a Merkle tree. A Merkle tree is a data structure that allows for safe and efficient content verification in large amounts of data.

FEATURES OF BLOCKCHAIN

Now, why does the need for using blockchain arises? Blockchains are expected to be incorporated by many businesses because of the different benefits it provides [13, 14].

Blockchain technology can be outlined into four key qualities on which it constructs its notoriety:

Low Expense

- Resources used to approve exchanges are principally figuring power that cost not exactly customary labor.
- Less utilization of mediators.
- No compromise work is required.

Reliable

- Transactions handled in the blockchain are permanent and unalterable.
- Blockchain innovation is strong and doesn't have any single purpose of disappointment.

Fast Exchange Settlement

- Ledgers are consequently refreshed.
- Both sides of the exchange are executed all the while.
- Transactions are prepared straightforwardly and distributed with less middle people.

Transparent and Auditable

- All exchanges are unmistakable to approved members and detectable inside the record.
- Blockchain is an open-source innovation.
- All accounts are recognizable on a pseudo-mysterious premise.

The blockchain wipes out the need of a third party among two entities that are willingly ready to exchange something. This helps in saving time as exchanges can be achieved without any outside interference. It saves money as it minimizes overhead and cost of intermediaries. It even reduces the risk of tampering, frauds, and cybercrimes because of its immutable nature [14].

TYPES OF BLOCKCHAIN

There are various forms of blockchain that can be used in the ecosystem:

1. Public: A permission-less blockchain is also known as a public blockchain. All can participate in this blockchain by walking as a node, mining a block, or making transactions inside the blockchain [11, 13]. Public blockchains include Bitcoin and Litecoin.
2. Private: Permissioned blockchain is another name for a nonpublic blockchain. Only members of the association and chosen participants are eligible to participate in the blockchain, so participation is limited or restricted. Personal blockchain projects such as Fabric and Sawtooth are examples of multichain and hyperledger initiatives [10, 11].
3. Consortium: Partially or semi-decentralized blockchains are defined as consortium blockchains. In comparison to public blockchain, which is owned by a single company, it is controlled by a group of companies. Members will participate by walking as a full node, mining, and so on. Consortium blockchains include R3 and the EWF (Energy Web Foundation).

BLOCKCHAIN'S ABILITY TO COMBAT COUNTERFEIT DRUGS

Blockchain innovation is exceptionally fit for monitoring the medication history all through the pharmaceutical supply chain. Two significant perspectives that makes blockchain information secure are that the blocks are immutable and timestamped which makes altering of data unimaginable [13].

Associations can have either an open blockchain or a private one. The associations will share a distributed ledger between the gatherings engaged with the assembling and appropriation of the medication on these blockchains. In addition, in these blockchains, just constrained access is given which relies upon the information-sharing agreement among the two gatherings [11, 13].

With blockchain, we can monitor the medications starting from makers to end customers as shown in Figure 5.2. Each time the medication heads out starting with one substance then onto the next, the information is put away on the blockchain-enabled supply chain. This makes the discernibility of medications a simple assignment and, hence, helps in battling fakes from the health industry.

The two fundamental issues which will be overcome by blockchain-empowered drug store network are initially, pharmaceutical organizations will have the option to follow their items all through the supply chain network and fabricating a sealed shut circuit forbidding the section of fake medications. Also, partners explicitly, labs will have the option to make posteriori move by identifying the specific area of their medications or drugs [10].

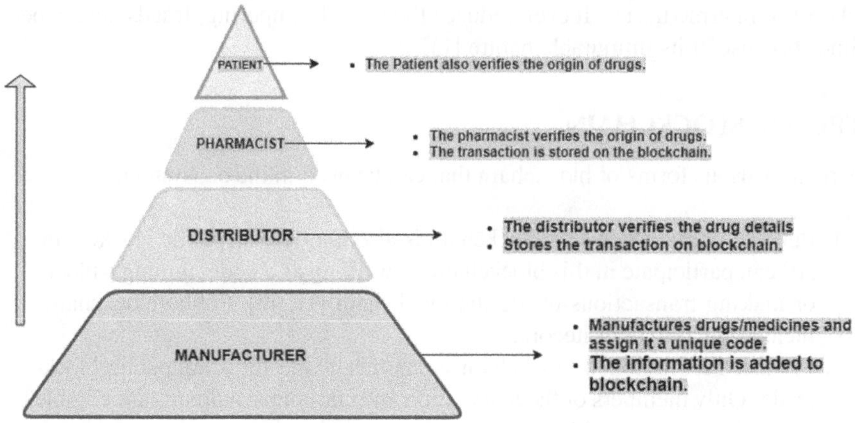

FIGURE 5.2 Medical supply chain hierarchical storage flow for drug safety.

ADVANTAGES OF USING BLOCKCHAIN IN PHARMA SUPPLY CHAIN

Blockchain technology helps in controlling the prime information which lead in building trust, brings flexibility in reacting issues as depicted in Figure 5.3. Further, Figure 5.3 also depicts how blockchain technology help in End-to-End visibility for observing the overall supply chain network.

- Reduced counterfeits-related misfortunes: blockchain can keep a clear track and follow record of whole drugs venture from producer to patient. In this way, tracing location of fake medications would turn out to be simple in the production network.
- The utilization of blockchain in the pharmaceutical inventory network can empower precise areas of meds to be distinguished. It is conceivable to send

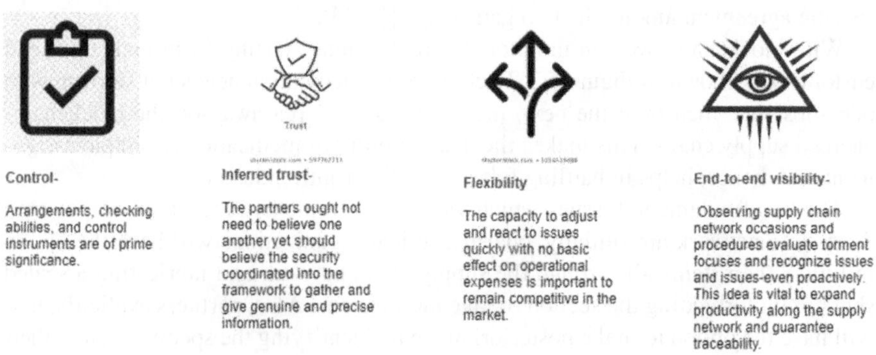

FIGURE 5.3 Key concepts of blockchain-enabled drug supply chain.

or play out the group updates productively and rapidly while keeping up expanded patient well-being security.

- The upgraded discernibility encourages the improvement of merchandise stream and an improved system of drugs stock management.

BLOCKCHAIN APPLICATIONS IN DRUG SUPPLY CHAIN

At present, one of the principle issues in medicinal services is that associations hold numerous and divided well-being records of patients. In Ref. [15], MedicalChain tackled these issues by putting clinical record exchanges on the blockchain to make a brilliant human services environment. In MedicalChain, a brilliant agreement is propelled to give time-restricted access to a patient's electronic well-being record. Specialists compose notes and output lab results, which are completely recorded as exchanges. The drug store apportions prescription and, furthermore, records the exchange on the blockchain. The patient gives a time-restricted access to their backup plan for check of treatment and installment settlement.. With shrewd agreements, patients permit specialists to remotely audit clinical cases and give guidance or a subsequent supposition. Patients offer access to their well-being record to safety-net providers to screen wellness advance and be compensated with tokens or decreased protection premiums. Patients are additionally remunerated for giving examination foundations time-restricted access to their well-being record for preliminary clinical purposes. MedicalChain issues prescription tokens, which patients use for putting away electronic well-being records on the blockchain, information from wearable wellness gadgets, and move worth and installments. MedicalChain will likewise be a stage that empowers designers to fabricate brilliant applications that investigate this information and give proposals, for example, nourishment and wellness schedules.

Blockchain is the one of the most upset advances of things to come. It utilizes circulated record innovation to record and transmit straightforward, secure, controllable, and deficiency-tolerant information. Blockchain has the capacity to make associations, which are decentralized, straightforward, productive, popularity-based, and secure. Throughout the years, numerous blockchain stages have been proposed in the writing. These blockchain applications could be isolated into three classes: open blockchain, private blockchain, and consortium blockchain [16]. Right now, the principle center is to cover health-related blockchain and medication store network in blockchain. Coming up next are not many of the ventures that have upset blockchain (e.g., inventory network the board, systems administration and web of things, determining, banking and installments, protection, estimating, private transportation, carpooling, online information stockpiling, casting a ballot, land, government, noble cause, well-being, vitality the executives, gauging, online music, and retail) [10, 11].

MedicoHealth is a blockchain-based venture intended to improve the divided human services framework. The MedicoHealth stage takes into account completely unknown and safe customer correspondence with world's driving doctors. Doctor certifications, together with permit legitimacy data, are refreshed in a changeless decentralized database. Tolerant information are secretly put away and gotten to just by chosen doctors for a restricted measure of time. Installments are completely tokenized and mysterious. Tokens run the framework and repay the specialist organization, stage, basic convention, and blockchain layer use [14, 17].

In Ref. [18], the creator presented MedRec, which is a blockchain-based decentralized disseminated record innovation for sharing and keeping up patients well-being records. The MedRec is a bitcoin-based arrangement that plans to determine issues like framework interoperability, slow access to clinical information, understanding, organization, and discontinuity. The tale blockchain-based arrangement furnishes patients with complete access to clinical data and unchanging logs across suppliers. The MedRec stage figures out how to keep the clinical records of the patients secure and gives classification, responsibility, and the constant sharing of heath record. The MedRec square information connote viewership and possession shared by the clients of a private, distributed system. The MedRec is a brilliant agreement-empowered stage that utilizes evidence of fill-in as an accord calculation in its working instrument [19]. The brilliant agreement utilizes a cryptographic hash capacity to make sure about the trustworthiness and protection of the health records of patients. The shrewd agreement structure of MedRec is ordered into three sections: register contract (RC), understanding supplier relationship contract (PPR), and a rundown contract (SC). The RC is dependable of character enrollment, PPR gives proprietorship, get to information, electronic medical record inquiries, and hashes, consents, and mining bounties, and SC is liable for keeping up the patient clinical history and furthermore gives insights concerning the patient's present status in the framework.

The "counterfeit medicine project" was as of late propelled by the Hyperledger. The Hyperledger venture plans to target medicate duplicating and its present-use cases. Large think tanks like IBM, Cisco, Accenture, Intel, Bloomberg, and Square Stream are right now associated with this exploration system of medication duplicating. As per this task, each medication which is fabricated is given with a timestamp on it. In this way, in a blockchain innovation, each medication which is created is detectable with its birthplace and maker subtleties. This undertaking diminishes sedate forging [20, 21].

MeFy is a membership-based model, in which the client of the Image Care pursues a yearly membership, permitting them any number of tests during the time for the expense of just consumables. Through its eConsult highlight, MeFy associates overall specialists to overall patients, in this way tackling availability issues, and with its Image Edge gadget, it gives validness to the test led. Image Edge fueled by artificial intelligence will have capacities to produce auto-prescription for off-the-rack medication by handling people's past well-being information, medicines, and natural variables affecting the strength of people of the region. Because of its eConsult work, MeFy interfaces overall specialists with overall patients, accordingly taking care of the availability issues, and utilizing the Image Edge gadget, it guarantees the realness of the test directed [22].

MediBloc's medicinal services data stage is an individual information environment for patients, suppliers, and specialists, based on blockchain innovation [23]. Our central goal is to streamline medication for patients, suppliers, and analysts by redistributing an incentive behind close-to-home human services information possession. Through MediBloc, you can viably claim your clinical information, suppliers can evacuate redundancies to give better mind, and your important information can assist scientists with pushing the headway of medication quicker than any time in recent memory.

CONCLUSION

Blockchain innovation demonstrates the huge ability to profit the present medicinal services. It gives a decentralized stage that shares any kind of exchange and that records data with a changeless and lasting authentic path. We trust it has a bright future in the pharmaceutical supply chain, as it vows to convey a proficient, straightforward, and communitarian arrange for associations to rapidly and safely share information over the assortment of production network divisions and procedures. This innovation permits drugs organizations to fabricate an increasingly adaptable and capable supply network and to heartily address new outside and inner difficulties. The conventional strategies for battling fake medications take a shot at outsider trust and, hence, need terms of security for the medication well-being. In contrast with these present techniques, the structure dependent on blockchain chips away at appropriated record stage and is subsequently profoundly secure and equipped for managing the phony medications danger.

REFERENCES

1. Tyndall, G, Gopal, C, Partsch, W, Kamauff, J. Supercharging supply chains. In *New Ways to Increase Value Through Global Operational Excellence*; 1998.
2. Poirier, CC. *Advanced Supply Chain Management: How to Build a Sustained Competition* Berrett-Koehler. 1999.
3. el Maouchi, M, Ersoy, O, Erkin, Z. TRADE: A transparent, decentralized traceability system for the supply chain. In: Proceedings of 1st ERCIM Blockchain Workshop 2018, European Society for Socially Embedded Technologies (EUSSET), 2018.
4. Chang, Y, Iakovou, E, Shi, W. Blockchain in global supply chains and cross border trade: A critical synthesis of the State-of-the-Art, Challenges and Opportunities. 5 Jan 2019. ArXiv preprint arXiv:1901.02715.
5. Release, IN. Maersk and IBM Unveil First IndustryWide CrossBorder Supply Chain Solution on Blockchain [Online]. 2017. Available from: https://www-03.ibm.com/press/us/en/pressrelease/51712.wss#feeds.
6. Allison, BI. Shipping Giant Maersk Tests Blockchain-Powered Bill of Lading. 2016. Available from: http://www.ibtimes.co.uk/shipping-giant-maersk-tests-blockchain-powered-bills-lading-1585929.
7. Deimel, M, Frentrup, M, Theuvsen, L. Transparency in food supply chains: Empirical results from German pig and dairy production. Journal on China and Network Science 2008;8(1):21–32.
8. Pant, RR, Prakash, G, Farooquie, JA. A framework for traceability and transparency in the dairy supply chain networks. Procedia-Social and Behavioral Sciences 2015;189:385–394.
9. Kshetri, N. 1 Blockchain's roles in meeting key supply chain management objectives. International Journal of Information Management 2018;39:80–89.
10. Dutta, S., Saini, K. Securing data: A study on different transform domain techniques. In WSEAS Transactions on Systems and Control, Volume 16, 2021. DOI: 10.37394/23203.2021.16.8
11. Saini, K. Next generation logistics: A novel approach of blockchain technology. In *Essential Enterprise Blockchain Concepts and Applications*. USA: CRC Press, 2020.
12. Dutta, S., Saini, K. Statistical Assessment of Hybrid Blockchain for SME Sector. In *WSEAS Transactions on Systems and Control*, Volume 16, 2021, E-ISSN: 2224-2856 2021, DOI: 10.37394/23203.2021.16.6

13. Saini, K., Chelliah, P. R., Saini, D. K. (Eds.). *Essential Enterprise Blockchain Concepts and Applications*. New York: Auerbach Publications, 2021.
14. Saini, K., Agarwal, V., Varshney, A., Gupta, A. E2EE for data security for hybrid cloud services: A novel approach. In IEEE International Conference on Advances in Computing, Communication Control and Networking (IEEE ICACCCN 2018) organized by Galgotias College of Engineering & Technology Greater Noida, 12–13 October, 2018. DOI:10.1109/ICACCCN.2018.8748782
15. Medicalchain. Medicalchain, Medicalchain Whitepaper 2.1. Tech. Rep. Medicalchain. 2018. Available from: https://medicalchain.com/Medicalchain-Whitepaper-EN.pdf (accessed on 14 March 2019).
16. Pilkington, M. 11: Blockchain technology: Principles and applications. In *Research Handbook on Digital Transformations*. London, UK: Edward Elgar Publishing, 2016; Volume 225.
17. MedicoHealth. MedicoHealth, MedicoHealth Whitepaper. 2018. Available from: https://medicohealth.io/supporters/documents/wp_beta.pdf (accessed on 15 March 2019).
18. Ekblaw, A, Azaria, A, Halamka, JD, Lippman, A. A case study for blockchain in healthcare: "MedRec" prototype for electronic health records and medical research data. In Proceedings of the IEEE Open & Big Data Conference, Vienna, Austria, 22–24 August 2016; Volume 13, p. 13..
19. Azaria, A, Ekblaw, A, Vieira, T, Lippman, A. Medrec: Using blockchain for medical data access and permission management. In Proceedings of the 2016 2nd International Conference on Open and Big Data (OBD), Vienna, Austria, 22–24 August 2016; pp. 25–30.
20. Arsene, C. Hyperledger Project Explores Fighting Counterfeit Drugs with Blockchain. 2019. Available from: https://healthcareweekly.com/blockchain-in-healthcare-guide/ (accessed on 20 March 2019).
21. Mettler, M. Blockchain technology in healthcare: The revolution starts here. In Proceedings of the 2016 IEEE 18th International Conference on e-Health Networking, Applications and Services (Healthcom), Munich, Germany, 14–16 September 2016; pp. 1–3.
22. Medicalchain. MeFy, MeFy Whitepaper. 2018. Available from: https://icosbull.com/whitepapers/3576/MeFy_whitepaper.pdf (accessed on 15 March 2019).
23. MediBloc. MediBloc, MediBloc Technical Whitepaper. 2018. Available from: https://github.com/medibloc/whitepaper/blob/master/old_whitepaper/medibloc_whitepaper_en.pdf (accessed on 15 March 2019)

6 Blockchain to Secure Data in Internet of Things (IoT)

Pramod Mathew Jacob, Prasanna Mani, R.L. Hariharan and Jisha Mariyam John

CONTENTS

Introduction ... 89
Blockchain Technology ... 90
Elements of Blockchain ... 91
Components of Blockchain ... 92
Properties of Blockchain Technology ... 93
Integration of Blockchain in IoT ... 94
Blockchain-Integrated IoT Model ... 95
Secure Communication ... 95
User Authentication ... 95
Identification of Trustable IoT Nodes ... 96
A Typical Secure IoT Model Consists of Four Layers ... 96
Algorithm for Adding New Block in Transaction Chain ... 97
Use-Case on Smart Farming ... 98
Related Works in Blockchain-Integrated IoT Models ... 99
Features of Blockchain Over Bitcoin ... 100
Conclusion ... 101
References ... 101

INTRODUCTION

The entire world is moving towards automation and smart computing. Internet of Things (IoT) is the prime cause for this revolutionary change. IoT is basically an internetworked collection of objects. An object can be any real-world entity. Objects are also tagged as 'things' in the IoT perspective. The typical IoT architecture is illustrated in Figure 6.1.

A typical IoT architecture consists of a central coordinator module, storage module, sensor-actuator module and a communication module. The central coordinator is usually a lightweight microcontroller or a microprocessor which act as the nodal point of the architecture. The central coordinator can be devices like Arduino Uno [1], Raspberry PI [2], Intel Galileo [3] and NodeMCU. Various peripheral devices like sensors and actuators are attached to the central coordinator. These components

DOI: 10.1201/9781003094210-6

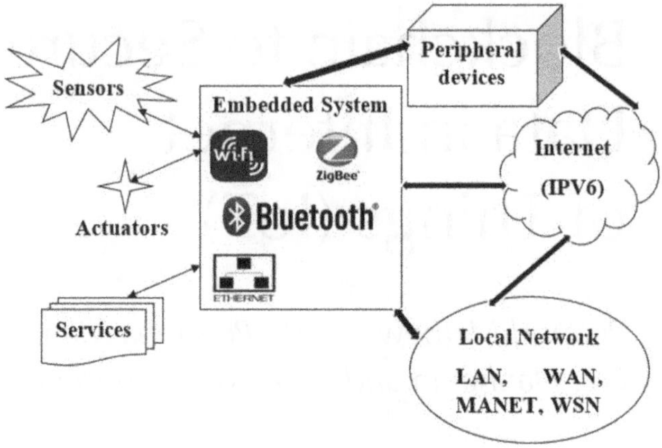

FIGURE 6.1 Architecture of Internet of Things (IoT).

or things are communicating with each other via wireless communication modes like Bluetooth, Zigbee and Wi-Fi (Wireless Fidelity). Usually the sensors act as a data collector (can be considered input module), and the central coordinator acts as a data processor. Based on the processed data, the central coordinator initiates actions with the aid of connected actuators. The data is usually stored in cloud storage so that it can be accessed and processed globally. Offline data storage is usually not preferred in IoT as a typical IoT device is lightweight in nature.

The major source of IoT data is the sensor data. A sensor may continuously fetch data, and it is stored in the cloud storage. The central coordinator accesses data from this cloud storage and processes it for decision-making. Though the decision-making is solely based on the sensed data, the authenticity of the stored data in the cloud is a prime concern in any IoT application. Any data tampering or data manipulation may lead to the entire failure of an IoT system. So, data security should have given a prime focus while designing a typical IoT system. The typical way to enhance data security is to encrypt the stored data using various standard encryption algorithms. But by the intervention of blockchain technology (BCT), data security standards are upgraded to the supreme level. The rest of this chapter discusses about how BCT can be used to secure IoT data in an efficient and effective manner.

BLOCKCHAIN TECHNOLOGY

Blockchain is a powerful and reliable technology which offers a secured mode for digital transactions. The core feature of blockchain is it acts as a 'distributed ledger' which accounts each and every transaction in an auditable, efficient, transparent and secure manner. This is conceptually new and can be applied in various business domains. Blockchain is typically a database system which holds a continuously growing distributed collection of data records. Every transaction is digitally verified and signed to ensure the authenticity. There is no master server which holds the

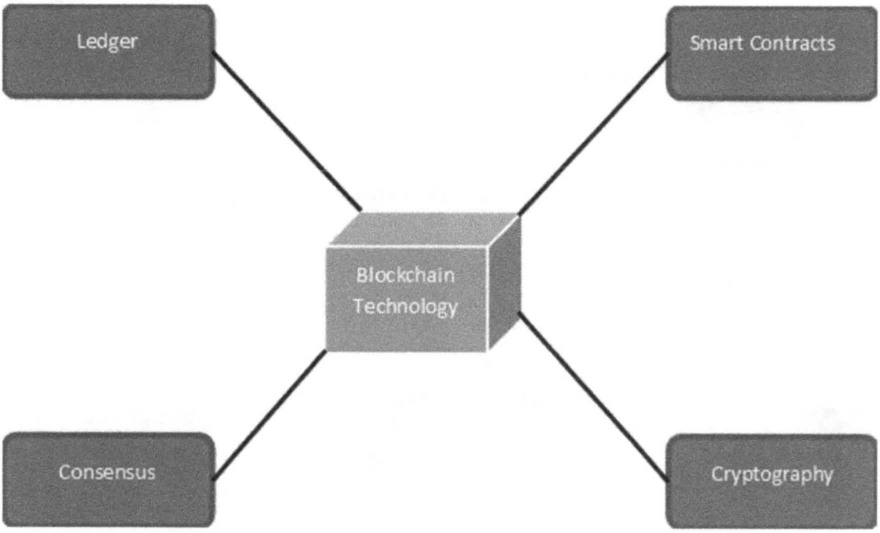

FIGURE 6.2 Four pillars of blockchain.

entire chain. All the participating computers (nodes) possess a copy of the transaction chain. The four pillars of blockchain are illustrated in Figure 6.2.

Consensus supplements the proof of work (PoW) and performs all sorts of verification in the network. Ledger holds the details of all the transactions that take place inside the network. Cryptography is the technique used to encrypt and decrypt the ledger data that is stored in the server or cloud. The data decryption can be performed only by the authorized personnel. Smart contract is a mechanism which is used to ensure the authenticity of all the participants in the network. Various verification and validation schemes are followed for the same.

Elements of Blockchain

A blockchain consist of two elements:

1. **Transactions:** It is any action performed by the participant in a blockchain.
2. **Blocks:** This component records all the transactions in the sequential manner and ensures that no block has been tampered. This is ensured by using a timestamp for all the transactions when and where it is added to the chain.

BCT prevents data tampering and, thereby, ensures the data security. IoT data is usually more critical as data tampering may result in the malfunctioning of the entire system. Though every transaction needs to be approved by the consensus, blockchain can be integrated with IoT to enhance data security. Figure 6.3 illustrates the working of typical blockchain architecture [4].

When a request for editing the transaction is initiated or a new transaction enters into the blockchain, the majority of the nodes that participate in the blockchain

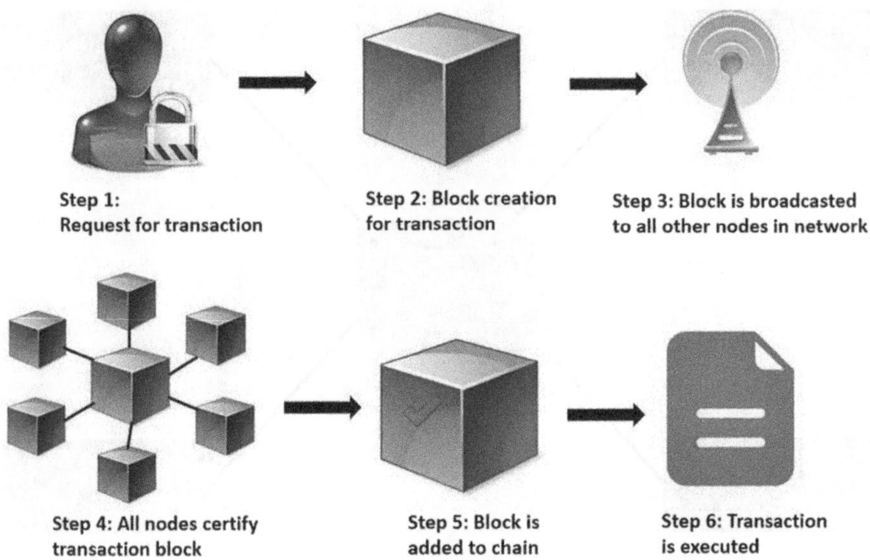

FIGURE 6.3 Illustration of working of blockchain technology.

process execute algorithms to check the authenticity of every blockchain block under consideration. If most of the participating nodes feel that the history and digital signature are valid, the new transaction module will be accepted in the distributed ledger and a new module will be added to the transaction chain. If most of the participating nodes do not perceive the digital signature as genuine, the request for change or addition will be rejected; else the new block is appended to the transaction chain. Therefore, this distributed consensus model allows blockchain to act as a distributed ledger which doesn't require centralized authority to verify records or transactions.

Components of Blockchain

A typical blockchain-based system [5] consists of four components as follows:

1. Networked nodes: All nodes are connected through the Internet where various transactions are taking place. During the initiation of a new transaction, its metadata is attached to previous transaction ledger, which is termed as 'mining'. All the new transactions are made authentic only if they are collectively approved by all the stakeholder nodes.
2. Distributed blocks: It is a distributed database which consists of distinct information blocks. This information is shared with every other node in the system. A block consists of metadata such as transactions list, timestamp and other information, which points to the previous link.
3. Shared distributed ledger: This is a publicly shared ledger which is updated during every transaction.
4. Cryptography: It is the technique of encrypting and decrypting of data using various algorithmic techniques to prevent data tampering.

Properties of Blockchain Technology

The three key properties of BCT are:

1. Decentralization
2. Immutability
3. Transparency

In previous days, there was a centralized system which may monitor and record all the transactions in a system. Any change can be initiated by the central coordinator. But the people who work with centralized system can tamper the data of various transactions without the intimation of other clients. This may lead to serious problems in case of a financial organization.

Blockchain overcomes this demerit by providing a decentralized system where the transaction chain is distributed among the participating clients or nodes. Whenever a node or a client tries to modify the data, it is intimated with all the other clients participating in that system. Thus, it is impossible to tamper the data without the consent of the majority of participating clients inside a blockchain. Thus, decentralization has become a key property of BCT.

The property 'transparency' is a bit confusing for a BCT as it is considered a secure system. Of course, the system is secure, and all the transactions and details of clients involved are stored in an encrypted form. But still, if any client tries to access or modify a transaction, it will be alerted to all the participating clients to achieve transparency.

Immutability in blockchain is the property which ensures that once a data is added to the system, it is impossible to tamper the same. This is one of the unique properties of blockchain compared to other similar techniques like bitcoin and centralized systems. Immutability is achieved in blockchain using some cryptographic hash function. Blockchain can be considered a linked list which includes data and a hash pointer. Hash pointer points to its previous block and thus generates a chain of blocks. Hash pointer is similar to a pointer in linked list, but instead of simply holding the address of previous block it also holds the hash of the data inside the previous block existing in the chain.

The blockchain network is simply a collection of nodes which are interconnected. The blockchain is maintained by peer-to-peer network architecture. In peer-to-peer model, there is no single centralized server. Every system participating in the network has equal priority. Every system can communicate with each other. Same system can work as both client and server in different instances. Thus, there are multiple distributed and decentralized servers. Though the system is using a peer-to-peer model, there is not a single point of failure.

A node in the blockchain can be categorized as follows:

1. **Light client:** A computer system which possess a shallow copy of blockchain.
2. **Full node:** A computer system possesses the full copy of blockchain.
3. **Mining:** A computer system which verifies the transactions.

Blockchain is a promising technology to ensure the data security and trustworthiness of the end user. Though IoT is incorporated in almost all aspects of human life, the security of personal data is the primary concern of every end user. As IoT uses lightweight architecture, it is not easy to use strong security algorithms to prevent data stealing. In this scenario, blockchain came to rescue IoT applications by providing a lightweight decentralized, distributed architecture to secure the data. The implementation of EdgeChain and LightChain proves that blockchain and IoT can go a long way ahead in the future years of computer technology.

INTEGRATION OF BLOCKCHAIN IN IoT

IoT is transforming and efficiently optimizing the manual processes to obtain huge volumes of data collected from various real-time systems. This collected data is processed accordingly, and the required information is extracted to derive conclusions. This model is used in weather forecasting, stock market prediction, smart farming, patient health monitoring etc.

The concept of cloud computing provides various functionalities to the IoT systems like data analysis and data processing. This unprecedented development in the IoT has paved way for new mechanisms to access and share information. But due to the transparent nature of IoT systems, end users lack confidence to share sensitive information through IoT systems.

Centralized architecture is used in most of the IoT applications where the network participants don't have a clear vision to the shared data through the network. The shared information may look like a black box, and the users don't know the authenticity and source of data. The need of blockchain in IoT is discussed in the next section.

Due to the distributed nature of IoT network, every node is a possible point of failure, which may be exploited by the cyber attackers (for example, distributed denial-of-service attack). An integrated class of nodes with multiple infected devices working simultaneously may lead to system collapse. Another key concern is the presence of central cloud service provider in an IoT environment. Any failure to this central node may lead to vulnerability which should be addressed. One of the most critical issues is data authentication and confidentiality. Lack of data security in IoT devices can be exploited and may be used in an inappropriate manner. Due to intervention of modern business models where the system can share or exchange data/resources autonomously, the need of data security is critical.

Another critical challenge in IoT is data integrity which has found some applications in the area of decision support systems (DSS). The collected data from the sensors can be used for generating timely instructions or decisions. Thus, it is mandatory to protect the system from injection attacks where the attackers inject false measures or values into the system which may seriously affect the accurate decision-making. Availability is critical for application domains like manufacturing plants, automated vehicular networks and smart grids where the real-time data is continuously monitored. Loss of data during a particular interval may result in the entire system failure. The integration of a security measure to publicly verify the audit trail will be beneficial for these sorts of systems. This can be easily achieved by the integration of blockchain.

The integration of various technologies like IoT, cloud computing and blockchain into a single system has proven to be incomparable as it ensures both performance and security [6]. The concept of implementing blockchain in IoT systems is a revolutionary step as it provides trusted data sharing services where the data is reliable and traceable [7]. The source of data being generated can be traced out at any stage, and at the same time, the data remains immutable.

In domains like smart cities and AI-based smart cars, reliable data is to be shared for the inclusion of new nodes (participants) in the system and, thereby, enhances the services. Thus, the implementation of blockchain can complement the IoT-based applications with increased reliability and enhanced security. Though the IoT functionalities can be improved with the aid of blockchain, there is still a great number of research constraints and issues that are to be resolved.

BLOCKCHAIN-INTEGRATED IoT MODEL

There are numerous ways to strengthen IoT security using the integration of BCT. The integration of blockchain is a prime concern in the following areas of IoT.

Secure Communication

The IoT devices have to communicate for data exchanging to process a transaction and store the same in the ledger. These ledgers are also used to store encryption keys to make the exchanges more secure and confidential. IoT device sends a message, which is encrypted, to the destination using a public key which is later stored in the blockchain network. The sender then requests its node to get the public key of receiver from the ledger. After that, the sender encrypts the message using the public key of receiver in such a way that only the receiver can decrypt the message using their private key.

User Authentication

The sender attaches digital signature to the message while sending to all other nodes. The receiver then receives public key from the distributed ledger. Receiver uses this public key to verify the received message's digital signature. The working of digital signature is explained as follows.

1. The sender generates a hash function and then calculates hash value of a message which is later encrypted using a private key.
2. The message is then transmitted along with the digital signature.
3. At the receiver side, the key stored in the shared ledger is used to estimate the hash value generated by the sender. Using that hash value, digital sign is decrypted.
4. The authenticity of the message is validated only if the generated hash and protected hash values are same.
5. To enhance the trust, the digital signature of all received messages is stored in the distributed ledger.

Identification of Trustable IoT Nodes

The identification of trustable IoT nodes is a herculean task for any IoT designer. Though there may be millions of IoT devices connected on the same network, there should be some reliable mechanism to ensure the trust of connected nodes. Whenever an IoT device starts, it initiates a request to the central server to provide the list of trustable nodes in the network. After that, the device gets registered itself in a trustable node and then starts communication between nodes. It can receive information from other trustable nodes and can send information to various peer nodes. DNSSec protocol has to be implemented to secure name resolution of various root servers and, thereby, prevent from spoof attacks. This sort of device enrolment can be easily performed in a public network. In private network, the root server has the responsibility of adding a new device to the blockchain by verifying the authenticity.

A Typical Secure IoT Model Consists of Four Layers

These layers are sensor layer, communication layer, data processing layer and data storage layer. It is illustrated in Figure 6.4.

The sensor layer consists of various sensors deployed in real-time environments. The sensors may be distributed in nature. The data fetched by various sensors is fed to the central coordinator module via firewall gateways. Firewall gateway ensures end-to-end connectivity between the sensors and central coordinator using TCP/IP connection management policies. Firewall gateway negotiates various firewall hops

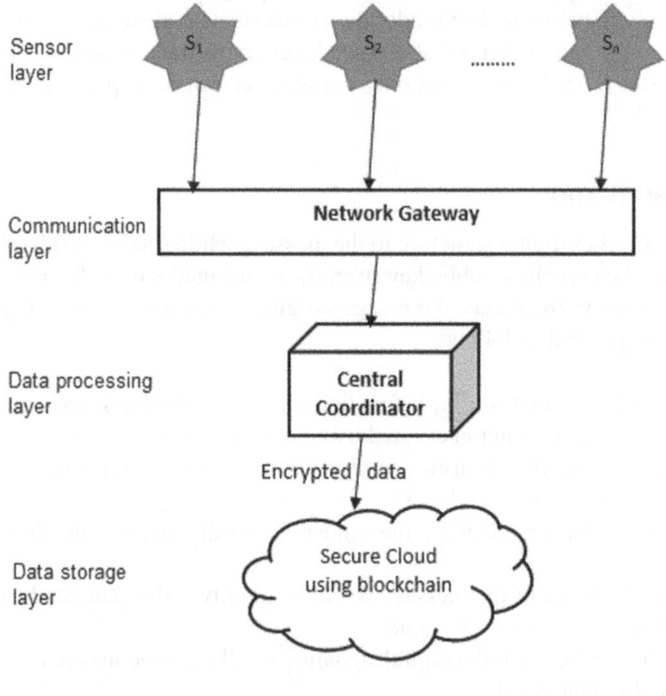

FIGURE 6.4 Blockchain-integrated IoT model.

and also supports network address translation. The data gathered by central coordinator is then encrypted using Twofish algorithm.

Twofish algorithm uses a block-ciphering system with a single key of length up to 256 bits. This encryption standard is efficient and can be integrated in an IoT device. This encrypted data from various gateways are stored in the cloud along with its gateway ID as a blockchain. These blocks are implemented as shared so that users can access it from anywhere at any time. The algorithm for creating a new block in the transaction chain is discussed as follows.

Algorithm for Adding New Block in Transaction Chain

1. Read the sensor input as a Transaction (T_i).
2. T_i is broadcasted to all nodes (N_1, N_2...N_n).
3. Every node gathers new transactions into a block and executes a consensus algorithm for its respective block.
4. When the node completes the consensus algorithm processing, it broadcasts the block and the processing results are mapped in blocks based on trust value.
5. Node N_i accepts the block only if all the transactions are valid.
6. If acceptance is successful, next block is created in the chain using hash function.

The blocks are interrelated in such a way that the parent block's hash is stored in the header field of child's block as shown in Figure 6.5.

Every updated sensor value is stored as a transaction. Transactions are properly hashed and stored. The hashes of two transactions are fetched and hashed together to

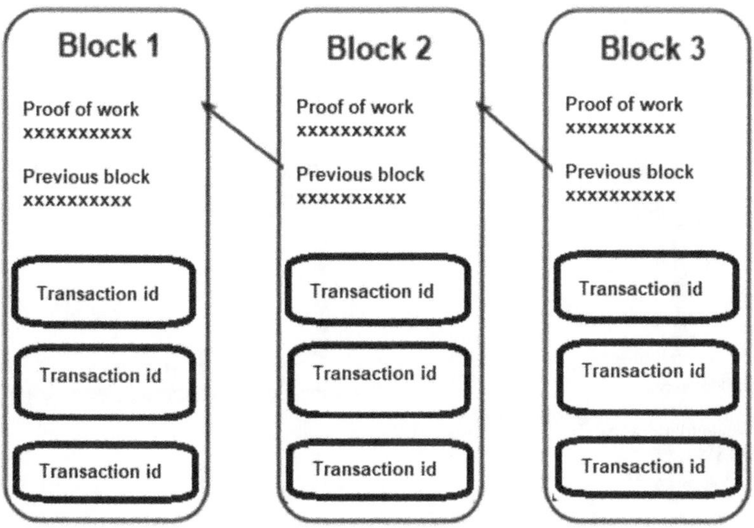

FIGURE 6.5 Hierarchy of related blocks.

generate the next hash. This process is repeatedly carried out and eventually generates a single hash from every transaction stored in a block. The hashing mechanism used here is transaction Merkle root hash [8].

The design of blockchain system is in such a way that it raises an objection when the data modification is initiated by anyone. Once the data is stored in the distributed ledger as block on the chain, it is impossible to tamper with the data without modifying all subsequent blocks. This exciting feature of blockchain is exploited in our proposed model to enhance the data security in the IoT systems. This feature of blockchain requires public verification for data modification and, thereby, enhances the trust. Ethereum is a generally used decentralized ledger which uses SHA256 for all the hashing processes.

USE-CASE ON SMART FARMING

Jacob et al. validated this integrated blockchain model by implementing a smart farming system using IoT [9]. They chose smart farming system as their experimental domain due to its lightweight architecture. It consists of various modules which require security and trust in every level of data storage.

The proposed smart farming system consists of the following four modules: Android app module, ML module, sensors module and a central coordinator module. The sensors are placed in the agricultural field to sense the required parameters. The sensors sent the data to the central coordinator which is managed by an Android application. This data is sent to a cloud database. The mobile app analyses the cloud data and alerts the farmer if any parameter exceeds its threshold limit. Node MCU acts as the central coordinator. The user can view all the data acquired from the sensors on the app, and necessary actions can be taken. The block diagram of smart farming system is shown in Figure 6.6.

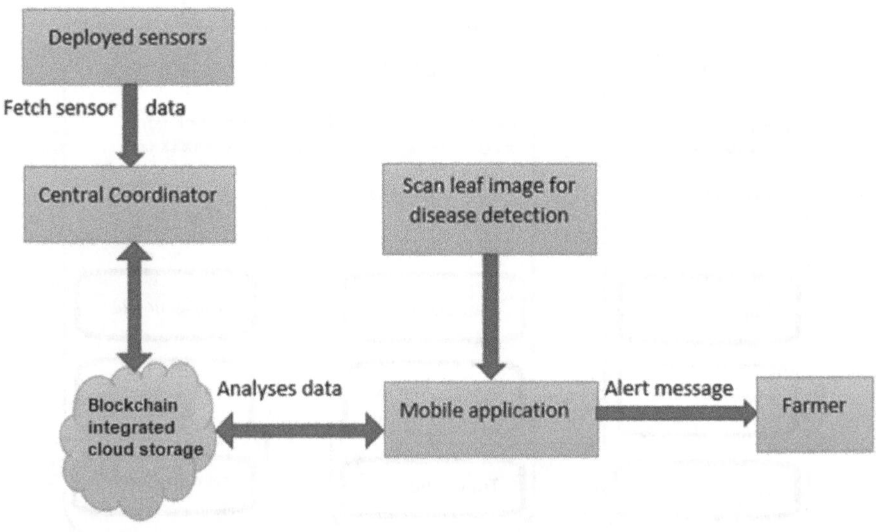

FIGURE 6.6 Block diagram of smart farming IoT system.

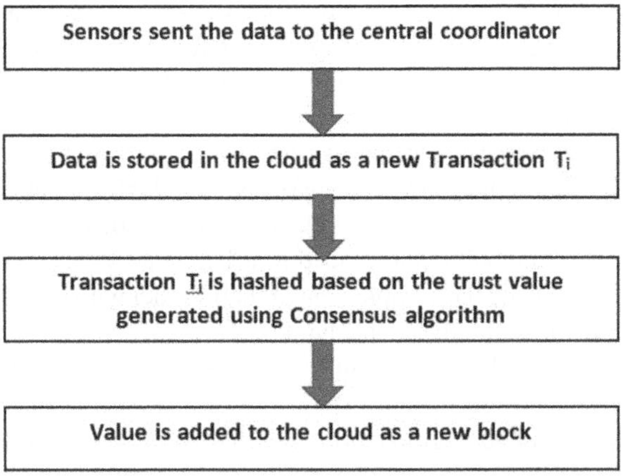

FIGURE 6.7 Workflow of blockchain-integrated smart farming system.

The workflow of our proposed model is illustrated in Figure 6.7. The sensor data is received by the central coordinator and stored in the central cloud in an encrypted form. Every transaction is added as a new block of data which should be approved by all the associated parties or stakeholders.

The automated watering process is initiated based on the stored data in the cloud which is fetched by the sensors. Whenever the moisture fetches the value, a transaction (T_i) is generated. It is hashed based on the trust value generated by the consensus algorithm. After the consensus algorithm processing the value is added to the cloud as a new block. Thus, the trust of data can be ensured in this system. The Android module decrypts these stored data and processes the information to initiate the necessary actions like watering, weather monitoring and fertilizing. Any tampering of data in these sensed values by any unauthorized person may affect the harvest of the crop. Thus, it is essential to ensure the stored value is accurate and trustable. The blockchain module in this system ensures and guarantees trust to the farmers.

RELATED WORKS IN BLOCKCHAIN-INTEGRATED IoT MODELS

There were many researchers who exploited the benefits of integrating blockchain in IoT. Securing the data exchanged between IoT devices is a critical challenge for every IoT service provider. Though various security measures are there, IoT requires a lightweight security model to ensure data integrity and security.

Kim et al. [10] proposed a taxonomy for securing IoT devices used in home and business applications. They encrypted the data shared in the distributed IoT architecture, and a smart contract is used to ensure the data integrity. They validated their system with a home automation system. Their experimental results prove that various security threats like man in middle attack, data stealing can be avoided with the help of blockchain.

Fakhri et al. [11] proposed a comparison model of a smart refrigerator system with and without BCT. They initiated explicit sniffing attacks to prove the validity of their model. Experiment results claims that blockchain has an upper hand over traditional security measure in an IoT system. They have observed the avalanche effect of encryption algorithms and the hash functions used. MQTT is used as the software pattern for application without IoT.

Oscar Novo [12] proposed a detailed clear-cut implementation of incorporating blockchain in IoT. This lightweight, transparent and scalable model introduces a new access control policy among the stakeholders using the benefits of blockchain. A node called management hub is introduced in IoT to store various distributed smart contract information. They have implemented their model with the help of Ethereum which is one of the most popular blockchain platforms.

Lv et al. [13] proposed a publish-subscribe-based IoT model over blockchains. This model mainly focuses on centralized IoT systems where all the data is stored at a single point. The failure of this node may lead to the entire failure of the system. The data integrity of this sort of system can be ensured by using BCT. They have implemented a lightweight, primitive key-based algorithm for ensuring the data security. They have validated their model with the help of Ethereum platform.

Viriyasitavat et al. [14] proposed a blockchain-based service handling operations in IoT. Their model claims that blockchain can be used for achieving interoperability of various services. They integrated together service-oriented architecture (SoA), BCT and various key performance indicators (KPI), which resolves both trust issues and interoperability challenges in the IoT system.

Doku et al. [15] proposed LightChain which is a dedicated blockchain architecture for IoT. PoW mechanism was initially used for verifying transactions. But the computational tasks and efforts required to resolve a PoW puzzle was enormously high which is not acceptable in a lightweight architecture like IoT. The PoW puzzle solving efforts are distributed among various nodes in the IoT system. Thus, the overhead of every single node can be drastically reduced, which improves the overall system performance and security.

Pan et al. [16] proposed EdgeChain which is an edge computing-based IoT architecture incorporating the BCT. The central node of the IoT architecture is excluded from the computational overhead of BCT. All these operations are performed in the edge-based cloud pool, which makes the architecture lightweight. Thus, it can ensure features like data security, integrity, scalability, interoperability and enhanced performance aspects.

FEATURES OF BLOCKCHAIN OVER BITCOIN

BCT has the following advantages over traditional bitcoin concept.

1. Decentralized control: There is no central authority to define or dictate rules. The authority is distributed in nature.
2. Data transparency: The metadata of all the transactions that take place inside the network is stored in the system and publicly available to all the peers.
3. Secure: Any data stored using blockchain concept is tamperproof. No one can modify or delete data without the knowledge of participants in the chain.
4. Decentralized consensus: The transactions are approved and validated by all the nodes in the network; not by a centralized authority.

5. Distribute information: Each node in the network stores a copy of the blockchain to avoid the overhead of centralized authority and privately stores the copy.

CONCLUSION

IoT is used in almost all areas of human life. The sensors gather the required data and store in a cloud database. The central coordinator processes this data to initiate necessary actions. Though the actuators are initiated based on stored data, the trust of this data is to be ensured. Any unauthorized person can gather this stored information, which may lead to the malfunctioning of the automation process. Thus, the entire IoT system may lead to failure due to data tampering. To resolve this, we proposed a blockchain-integrated secure IoT model. Whenever the sensor fetches a data, a transaction is initiated and the hash function is estimated based on the previous data and the new block is added only if the transaction is validated. Thus, we can control the unauthorized access to the IoT data and, thereby, resist tampering of data. We have validated our model by implementing it in a smart farming system which automates watering and fertilizing in an agricultural field. Experimental results prove that our model can be used in lightweight IoT models to ensure the data security and trust.

REFERENCES

1. "Arduino," March 2017. [Online]. Available: https://www.arduino.cc [accessed 4 April 2018].
2. "Raspberry PI," March 2017. [Online]. Available: https://www.raspberrypi.org/ [accessed 16 March 2018].
3. "IntelGalileo," April 2017. [Online]. Available: https://www.arduino.cc/en/Arduino Certified/IntelGalileo [accessed 6 May 2018].
4. "BlockGeeks," 2018. [Online]. Available: https://blockgeeks.com/guides/what-is-block chain-technology/ [accessed 14 6 2020].
5. S. Jain, "Blockchain to Secure IoT Data," GeeksforSeeks, 1 August 2020. [Online]. Available: https://www.geeksforgeeks.org/blockchain-to-secure-iot-data/ [accessed 2 August 2020].
6. Y. Lee, S. Rathore, J. H. Park, J. H. Park, "A Blockchain-Based Smart Home Gateway Architecture for Preventing Data Forgery," *Human-centric Computing and Information Sciences*, vol. 10, no. 9, 2020.
7. C. AnaReyna, "On Blockchain and its Integration with IoT. Challenges and Opportunities," *Future Generation Computer Systems*, vol. 88, pp. 173–190, November 2018.
8. N. Tapas, F. Longo, G. Merlino and A. Puliafito, "Experimenting with Smart Contracts for Access Control and Delegation in IoT," *Future Generation Computer Systems*, vol. 111, pp. 324–338, 2020.
9. P. M. Jacob, J. M. John, S. Suresh, P. Nath H and P. Nandakumar, "An Intelligient System for Monitoring and Managing Agricultural Fields," *International Journal of Recent Technology and Engineering*, vol. 8, no. 4, November 2019.
10. M. Singh, A. Singh and S. Kim, "Blockchain: A Game Changer for Securing IoT Data," in *2018 IEEE 4th World Forum on Internet of Things (WF-IoT)*, Singapore, 2018.
11. Mutijarsa and D. Fakhri, "Secure IoT Communication using Blockchain Technology," in *2018 International Symposium on Electronics and Smart Devices (ISESD)*, Bandung, 2018.

12. O. Novo, "Blockchain Meets IoT: An Architecture for Scalable Access Management in IoT," *IEEE Internet of Things Journal*, vol. 5, no. 2, pp. 1184–1195, April 2018.
13. P. Lv, L. Wang, H. Zhu, W. Deng and L. Gu, "An IOT-Oriented Privacy-Preserving Publish/Subscribe Model Over Blockchains," *IEEE Access*, vol. 7, pp. 41309–41314, 2019.
14. W. Viriyasitavat, L. D. Xu, Z. Bi and A. Sapsomboon, "New Blockchain-Based Architecture for Service Interoperations in Internet of Things," *IEEE Transactions on Computational Social Systems*, vol. 6, no. 4, pp. 739–748, August 2019.
15. R. Doku, D. B. Rawat, M. Garuba and L. Njilla, "LightChain: On the Lightweight Blockchain for the Internet-of-Things," in *2019 IEEE International Conference on Smart Computing (SMARTCOMP)*, Washington, DC, USA, 2019.
16. J. Pan, J. Wang, A. Hester, I. Alqerm, Y. Liu and Y. Zhao, "EdgeChain: An Edge-IoT Framework and Prototype Based on Blockchain and Smart Contracts," *IEEE Internet of Things Journal*, vol. 6, no. 3, pp. 4719–4732, June 2019.

7 Blockchain IoT Concepts for Smart Grids, Smart Cities and Smart Homes

Shriyash Mohril, Mahipal Singh Sankhla, Swaroop S. Sonone and Rajeev Kumar

CONTENTS

Introduction 104
Overview of Smart City Model 105
Aims of Smart City 105
Smart City: Scope 105
Scope of Smart Cities Comprises the Following 105
Internet of Things for Smart Cities 107
IoT Applications for Smart Cities 109
Smart Homes 109
Online Monitoring of Power Lines 110
Smart Parking Lot 110
Demand-side Energy Management 111
Integration of Distributed Energy Sources 111
Integration of Electric Vehicles 112
Healthcare 112
Weather and Water Systems 112
Surveillance Systems 113
Smart Cities and Communities 114
Blockchain-Based Smart Cities 114
Blockchain Solutions and Smart Contracts 115
Blockchain Model and its Application in Smart Grid 116
Challenges 117
Impacts of Block Size 117
Security 117
Data Ownership and Privacy 117
Trust 117
Social Issues 118
Central Control 118
Costs in Updating Present Towns 118
Conclusion 118
References 118

DOI: 10.1201/9781003094210-7

INTRODUCTION

In today's scenario, the rate at which new technologies are developing is very fast. Science and technology provide us new devices and studies every day. Such improvements were unthinkable 20 years ago; the cloud computing, Internet of Things (IoT), the existence of smartphones, and smart towns was far from realism. There are specimens of advancements that take wholly novel ways such as shared computation that uses sensory grids containing many smart detectors, meters, and counters (Kushch, S. et al. 2017). The IoT is a high-tech improvement focused on the assimilation of instruments in a varied series of surroundings over the Internet (Javaid, U. et al. 2018). The combination of data and contact technologies in the energy industry has directed to an innovation called the smart grid (SG). Via these techniques, the complete employing of the SG bionetwork reaching from distribution, transmission, power production, utilization, and transfer to consumption is handled actively with better quality efficiency, scalability, and reliability (Jingcheng, G. et al. 2012). Due to the speedy growth of the resident's concentration in city surroundings, services and substructures have been required to fund the necessities of the civilian. Thus, there is a significant progress of digital instruments, such as actuators, smart appliances, sensors, and mobile phones, which get-up-and-go to massive marketable purposes of IoT, since it is likely to interrelate all instruments and generate interactions among themselves over the Internet. In-house applications, it offers simulated entertainment as well as actual relationships. IoT makes houses better energy efficient by controlling devices like washing machines and refrigerators. Over the enlargement of area grids at houses, it is conceivable to govern the fitness conditions of the elders, and this decreases action prices. Some social media apps like Facebook help gather the information of the people for an occasion (Talari, S. et al. 2017). As the civilians have fully grown to rely on the data, communication, and important sources of the Internet, there is an increased desire to have all things connected to the Internet. These markets consist of devices in furniture, vehicles, and appliances to deliver more information and accessibility from our day to day lives to our world of Internet. Providing sensors to varied backgrounds, there is an assumption that our life develops to be extra safe, convenient, and efficient. This approach is well defined as the IoT (Atzori, L. et al. 2010). The generation of IoT and wireless message systems add the frame of the idea of smart cities that is a usual outcome of the city development and the growing residents, as well as the reserve consumption optimism. Still, with the expansion of smart city system supplementary available and relevant to the real life of residents, safety and secrecy worries rise as well. Open information admittance happens where there are smart terminals such as self-service machines for vending or rentals. These information admittances are confronted with truth and privacy dangers as maximum information is related to individuality and monetary data. With this idea, novel outbreak exteriors are being recognized, but safety answers are still being investigated (Suo, H. et al. 2012). Due to social and practical growths, it will be unavoidable that energy production from reusable energy sources will show an added dynamic part to fulfil the energy request. Of all reusable energy sources, wind and solar energy will donate to a huge portion in the present and upcoming groups. Equated to old-style power production arrangements, these dispersed energy sources have precise features that direct new tasks to the existing distribution scheme (Muyeen, S.M. et al. 2017).

OVERVIEW OF SMART CITY MODEL

Elevated opinion of the smart town prototype depicts how the numerous objects in a smart town interact within themselves to offer facilities in smart towns (Rameshwar, R. et al. 2020, Krishnamurthi, R. et al. 2019, Das, S. et al. 2019, Nayyar, A. et al. 2019, Solanki, A. et al. 2019). Diverse parts of smart cities cooperate with one another over telephonic amenities or net facilities like Wi-Fi, ZigBee, and 3G/4G/5G/6G. The SG, smart power, and clever movement are the dissimilar facilities in the smart town situation. Micro- or macrocells are interaction devices utilized to offer on-demand facilities (Singh, P. et al. 2020).

AIMS OF SMART CITY

Smart city offers an important medium for the movement of info on knowledge and expertise. Its aim is to inspire experts to publish their theoretical and experimental consequences in a detailed manner. There is no binding in lengths to produce an experimental work. Articles concerning research applications and research philosophies are always welcomed. One of the unique characteristics is that software and digital files, giving all particulars of the summing and experimental processes, can be accumulated as accompanying material (Siano, P. et al. 2018). There is a great hope that IoT will be effective in partaking smart appliances and homes similar to smart refrigerators, lighting control, home temperature monitoring, smart TVs, fire detection, and security systems. These appliances and systems include actuators and sensors that govern the surroundings and direct investigation information to a regulator unit. The controller unit allows the homeowners to uninterruptedly govern and regulate the electrical devices extensively. It practices surveillance statistics to forecast forthcoming events to be ready in advance for a more suitable, relaxed, safe, and well-organized existing situation. A cluster of smart homes in a neighbourhood is linked by a NAN or Neighbour Area Network to arrange a smart society (Li, X. et al. 2011). Houses share the consequences of their open-air scrutiny cameras to sense slight misfortune and notify police posts in a smart community. More devices of the smart society approach are in handling communal sources, healthcare, and allowing sustenance to social networking. The idea of smart society is protracted to progress smart city (Stratigea, A. 2012). In the smart town, a complete observation system is established to regulate diverse doings in the full city or a nation (Jaradat, M. et al. 2015).

SMART CITY: SCOPE

Scope of Smart Cities Comprises the Following

- Electrical manufacturing for smart cities – blockchain, smart networks, and power electronics for smart cities, renewable energies, smart lighting, smart homes, energy market, and smart buildings.
- IT engineering and computer engineering for digital towns and smart initiatives. Information management and information communication technology

set-up in smart cities, IoT devices, IoT constructions, procedures and processes, cloud computing, IoT network technologies; autonomic computing; statistics management; smart data processing and immediate and semantic web facilities, big data management for smart cities, and situation-based structures for cities and industries.

- Cyber networking structures.
- Virtual reality.
- Smart hospitals and informatics for cities – e-fitness, digital health, telehealth, telemedicine, and smart health.
- Mobility and transport – smart transport structures and electric mobility, vehicular systems, mobility, traffic congestion, parking, people mobility, and logistics.
- Engineering dimensions for towns – communications and networks, developments in sensor interface, SG detection and management in grids, multi sensor data combination models for SGs and smart cities, standardization of dispersed detecting networks and traceability, distributed and networked sensors for smart cities, ubiquitous sensing, radio frequency identification (RFID), embedded sensing and actuating, wireless sensor networks, and mobile internet.
- Civil manufacturing for smart cities, environmental engineering for cities, city constructions and substructures, maintainable areas and town growth, smart water administration, agriculture, waste managing for cities, and greenhouses.
- Flood management, predicting, broadcasting, and weather analysis for cities.
- Automobile engineering and power-driven sciences for smart cities.
- Humanities and practical science for cities.
- Retail for cities, smart product management, Near Field Communication Payments, smart shop requests, supply chain control, etc. Emergencies, safety, and confidentiality in cities, identity management, and cryptography.
- Living: community security, well-being, and public spaces for communal novelty, ethos, and pollution control.
- E-government and smart urban governance for cities.
- Social and business issues for smart cities: commercial archetypal novelty in smart towns advertising plans for the contribution of the company for novel facilities in smart cities, smart economy, and green and blue economy.
- Deployments and experimentation: system design, real answers, pilot deployments, evaluation, and modelling for smart cities and act assessment.
- Challenges and trends in cities.
- Data analysis, big data, data storage, visualization, and governance.
- Sensors for designing, usage, and transmission of data.
- Social sciences like privacy, governance, social acceptability, law, innovation, and economic model.
- E-governance smart services.
- Smart care (Siano, P. et al. 2018).

INTERNET OF THINGS FOR SMART CITIES

IoT can be a broadband interface that uses standard transmission rules (Atzori, L. et al. 2010, Internet of Things 2020), whereas the web would be its meeting point. IoT is the broad presence of things that can be estimated and incidental, also because it's in a position to transform objects. Accordingly, IoT uses an extension of numerous object and transmission modes. IoT includes smart equipment like smartphones and other amenities as well as appliances, landmarks, and foodstuff (Six Technologies with Potential Impacts on US Interests 2017, Alamri, A. et al. 2013). This will help to receive a common aim. The most typical feature of the IoT is its impact on the living of the users (Strategic Opportunity Analysis of the Global Smart City Market 2017). The idea of IoT is that as the wiring price is high for many detectors, the interaction among the sensors that is wireless. The low-energy standard transmission is appropriate for communications in most gadgets. Some systems are described as follows based on consistency with surface and area coverage:

1. HAN commonly known as Home Area Networks uses short ranged standard like Wi-Fi, Dash7, and ZigBee. All regulating and controlling elements between houses are connected through the HAN.
2. WAN or Wide Area Networks create a connection between customers and distribution utilities that need a wider coverage than HAN and require fibre broadband or cable wireless such as 3G and LTE for implementation.
3. Field Area Networks are utilized for connection among consumers and substation (Hancke, G. et al. 2012).

In IoT, both functions involving detecting and processing the information have been implemented, but they are not integrated from the WSN or wireless sensor network perspective. Combined answers are iOBridge and Speakthing. Speakthing is an analytics IoT platform for the collection, imagining, and examining the live information directly in the cloud, and you're equipped to check the information by coding in MATLAB. In difference, iOBridge has computer hardware modules attached to clouds that can be retrieved through web interfaces and indented up data are often combined to other web facilities. It's striking that the clouds are notably significant in smart towns for data storage and processing. An IoT-associated technology is described during this unit (Talari, S. et al. 2012).

One of the main challenges and perhaps many of us may be wondering how IoT usually cannot establish and build a wise city. That is why we have come up with the right explanation and solution to the current question. IoT is named the interconnecting of various devices together on the web. We are heading to the smart age houses and towns. So, we start thinking about what is available in homes and, therefore, link to the web for faster access. To identify our targets, we collected information using a variety of sensors in different locations and interpreted that data to make greater use of the meaning. The ultimate goal is to be aware of smart houses, smart places, climate and water structures, vehicle control, atmospheric attributes, and closed-circuit television. In a smart home, there is a constant monitoring of the data transmitted by the sensors which obtain them by measuring smoke and temperature. Similarly, it is used in power and gas facilities to efficiently accomplish gas and water supply to homes and several regions of the town to detect fire at an important time. Similarly, controlling pollution helps to care about the health of citizens and warns them when the contamination exceeds a certain verge. The smart parking assists to check automobiles arriving and going out of various car parking zones. Therefore, sensitive parking is often premeditated keeping in mind the various vehicles in an area. Novel parking lots are being advanced in area of vehicles. Likewise, the smart vehicle parking information produces a large number of facilities that are created for residents as well as traders as a part of smart towns. The residents can effortlessly get knowledge of free slots near the parking lot. Equally, citizens can get knowledge from the smart town in a more appropriate place to park the vehicle. Such technique decreases the fuel ingesting of cars. In addition, another application may consist of the security of wasting time and an individual may spend more time in the market or other actions. Climate and aquatic knowledge also upsurge the effectiveness of the smart town by implementing climate-associated data like heat, rainfall, wind speed, pressure, humidity, and water levels at dams, lakes, rivers, and other tanks.

This complete data is gathered by fixing the sensors in the reservoir of water and other open areas. Most of the floods occur in the world because of the rainfall and few by snow melting and dam breakage. Therefore, we use rain-calibrating sensors and snow-melting parameters to predict the flood earlier. We will also predict the water reservoirs to meet the necessity of the water to the residents. Vehicle traffic information is the most important source of a smart city. The citizens and government can similarly get the information from the smart city about more suitable places to park their vehicles. This system decreases the fuel burning of vehicles. Moreover, other applications may include the safety of time wastage and a person can waste more time in a marketplace or other activities. Weather and water information also enhances the effectiveness of the smart city by producing weather-related information like temperature, rain, humidity, pressure, wind velocity, and water levels at rivers, lakes, dams, and other reservoirs. All this data is collected by putting the sensors in water reservoirs and other open places. In the world, most of the flood occurs due to the rain and similarly few by snow melting and dam breakage. Therefore, we use rain-mapping sensors and snow-melting parameters to predict the flood earlier. We can also predict the water reservoirs in advance to meet the need of the water to the citizens. Vehicular traffic information is the most important source of a smart city. Citizens and the government can be more civilized through this type of knowledge source and with real-world analysis. Through this sort of information source and with useful real-time analysis, the citizens can get to the destination based on the current intensity of traffic and the average speed of the vehicles. The traffic in all the cities can be diverse and this will reduce fuel consumption as well as reduce pollution caused by congested traffic. Government authorities can also get real-time data about the blockage of the road due to the accident or other things. They can take significant action in real time to manage the traffic. In our smart city system, we are getting the traffic information by GPRS, vehicular sensors, as well as the sensors placed on the front screen of the car. We get the number of vehicles between two pairs of sensors at different places in the city where each vehicle is located. The front screen will be broken and the sensor will send a warning to the police, traffic authorities, and hospital. Similarly, in real time, we can do many things to make these things more effective. It is also important for the health of the people to control the pollution of the environment and to disseminate information to the people. A city is smart with its healthy citizens. So, while outlining a smart city, we put a separate module to get environmental information which includes gas information, such as particular metals, carbon monoxide sulphur dioxide, ozone, and noise. These gases are extremely dangerous to human well-being and cause liver disordering, coughing, and heart diseases. People should not go outside when these gases are at a high level in the atmosphere. Particularly the children, old-age people, people for physical exercise, already sick people, should not go outside from their homes when the polluted gas is more in the environment. People will have access to all this information in real time and it is possible to be cautious when any particular threshold of gas is crossed. Moreover, in a place where there is a higher population, the government should decrease the problems of pollution, like moving industries to other areas and diverting traffic to other routes. The most important thing for the people of the smart city is safety concerns. Security is achieved through the proposed system by constantly monitoring the video throughout the city. However, analysing video and detecting any mishap with anyone through the system in real time is very challenging. To overcome this limit, we propose new conditions that increase the security of the entire city. We have placed various emergency buttons with microphones at various places in the city along with surveillance cameras. When any accident happens to someone like robbery, car theft, purse theft, fighting, or someone watching some unlawful activity, he can just push the emergency button at any nearby place, and it will transmit the message to the nearest police station. In this way, the police or security agencies can monitor nearby places through surveillance cameras and can quickly find the imposter. Furthermore, the data assembled from various sensors can be used to avoid future safety issues. The proposed smart city provides a safe environment for the citizens. There is a combination server that gathers and aggregates the information from all smart systems. The information is welcomed at high rapidity. So, the collection process is sufficient to collect data and transfer it for analysis through the IoT system (Rathore, M.M. et al. 2016).

IoT APPLICATIONS FOR SMART CITIES

IoT practices the web to combine numerous mixed possessions. So, and for giving the convenience of entree, all present things need to be associated to the web. The rationale behind this is often those cities that comprise these systems and linking of smart devices to the web is important to at all regulate their action like energy-use regulation to enhance the electric usage, light administration, and air conditioning organization. To urge this goal, detectors are ready to be positioned at several sites to collect and analyse information for consumption enhancement (Botta, A. et al. 2016).

SMART HOMES

By using the info that is shaped by numerous detectors, smart homes are often practical (Shafie-Khah, M. et al. 2016). For instance, new demand response (DR) systems are often functional, and clients are often warned in a situation where contamination is over its permissible border and about the regulation of the contamination. IoT technology consists of smart homes and devices counting smart TVs, home safety systems, fire detection, lighting control, and temperature regulation. The detectors of those devices regulate the circumstances and setting and send investigation information to a vital supervisor reception which allows the homeowner to uninterruptedly regulate and control the house from the outdoor and make the simplest choice below each condition (Li, X. et al. 2016). Similarly, these investigation information help to forecast upcoming actions to be ready beforehand by getting an effectual dimension to stop trailing behind with respect to suitability, safety, luxury, and a high status of living. Furthermore, smart homes in a neighbourhood are often associated over NAN to make a sensible public (Stratigea, A. 2012). During this situation, homes are ready to share some shadowing statistics like outdoor cameras to seek out a chance or describe actions to a police headquarters. Healthcare, management of common sources, and allowing care for social networking are other functions of the societies. Hence, this idea is not only about being connected to the neighbours but also way for the growth of a complete smart city which may regulate and resist the actions while being a smart town (Jaradat, M. et al. 2016).

Online Monitoring of Power Lines

As more constructions and zones are being electrified, the amount and strictness of power usages become more complicated, resulting in lower system reliability (Amin, M. 2008). Dependability is vital because its absence originates grave undesirable influences on the community and financial systems. Incorporation of IoT technique alongside the facility network goals enhances the dependability of power networks over endless regulation of the status of broadcast lines; additionally, to ecological behaviours and the actions of the shoppers to send intervallic information to the network regulator units. The regulator unit's procedure and excerpt info from the described statistics to sense liabilities separate the burden and then resolve faults intelligently. Executing energy refurbishment during a smart network must take into account the situation cruciality of shutdowns. For instance, it's serious to ensure great dependability for health and manufacturing organizations. The renovation issue converts a multifaceted problem when taken into consideration the massive amount of mixtures of swapping processes which suddenly upsurge with the rise in system's apparatuses (Solanki, J. et al. 2007, Zidan, A. et al. 2011). Scheming the smart network during a graded model 15 separates the matter into numerous regulator units responsible for reinstating power inside its area or choice. This improves the time required to progress the info and accelerates the refurbishment process. If any control units flop to recover power in some areas within their possibility, they advance the matter to higher stages for improved deed and management as advanced planes have a bigger system's opinion (Jaradat, M. et al. 2016).

Smart Parking Lot

By permitting smart parking, incoming and departure periods of various vehicles are outlined everywhere in the town (Neyestani, N. et al. 2015a). Therefore, these car parks need to be prearranged in such a mode to require a variety of cars in each area under consideration (Yazdani-Damavandi et al. 2016). Besides, novel car park lots where there are extra vehicles need to be found out (Neyestani, N. et al. 2015b). So, the information of smart parking lots is ready to offer benefits to everyday lives of both clients and dealers within the smart cities. This facility supports road devices and smart displays which direct motorists to the simplest way for car parks within the town (Lee, S. et al. 2008). Many profits of this facility are discovering a space quicker which suggests lower CO releases from vehicles, lower road traffic, and better lived residents. It is often combined into city IoT substructures. Furthermore, through short-range interaction machineries like NFC and RFID, it's likely to understand an electric confirmation of car parks licenses and permits for presenting improved facilities to inhabitants (Zanella, A. et al. 2014).

Demand-side Energy Management

DSM or demand-side energy management is the alteration in the energy feeding profiles of customers consistent with changing power prices over a period, and other payment inducements from effective businesses (Balijepalli, V. et al. 2011). Request retort is employed to attenuate customer's electricity bills, shift peak's load request, lessen process price of the facility network, and diminish energy damage and greenhouse gas releases (Siano, P. 2014, Koutsopoulos, I. et al. 2011). IoT elements gather energy necessities of various house devices and direct them to meters. The regulator unit into smart system timetables energy feeding of houses devices consistent with the operator's favourites during a plan that diminishes the bill. The DSM problems are often solved at different levels of the hierarchical SG infrastructure. It is often solved at the extent of home premises to preserve consumer privacy. Also, it is often explained at advanced stages to get simpler arrangement plans that don't only profit customers but also the useful company (Nguyen, H.K. et al. 2012, Molderink, A. et al. 2010).

Integration of Distributed Energy Sources

Reusable energy producers are being combined into the nowadays power system due to ecological reasons, global climate alteration, and its short price. This lessens discharges of greenhouse vapours that raise the Earth's temperature. In current centuries, many administrations, establishments, and people progressed to establish wind turbines and solar cells to please part of their power necessities. Germany, for instance, strategies to completely accomplish its power stresses using reusable energy resources by 2050 (Economic, U.N.D., Social Affairs 2014). Reusable energy agonizes from availability which has led to great enhancements in loading technology. IoT technology uses wireless sensors to gather present climate data to assist in forecasting energy obtainability within the upcoming future. Correctness of the predicted power quantities through the next time interlude is critical for energy arrangement replicas (Potter, C. et al. 2009). Dissimilar plans and optimization explanations have been advanced in study to professionally succeed reusable energy resources inside the smart network (Jarrah, M. et al. 2014).

Integration of Electric Vehicles

EVs or Electric Vehicles are utilized as power-storing strategies when they are shiftless. Similarly, they deliver competent and green transport facilities. Making effectual preparation methods for discharging and charging of EVs can possibly be central to diminished releases, shear peak storage, and surge the utilized fraction of produced reusables (Saber, A. et al. 2011). Perception appliances gather info about EV individuality, battery status, position, etc. to advance the effectiveness of discharging and charging scheduling processes (Jaradat, M. et al. 2015).

Healthcare

IoT methods have numerous benefits in the healthcare domain of smart cities. Few of these devices are tracing individuals and items including victims, operators and ambulance, detection of individuals, and involuntary information collection and detection. In words of persons and unbiased tracing, the position of patients in a health centre or hospital is supervised to offer improved and quicker workflow in the clinic. The positions of the ambulance, blood stuff, and many organs for replacement are regulated to check the accessibility on-line. In terms of people identification, in a directory, patients are known to diminish the risk of errors for the prevention of receiving wrong medications, amounts, and trials (Niyato, D. et al. 2009). The verification of members targets to advance the worker's behaviour to affected ones. Concerning the information gathering and sense, it assists to save time for information processing and avoiding person's faults. By sensor applications, analysing patient situations, offering actual data on the affected's well-being signals such as medicine obedience by the patient, is applied. By utilizing bio-signal regulators, the patient illness is inspected over varied wireless access-based approaches to allow receiving the patient information anyplace (Atzori, L. et al. 2009).

Weather and Water Systems

Weather structures utilize varied devices to provide correct data like rain, temperature, wind speed, and solar irradiation and also aid to improve the competence of a sensible town (Botta, A. et al. 2016). Along with electricity, water supply structures are vital portions of every smart town. Traditional approaches of water delivery from the water foundation to the purchaser grounds aren't appropriate and effective, particularly for analysing any escape inside the tube or other portions of the structure. By positioning devices at correct places of the supply structure, it develops a progressive stance for the uncovering of any silent faults or other applications. WDS have some fragments consisting of water resource, kind of a river or a lake, storing services like tanks and supply grids like underground- or ground pipelines. Discovery of accountabilities like leak, the superiority of water and the level of lake water can be applied over employing sensors in an IoT-based setting. The superiority of water is frequently calculated both after and before the tank at tactical sites by a glass electrode for gauging water pH. The outflow is often sensed in tubes through three diverse sensors consisting of sound (ultrasonic sensor), vibration (using dual-axis accelerometers), and pressure (piezo-resistive sensor) monitoring (Hancke, G. et al. 2012). Besides, when a city faces an excessive amount of or insufficient shower, countless people experience several water-related problems. According to the necessities of an area, resident services can develop advanced approaches to plot and accomplish irrigation, resolving extreme water usage, upgrading of water preservation, assigning their scarce sources more professionally, wastewater management, and addressing flooding during a hurricane through IoT. Discarding raw mess into the local channels will happen inescapably in an area without any supervision and strategy. IoT devices are used locally and established for administration and plan all things concerning water like regulating a huge quantity of raw waste and simpler training for storms. Towns via systems that regulate the meteorological situations and people that regulate the rainwater storage are ready to collect data for resolving the position of water supplies. With an appropriate technique, towns will lessen the excess of gutters and diminish water pollution. Additionally, utilizing a structure of sensors for collecting information on the liquid level of water resources and streams, it is likely to forestall flood events. These structure devices are built on ultrasonic variety finders and positioned overhead home-grown channels to measure the alterations in water level and forecast the flood dangers. IoT through TV whitespace networks, which resident telecom suppliers made accessible, permits towns to make community alertness statements about the flood in present situations (The Urban Internet of Things 2017).

Surveillance Systems

Safety is the greatest vital component of smart towns from the residents' point of interpretation. In the end, the whole smart town needs to be consistently regulated and watched, but analysing the data and finding out criminal activities are greatly difficult. Rathore, M.M. et al. (2016) gave new conditions to upgrade the safety of smart cities. Conventional television (CCTV) systems offer a structure for smart investigation arrangements. Though, they are linked to a tape recorder; they don't have the ability of smart dispensation. Furthermore, individual workers may fail towards few scenarios and create a mistake. Through smart investigation, it's conceivable to observe an individual's movements to seek out any ferocious actions and find out the persons involvements. These systems can initiate a situation of attention. It is frequently utilized as supervision for the extended run project of ordinary amenities or its alteration through regulating people's thinking's and discovering sidewalk road traffic designs. In a performance or a community location like landing field where there is a vast quantity of peoples, a regulator arrangement for sidewalking, troop nursing, and emergency administration systems is significant. For uncovering and tracing of persons at evening-time, IR cameras are handled because they work built on temperature (Wang, J. et al. 2012). Additional feature of this method is to identify what quiet items people are taking to find out any unlawful or excluded materials. To end this, video sequence outlines are made functional (Damen, D. et al. 2012), which suggests founded on seeing any indiscretions in commons silhouettes. This is doing by comparation a pattern of a usual person walking in the same way and in the situation of any lumps and nonconformity, measured as likely pixels for resonant objects (Hancke, G. et al. 2012). Few of these camera surveillance systems can sense irregular circumstances including pedestrians crossing the street deprived of crossings and cars moving in the incorrect way by running motion detection algorithms to extract video data and format it in XML, aggregating several frames for performing regular detection. Last, a module categorizes reasonable statistics and interprets it to find any irregularities (Calavia, L. et al. 2012). This structure can be organized for dissimilar goals by just familiarizing it to the laws of that situation (Talari, S. et al. 2009).

SMART CITIES AND COMMUNITIES

Cloud IoT is central to the production of facilities that interrelate with the nearby situation, thus producing novel occasions for contextualization and geo-cognizance. Maintainable growth of town ranges may be a test of main significance and needs innovative, effective, and accessible technologies and facilities. The difficulty is to attach the cooperative power of ICT grids (networks of persons, of information, of devices) to make a shared and distinct alertness about the numerous sustainability dangers which our civilization is fronting now at communal, ecological, and radical heights. The finishing shared intellect will cause better detailed policymaking procedures and allow people, through partaking and communication, to accept the more frequent separate and shared behaviours and lives (Horizon 2020 Work Programme 2014). Cloud IoT can offer a mutual middleware for the future concerned with smart city amenities (Ballon, P. et al. 2011, Cloud Project 2014, Suciu, G. et al. 2013). Getting data from dissimilar varied sensing structures, retrieving all types of geo locations and IoT technologies, for example, 3D symbols through RFID sensors and geo-tagging and steadily revealing information (e.g., by an animatedly marked chart). Agendas classically contain a sensor stage with APIs for detection and activating and a cloud stand that gives climbable and long-lasting storing and processing sources for the automatic administration and regulation of practical sensing instruments throughout an extensive placement. Troop-sourced and status-dependent outlines also occur (Kantarci, B. et al. 2014a,b). Proposing an outline applying sensing as a frontline example in the background of smart cities is targeted at public security. Antonic, A. et al. (2014) and Podnar Zarko, I. et al. (2013) presented an ecology for mobile crowd-detecting gadgets that depend on the cloud-based publish/subscribe software to credit sensor information from mobile gadgets in a framework-cognizant and power-efficient way (Xiao, Y. et al. 2013). Concentration on app creators and end-product handlers is shaped by the need to deal with bulky settings. Meanwhile the IoT situation is very uneven; sensor virtualization is often worked to scale back the difference among current mixed technologies and their possible users, letting them interrelate with sensors at diverse layers (Petrolo, R. et al. 2014).

BLOCKCHAIN-BASED SMART CITIES

Blockchain is a dispersed record technology that grew after bitcoin (Nakamoto, S. 2019) and other cryptocurrencies. Blockchain is primarily useful to Bitcoin and was formed by Satoshi Nakamoto. Blockchain is an unchallengeable, dispersed, and publicly accessible common database. In blockchain, all connections are logged and anybody in the organization is permissible to contact, direct, and authenticate these dealings. Applying BT to smart town can fetch numerous respectable characteristics, such as belief-free, opacity, false nymity, republic, computerization, devolution, and safety. Belief less means that the scheme can function usually in a person-to-person means deprived of a dependable third party (Gensollen, N. et al. 2018, Yolda, Y. et al. 2017). BT allows everybody to monitor all deal records, which makes it crystal clear. The pseudonymity can be understood by footage transactions using community pseudonymous addresses and possessing the unseen real-world individualities of the nodes. In blockchain, choices are made by all nodes in a man-to-man method, which makes it democratized. Smart contracts towards blockchain can complete transaction production, choice creation, and information storing robotically. The devolution of blockchain structure makes it essential to guarantee steadiness by successively consensus procedures among dispersed nodes. Safekeeping in the blockchain is associated with honesty, privacy, and permission. Though smart cities and blockchain have been considered widely in preceding works, these two significant zones have conventionally been studied distinctly in the prevailing revisions. As finest of our information, there is no current effort to review the combination of these two significant extents. To complete this slit, the state-of-the-art blockchain technology can be functional in smart cities. Study on accepting BT as to advance the action, elegance, effectiveness, and safety of smart cities is needed. Also, we discuss future research directions in related areas with proper depth and sufficient breadth. It is believed that conversation and search can give a complete thoughtful knowledge of this arena, and stand in more succeeding educations on this subject. How BT is functional within the dominion of smart cities from the viewpoints of the smart healthcare, smart cities, smart transportation, SG, and supply chain administration and offers a thorough clarification of how blockchain can be useful inside respective group (Xie, J. et al. 2019).

BLOCKCHAIN SOLUTIONS AND SMART CONTRACTS

Immutability of authorized records is ensured through blockchain technology. Computer networks collaboratively keep a rising list of assembled accounts which are connected to the former blocks using cryptography. Blockchain is primary identified as a mainstay of BC Tech (Nakamoto, S. 2008), the first common cryptocurrency, that agree for internet operators to handover money to the respectively supplementary in a person-to-person way deprived of the trusted in-between. The blockchain, as applied in Bitcoin, assimilates cryptoanalysis and spreading of data to make it hard to delay with the businesses that have established their efficiency as Bitcoin is in action from 2009 and no important threat has been fruitful. Although Bitcoin is a precise request of BC as a community economic application which helps the transfer of value from one participant to another, blockchain has been extended to use in other contexts. In the crossway between SGs and smart cities, the blockchain enables transactive energy solutions that also include energy losses (Sanseverino, E.R. et al. 2017) and permit the technical operation of the distribution network (Silvestre, M.D. et al. 2018). The use of blockchain is extended with the idea of "smart contracts". One of the main functions in Bitcoin is the automatic verification of the availability of funds before a transaction. This validation comes under "smart contracts", which are lines of code that are stored on a blockchain and automatically execute when predetermined terms and conditions are met. One example of "Smart contract" is the reason in selling machineries. A selling engine confirms order only after the user put cash in device or machine. If the money inserted is not adequate to shelter the price of the order, the machine statements the money inserted, otherwise it proclaims the stated order and the quantity that surpasses the price. Similarly, smart contracts require to be decided upon by the members of the grid, this can't be interfered with and this can be performed on all the active bulges (Gallo, P. et al. 2018). Participants of block-chain are required to decide upon the contented of the record, which is done by a consensus method. In its place of believing an expert to choose which content is the fact in a central way, blockchain parts the content amongst everybody. This method involves that the system continues accord everywhere the recorded info on the blockchain. Several agreement methods have been planned and organized. Each agreement mechanism has diverse trade off and linked the safety of the information and the financial presentations of the organization. Bitcoin uses PoW or Proof of Work that is extremely protected but accomplishes gradually and wastelands. Instances of additional common agreement apparatuses comprise PoS or Proof of Stake and PBFT or Practical Byzantine Fault Tolerance (Castro, M. et al. 2002).

BLOCKCHAIN MODEL AND ITS APPLICATION IN SMART GRID

Application of P2P energy trading is addressed by dispersed power trade among consumers and promotion of reusable energy garnering. It's blockchain architecture is of consortium blockchain. Sample block content can be used for consumer meter ID, Transaction ID, quantity of energy demanded, and power approved, a digital signature of vender and node. Here technologies used are virtual currencies, smart contracts, and points-based e-wallets. Energy trade between EVs is addressed by purchasing and marketing of extra energy between EVs, privacy preserving of EVs by using architecture of consortium blockchain. Sample block content implied is EV's meter ID, Transaction ID, a digital signature of the charging station, charged energy, and the processing protuberance. Technologies used are smart contracts and power coins. Privacy and security preservative methods are used to defend the app usage pattern and the confidentiality info of user. The architecture that can be used by a private blockchain consists of energy-transferred Sample Block Content, Transaction ID, digital signature of vender, and LAGs. Technologies applied are of data aggregation, bloom filter, and verification methods. Energy generation and supply can be carried out by dApps, contract, and remote regulator of misrepresentation utilizing electrical appliances using consortium blockchain. One can address the issue of defence from cyber-attacks, combination of irregularity-control events by the factors of time of measurement, voltage and current, measurement of frequency, switch states, etc. Secure equipment maintenance can be addressed by creating a stage for communication between seller and customer for apparatus analysis and secrecy safeguarding. Technologies required are smart contracts, user communication using mobile phone application. This can be achieved using consortium blockchain by the use of device ID, service files, transaction value, and credits, mode of maintenance, etc. (Alladi, T. et al. 2019, Mohril, S. et al. 2020).

CHALLENGES

There are numerous encounters associated to detect in smart towns, both of a mechanical and communal behaviour.

Impacts of Block Size

As blockchain size rises, it is a matter of worry for contenders departing that surges the centralism danger. The output of the blockchain is the amount at which dealings are authenticated. The output is restricted by the size of block and time between blocks. Block dimensions is a purpose of transactions encoded. The programming of transactions is exact to the application domain. In Bitcoin, the contract authentication time needed is about 10 minutes. The bootstrap period denotes to the total time a new confirmatory node in the system that would take to progression in past to authenticate the present state. This period is stereotypically a purpose of the dimensions of the blockchain. There is a necessity to recognize the price of the incomes essential to settle a deal. The possessions are required to implement transaction validating, storage, block mining, and network bandwidth. Block mining involves computational resources to produce evidence, reliant on the accord procedure. Transaction authentication needs widespread computational properties if the cryptographical rigidity is amplified. The confirmative nodes in the grid should continuously be tangled with the exchange of blocks, which emphasizes the obtainability of network range. Last, here is a necessity to assign storing to sustain block mining, transaction authentication processes, and stowage of past data to assist new bulges (Liang, X. et al. 2018).

Security

Allowing machineries for identifying apps have several issues that have to be careful inside the situation of smart towns. These systems are going to be susceptible to cyber terrorism and cyber vandalism (Hancke, G.P. et al. 2010, 2011).

Data Ownership and Privacy

Rights for all information gathered using these identifying apps are owned by whom? For Example, as the electric usage has admittance to a person's energy feasting statistics, can it be utilized without one's permission? (Hancke, G.P. et al. 2013).

Trust

Could people believe the units accountable for combining and accessing their information? As an example, cloud can be taken as a dominant data system wherever admittance to information is characteristically regulated by the corporation which retains the organization. Can these corporations be considered reliable? (Hancke, G.P. et al. 2013).

Social Issues

Citizens have forever been proactively associated with a town. As an example, there are cooperative drives that personages close and aid to keep the town clear by increasing no scattering, etc. Will smart towns find any sort of separate among the characters further therefore the city? Then there is the matter of knowledge as well. Is the human trained sufficient to practice and learn all these operations? (Hancke, G.P. et al. 2013).

Central Control

This is obvious from the content of this article that we are running in the direction of a central control system, where complete sermons are living increasingly combined, to get controlled by one great primary way. This changes to whole power by the administrative frames that can be utilized to illiterately follow individuals or occupy somebody's security. It is relevant to support and secrecy concerns earlier discussed (Hancke, G.P. et al. 2013).

Costs in Updating Present Towns

How costly will it be to update present towns to transform themselves into smart towns? It will surely be very costly to upgrade all the present systems. These cities are mostly dependent on infrastructures and communications (Gungor, V. et al. 2010, Hancke, G.P. et al. 2013).

CONCLUSION

Technology of blockchain is implemented in the dimension of smart cities and consists of SG, viewpoints of smart citizens, supply chain management, smart transportation, and smart healthcare. We have described few important research objections and upcoming techniques in blockchain technology-based smart cities, consisting of storage, safety and confidentiality, cost, energy efficiency, punishment mechanisms inducement, and regulation. The acceptance of blockchain in IoT surroundings can fetch vital aids in varied parts, for instance, welfare, transportation, financial, health. These assistances are similarly imported to a somewhat result using blockchain, like non-repudiation of the generated information by the nodes, high availability, no lucidity of processes done in the system, and a single point of failure.

REFERENCES

Alamri, A., Ansari, W.S., Hassan, M.M., Hossain, M.S., Alelaiwi, A., Hossain, M.A. A survey on sensor-cloud: architecture, applications, and approaches. *Int. J. Distrib. Sens. Netw.* **2013**, *9*, 917923.

Alladi, T., Chamola, V., Rodrigues, J.J., Kozlov, S.A. Blockchain in smart grids: A review on different use cases. *Sensors* **2019**, *19*(22), 4862.

Amin, M. Challenges in reliability, security, efficiency, and resilience of energy infrastructure: Toward smart self-healing electric power grid. In Power and Energy Society General Meeting – Conversion and Delivery of Electrical Energy in the 21st Century, 2008, IEEE, 2008; pp. 1–5.

Antonic, A., Roankovic, K., Marjanovic, M., Pripuic, K., Zarko, I. A mobile crowdsensing ecosystem enabled by a Cloud-based publish/subscribe middleware. In Future Internet of Things and Cloud (FiCloud), 2014 International Conference on, August 2014, pp. 107–114.

Atzori, L., Iera, A., Morabito, G. The internet of things: A survey. *Compu. Netw.* **2010**, *54*(15), 2787–2805.

Balijepalli, V., Pradhan, V., Khaparde, S., Shereef, R.M. Review of demand response under smart grid paradigm. In Innovative Smart Grid Technologies – India (ISGT India), 2011 IEEE PES, 2011; pp. 236–243.

Ballon, P., Glidden, J., Kranas, P., Menychtas, A., Ruston, S., Van Der Graaf, S. Is there a need for a Cloud platform for European smart cities? In eChallenges e-2011 Conference Proceedings, IIMC International Information Management Corporation, 2011.

Botta, A., de Donato, W., Persico, V., Pescapé, A. Integration of Cloud computing and Internet of Things: A survey. *Future Gener. Comput. Syst.* **2016**, *56*, 684–700.

Calavia, L., Baladrón, C., Aguiar, J.M., Carro, B., Sánchez-Esguevillas, A. A semantic autonomous video surveillance system for dense camera networks in Smart Cities. *Sensors* **2012**, *12*, 10407–10429.

Castro, M., Liskov, B. Practical byzantine fault tolerance and proactive recovery. *ACM Trans. Comput. Syst. (TOCS)* **2002**, *20*(4), 398–461.

Cloud Project, Cloud of Things for empowering the citizen clout in smart cities. 2014. http://clout-project.eu/.

Damen, D., Hogg, D. Detecting carried objects from sequences of walking pedestrians. *IEEE Trans. Pattern Anal. Mach. Intell.* **2012**, *34*, 1056–1067.

Das, S., Nayyar, A. Innovative Ideas to Manage Urban Traffic Congestion in Cognitive Cities. In *Driving the Development, Management, and Sustainability of Cognitive Cities*; IGI Global: Hershey, PA, 2019; pp. 139–162.

Economic, U.N.D., Social Affairs, D.f.S.D. 2014. http://sustainabledevelopment.un.org/index.html.

Gallo, P., Pongnumkul, S., Nguyen, U.Q. BlockSee: Blockchain for IoT video surveillance in smart cities. In 2018 IEEE International Conference on Environment and Electrical Engineering and 2018 IEEE Industrial and Commercial Power Systems Europe (EEEIC/I&CPS Europe), IEEE, June 2018, pp. 1–6.

Gensollen, N., Gauthier, V., Becker, M., Marot, M. Stability and performance of coalitions of prosumers through diversification in the smart grid. *IEEE Trans. Smart Grid* **2018**, *9*(2), 963–970.

Gungor, V., Lu, B., Hancke, G.P. Opportunities and challenges of wireless sensor networks in smart grid. *IEEE Trans. Ind. Electron.* **2010**, *57*, 3557–3564.

Hancke, G.P. Practical eavesdropping and skimming attacks on high-frequency RFID tokens. *J. Comput. Secur.* **2011**, *19*, 259–288.

Hancke, G.P., Hancke Jr, G.P. The role of advanced sensing in smart cities. *Sensors* **2013**, *13*(1), 393–425.

Hancke, G.P., Markantonakis, K., Mayes, K. Security challenges for user-oriented RFID applications within the 'Internet of Things'. *J. Internet Technol.* **2010**, *11*, 307–313.

Hancke, G., Silva, B., Hancke, G., Jr. The role of advanced sensing in smart cities. *Sensors* **2012**, *13*, 393–425.

Horizon 2020 Work Programme 2014–2015. Industrial leadership. Leadership in enabling and industrial technologies. Information and communication technologies, 2014. https://ec.europa.eu/research/participants/data/ref/h2020/wp/2014_2015/main/h2020-wp1415-leit_en.pdf.

Internet of Things in 2020: Roadmap for the Future. Available online: http://www.smart-systemsintegration.org/public/documents/publications/Internet-of-Things_in_2020_EC-EPoSS_Workshop_Report_2008_v3.pdf (accessed on 24 February 2017).

Jaradat, M., Jarrah, M., Bousselham, A., Jararweh, Y., Al-Ayyoub, M. The Internet of energy: Smart sensor networks and Big Data management for smart grid. *Procedia Comput. Sci.* **2015**, *56*, 592–597.

Jarrah, M., Jaradat, M., Jararweh, Y., Al-Ayyoub, M., Bousselham, A. A hierarchical optimization model for energy data flow in smart grid power systems. *Inf. Sys.* **2014**, doi: http://dx.doi.org/10.1016/j.is.2014.12.003.

Javaid, U., Aman, M.N., Sikdar, B. Blockpro: Blockchain based data provenance and integrity for secure IoT environments. In Proceedings of the 1st Workshop on Blockchain-enabled Networked Sensor Systems, 2018.

Jingcheng, G., Xiao, Y., Liu, J., Liang, W., Chen, C.L.P. A survey of communication/networking in smart grids. *Future Gener. Comput. Syst.* **2012**, *28*(2), 391–404.

Kantarci, B., Mouftah, H. Trustworthy sensing for public safety in Cloudcentric Internet of Things, 2014a.

Kantarci, B., Mouftah, H.T. Mobility-aware trustworthy crowdsourcing in cloud-centric internet of things. In Computers and Communication (ISCC), 2014 IEEE Symposium on, IEEE, 2014b; pp. 1–6.

Koutsopoulos, I., Tassiulas, L. Control and optimization meet the smart power grid: Scheduling of power demands for optimal energy management. In Proceedings of the 2Nd International Conference on Energy-Efficient Computing and Networking; e-Energy '11, ACM, New York, NY, 2011; pp. 41–50.

Krishnamurthi, R., Nayyar, A., Solanki, A. Innovation Opportunities through Internet of Things (IoT) for Smart Cities. In *Green and Smart Technologies for Smart Cities*; CRC Press: Boca Raton, FL, 2019; pp. 261–292.

Kushch, S., Castrillo, F.P. A review of the applications of the block-chain technology in smart devices and dis-tributed renewable energy grids. *ADCAIJ: Adv. Distrib. Comput. Artif. Intell. J.* **2017**, *6*(3), 75–84.

Lee, S., Yoon, D., Ghosh, A. Intelligent parking lot application using wireless sensor networks. In Proceedings of the 2008 International Symposium on Collaborative Technologies and Systems, Irvine, CA, 19–23 May 2008; pp. 48–57.

Li, X., Lu, R., Liang, X., Shen, X., Chen, J., Lin, X. Smart community: An internet of things application. *IEEE Commun. Mag.* **2011**, *49*(11), 68–75.

Liang, X., Shetty, S., Tosh, D. Exploring the attack surfaces in blockchain enabled smart cities. In 2018 IEEE International Smart Cities Conference (ISC2), IEEE, September 2018; pp. 1–8.

Mohril, S., Sankhla, M.S., Sonone, S.S. Adverse impacts of mobile phone tower radiation on human health. *Int. J. Radiol. Radiat. Ther.* **2020**, *7*(5), 163–166.

Molderink, A., Bakker, V., Bosman, M.G.C., Hurink, J., Smit, G.J.M. Management and control of domestic smart grid technology. *IEEE Trans. Smart Grid* **2010**, *1*(2), 109–119.

Nakamoto, S., Bitcoin: A Peer-to-Peer Electronic Cash System, 2008.

Nayyar, A., Jain, R., Mahapatra, B., Singh, A. Cyber Security Challenges for Smart Cities. In *Driving the Development, Management, and Sustainability of Cognitive Cities*; IGI Global: Hershey, PA, 2019; pp. 27–54.

Neyestani, N., Damavandi, M.Y., Shafie-khah, M., Catalão, J.P.S. Modeling the PEV traffic pattern in an urban environment with parking lots and charging stations. In Proceedings of the 2015 IEEE Eindhoven PowerTech, Eindhoven, The Netherlands, 29 June–2 July 2015a; pp. 1–6.

Neyestani, N., Damavandi, M.Y., Shafie-Khah, M., Contreras, J., Catalão, J.P.S. Allocation of plug-in vehicles' parking lots in distribution systems considering network-constrained objectives. *IEEE Trans. Power Syst.* 2015b, *30*, 2643–2656.

Nguyen, H.K., Song, J., Han, Z. Demand side management to reduce peak-to-average ratio using game theory in smart grid. In Computer Communications Workshops (INFOCOM WKSHPS), 2012 IEEE Conference on, 2012; p. 91–96.

Niyato, D., Hossain, E., Camorlinga, S. Remote patient monitoring service using heterogeneous wireless access networks: Architecture and optimization. *IEEE J. Sel. Areas Commun.* **2009**, *27*, 412–423.

Petrolo, R., Mitton, N., Soldatos, J., Hauswirth, M., Schiele, G., et al. Integrating wireless sensor networks within a city Cloud. In SWANSITY Workshop in Conjunction with IEEE SECON 2014, 2014.

Podnar Zarko, I., Antonic, A., Pripužic, K. Publish/subscribe middleware for energy-efficient mobile crowdsensing. In Proceedings of the 2013 ACM Conference on Pervasive and Ubiquitous Computing Adjunct Publication. UbiComp'13 Adjunct, ACM, New York, NY, 2013, pp. 1099–1110. URL http://doi.acm.org/10.1145/2494091.2499577.

Potter, C., Archambault, A., Westrick, K. Building a smarter smart grid through better renewable energy information. In Power Systems Conference and Exposition, 2009, PSCE '09, IEEE/PES, 2009; pp. 1–5.

Rameshwar, R., Solanki, A., Nayyar, A., Mahapatra, B. Green and Smart Buildings: A Key to Sustainable Global Solutions. In *Green Building Management and Smart Automation*; IGI Global: Hershey, PA, 2020; pp. 146–163.

Rathore, M.M., Ahmad, A., Paul, A., Rho, S. Urban planning and building smart cities based on the internet of things using big data analytics. *Comput. Netw.* **2016**, *101*, 63–80.

Saber, A., Venayagamoorthy, G. Plug-in vehicles and renewable energy sources for cost and emission reductions. *IEEE Trans. Ind. Electron* **2011**, *58*(4), 1229–1238.

Sanseverino, E.R., Silvestre, M.L.D., Gallo, P., Zizzo, G., Ippolito, M. The blockchain in microgrids for transacting energy and attributing losses. In 2017 IEEE International Conference on Internet of Things (iThings) and IEEE Green Computing and Communications (GreenCom) and IEEE Cyber, Physical and Social Computing (CPSCom) and IEEE Smart Data (SmartData), June 2017, pp. 925–930.

Shafie-Khah, M., Heydarian-Forushani, E., Osório, G.J., Gil, F.A.S., Aghaei, J., Barani, M., Catalão, J.P.S. Optimal behavior of electric vehicle parking lots as demand response aggregation agents. *IEEE Trans. Smart Grid* **2016**, *7*, 2654–2665.

Siano, P. Demand response and smart gridsa survey. *Renewable Sustainable Energy Rev.* **2014**, *30*, 461–478.

Siano, P., Shahrour, I., Vergura, S. Introducing smart cities: A transdisciplinary journal on the science and technology of smart cities. *Smart Cities* **2018**, *1*(1), 1–3.

Silvestre, M.D., Gallo, P., Ippolito, M.G., Sanseverino, E.R., Zizzo, G. A technical approach to the energy blockchain in microgrids. *IEEE Trans. Ind. Inform.* **2018**, *14*(11), 4792–4803.

Singh, P., Nayyar, A., Kaur, A., Ghosh, U. Blockchain and fog based architecture for internet of everything in smart cities. *Future Internet*, **2020**, *12*(4), 61.

Six Technologies with Potential Impacts on US Interests Out to 2025. Available online: https://fas.org/irp/nic/disruptive.pdf (accessed on 24 February 2017).

Solanki, A., Nayyar, A. Green Internet of Things (G-IoT): ICT Technologies, Principles, Applications, Projects, and Challenges. In *Handbook of Research on Big Data and the IoT*; IGI Global: Hershey, PA, 2019; pp. 379–405.

Solanki, J., Khushalani, S., Schulz, N. A multi-agent solution to distribution systems restoration. *IEEE Trans. Power Syst.* **2007**, *22*(3), 1026–1034.

Strategic Opportunity Analysis of the Global Smart City Market. Available online: http://www.egr.msu.edu/~aesc310web/resources/SmartCities/Smart%20City%20Market%20Report%202.pdf (accessed on 24 February 2017).

Stratigea, A. The concept of "smart cities". Towards community development? *NETCOM: Réseaux Commun. Territ.* **2012**, *26-3/4*, 375–388.
Suciu, G., Vulpe, A., Halunga, S., Fratu, O., Todoran, G., Suciu, V. Smart cities built on resilient Cloud computing and secure Internet of Things. In Control Systems and Computer Science (CSCS), 2013 19th International Conference on, IEEE, 2013, pp. 513–518.
Suo, H., Wan, J., Zou, C., Liu, J. Security in the internet of things: A review. In Computer Science and Electronics Engineering (ICCSEE), international conference on, vol. 3. IEEE, 2012, pp. 648–651.
Talari, S., Shafie-Khah, M., Siano, P., Loia, V., Tommasetti, A., Catalão, J.P. A review of smart cities based on the internet of things concept. *Energies* **2017**, *10*(4), 421.
The Urban Internet of Things. Available online: http://datasmart.ash.harvard.edu/news/article/the-urbaninternet-of-things-727 (accessed on 24 February 2017).
Wang, J., Chen, D., Chen, H., Yang, J. On pedestrian detection and tracking in infrared videos. *Pattern Recognit. Lett.* **2012**, *33*, 775–785.
Xie, J., Tang, H., Huang, T., Yu, F.R., Xie, R., Liu, J., Liu, Y. A survey of blockchain technology applied to smart cities: Research issues and challenges. *IEEE Commun. Surv. Tutorials* **2019**, *21*(3), 2794–2830.
Xiao, Y., Simoens, P., Pillai, P., Ha, K., Satyanarayanan, M. Lowering the barriers to large-scale mobile crowdsensing. In Proceedings of the 14th Workshop on Mobile Computing Systems and Applications, HotMobile'13, ACM, New York, NY, 2013; pp. 9:1–9:6. URL http://doi.acm.org/10.1145/2444776.2444789.
Yolda, Y., Önen, A., Muyeen, S.M., Vasilakos, A.V., Alan, İ. Enhancing smart grid with microgrids: Challenges and opportunities. *Renew. Sustain. Energy Rev.* **2017**, *72*, 205–214.
Yazdani-Damavandi, M., Moghaddam, M.P., Haghifam, M.R., Shafie-khah, M., Catalão, J.P.S. Modeling operational behavior of plug-in electric vehicles' parking lot in multienergy systems. *IEEE Trans. Smart Grid* **2016**, *7*, 124–135.
Zanella, A., Bui, N., Castellani, A., Vangelista, L., Zorzi, M. Internet of things for smart cities. *IEEE Internet Things J.* **2014**, *1*, 22–32.
Zidan, A., El-Saadany, E.F., El Chaar, L. A cooperative agent-based architecture for self-healing distributed power systems. In Innovationsin Information Technology (IIT), 2011 International Conference on, 2011; pp. 100–105.
Talari, S. A., Talari, M. R., Behzadi, Z., Hooshyar, H., Soltani, R., & Ehteram, H. (2012). The relationship of zoonotic cutaneous leishmaniasis to ABO blood group. *IIOAB Journal*, *3*(2), 42–44.

8 SabPay

A Biometric-Based Blockchain-Enabled Payment System

Shubham Rawal, Yashvardhan Singh and Rakshit Singh

CONTENTS

Introduction 123
Background: A Look at the Expansion and Inevitable Contraction of the Future of Payments 124
Origins and Expansion 124
Securing Digital Payments 125
Objective of Proposed Payment System 127
Methodology 127
Technology is the Future 128
  Convenience is the Key 128
  E-commerce Boom 128
  Demonetization Upshot 128
  Understanding Digital Payment Models 128
Conclusion 129
Bibliography 129

INTRODUCTION

Digital payments have a promising future given the convenience and ongoing digital transformation of numerous industries. They also provide a secure way to store and use the money and are more easily protected than other payment modes because they can incorporate encryption, biometric safeguards and multifactor authentication. Still, digital wallets are an attractive target for hackers and stand the risk of security breach and fraud. As the industry continues to evolve, providers will need to find the delicate balance between strong security measures and usability, to ensure the inherent convenience is maintained, without compromising the devices, private information and financial assets of the customers.

Blockchain made its way to securely authenticate and transact users from one wallet address to other wallet address. Blockchain characteristics include decentralization,

DOI: 10.1201/9781003094210-8

immutability and transparency. In traditional ways, each service provider keeps some portion of individual's identity information for identity verification. Hackers are constantly attacking these systems to steal identity information, but when we talk about the use of Distributed Ledger Technology (DLT), we break the barrier of storing sensitive information onto a central location which prevents the chance of suspected data breach.

BACKGROUND: A LOOK AT THE EXPANSION AND INEVITABLE CONTRACTION OF THE FUTURE OF PAYMENTS

What's happening these days with mobile/digital/e-wallets brings to mind the Big Bang theory. Scientists tell us that all the matter in the universe is speeding outward from a momentous explosion that occurred 14 billion years ago—and, eventually, it will all fall back inward. A somewhat similar, if less dramatic, fate is befalling the universe of digital wallets: it has expanded rapidly but is expected to contract.

From barter exchange to commodity money to metallic and paper money, it subsequently gave way to plastic in the form of debit and credit cards. Now, an increasing number of people are turning to digital money: mobile wallets/applications that enable today's tech-savvy generation to operate without real cash.

Industry reports show the digital payments industry accounted for a total transaction value of $51,756M USD in 2018. There are several factors, pushing the industry towards a growth trajectory. "An explosion of payment options has been ignited by the [mobile payment] market's rapid growth to $180 billion—tripling in only three years," according to a report by Daniel Van Dyke, an analyst at Javelin Strategy & Research. "However, from 2019 to 2021, Javelin expects the explosion will give way to an implosion, as the number of payment providers contracts."

ORIGINS AND EXPANSION

The history of mobile wallets begins in July 2008, when Apple started an app store and opened it to third-party developers, says Russ Jones, an analyst at Glenbrook Partners. "The opening gave just about everyone the opportunity to develop an app that held payment data," he says.

It also led to a period lasting until about 2011 when the industry was "up for grabs," as uncertainty reigned about how the early mobile wallets would communicate payments data, Jones says. But the questions didn't end there. "The back-and-forth in the industry was about what a mobile wallet was, how many wallets did you need, how many wallets would there be, and would they all be on your phone at the same time," he says.

During that time, the payments industry was leaning towards storing transaction data in smartphones while the rest of the world was enthusiastically embracing storage in the cloud, according to Jones. Players who owned handsets thought the data should reside there, those who owned the SIM cards wanted data to live there, and those who controlled neither the handset nor the SIM card tended to believe the cloud should store the data, he explains.

The first working demonstration of how the technology could converge came in May of 2011 with the introduction of the Google Wallet. Google had aligned partners who thought the smartphone should contain the data. It was under the control of the wireless carrier, and the wallet was an app on the phone that Google developed. Bank participation was limited. "So they were off to the races with that," Jones adds.

The Google offering proved mobile wallets could work, but its system was flawed because it was based on a laundry list of requirements that few consumers could fulfil, Jones explains. First, users had to have the right device—one of only a few that contained near-field communication (NFC) chips at the time. They also had to have the right Android operating system and a data plan with Sprint. They had to have a card that not only came from one of just a couple of participating issuers but also had been designated for use in the mobile wallet, he says.

Not surprisingly, the planets seldom aligned in just the right way to enable Google Wallet. And further complications ensued, Jones explains: "When you walked into a store, you had to unlock your phone and unlock the app. Now, we would laugh at that with simple biometric identification."

Other missteps have occurred, too. "The graveyard of mobile wallets is filled with some high-profile names," Grover observes, citing the demise of Softcard, which was backed by wireless providers AT&T Mobility, T-Mobile, and Verizon.

SECURING DIGITAL PAYMENTS

Securing digital payments in this ever-growing world has become challenging day by day. Cyberthreats on payment ecosystem are increasing according to a report published by the security council of India.

Digital payments is a complex ecosystem that has many challenges both in terms of data protection and enterprise security. In India, due to lack of proper security standards and technology compliances, one lacks for choosing flexible payment infrastructure according to enterprise's needs.

European Union's General Data Protection Regulation deals with privacy and strong laws which have been lacking across globe. Many experts believe as payment systems are linked worldwide and have scopes across industries. This conclusion also backed with a thought that there should be some globally accepted security standards and laws to create a better payment ecosystem.

Today we see most of the payment crimes in locations where there are poor legislation and privacy laws. As we are progressing towards doing business together globally, we are getting apart legislatively.

Here are some of the steps listed below which can ensure the security of cashless payments:

- Establishing long-term strategy for global security.
- Standardizing data security laws and framework.
- Creating guidelines and framework for risk policies and payment security.
- Building dedicated testing environment.
- Prioritizing cybersecurity and data protection in companies.

Due to demonetization, India has been successfully shifted to cashless transactions. Mobile wallets and payment gateways have been a major breakthrough in facilitating this cashless era. India hasn't launched any efforts to secure and process this much data and payments.

The fintech space in India has been hindered greatly due to the lack of minimum-security frameworks and security laws. If in case of disruption in this ecosystem, it would lead to catastrophic events.

These minimum frameworks not only ensure smooth working of the ecosystem but also create strict penalties for those who deliberately break rules. This will be ensured only if legislative powers collaborate to create a stronger framework.

New frameworks should be carefully designed and developed for a sustainable practice as with the case of Payment Card Industry Data Security Standard (PCI DSS) compliances, there are now over 25 security standards that have covered up the command of payment technology.

To create these results, we must put great effort on building trust, transparency and information sharing and to encourage active participation from government and private players to secure ecosystem and build consumer trust.

Now our digital wallet SabPay (Sab meaning everyone can pay) comes into picture keeping all the needed points and the changes required for a future digital wallet and keeping up with the need of the society and future. SabPay would be a personalized digital wallet being different than others in the below-mentioned points:

- SabPay makes payment device independent.
- A blockchain/biometrics-enabled wallet.
- No password login.
- Peer-to-peer connection.
- Single-point access.
- Your login ID and password is your fingerprint.
- Being consumer oriented as other e-wallets are seller oriented.
- Phishing free.
- Convenient cashless method.
- Double-finger-enabled wallet for added security.
- Not relying on third parties for transactions.
- No QR code, credit or debit card needed for transaction.
- SabPay would be following guidelines and security protocols.
- The wallet would be linked with Aadhaar/KYC.
- Using phone fingerprint scanners for prototypes.
- Using finger vein recognition system (FVRS).
- Using RBI-issued fingerprint scanner for best accuracy on large-scale implementation.
- We would be using PCI & DSS-certified third-party security.
- Blockchain security level implemented with TLS 3.0.
- A preset pin and two-finger security for access and locking out of the wallet in case of theft and accidents.

As we already know, the steps involved in online payment processing have significantly reduced the waiting period and hassle when purchasing commercial products and services. With new technologies and payment processes, people can easily purchase products and one-time services, set up recurring payment, and streamline payments that allow sellers to accept new orders 24/7. With SabPay, we want to do just that. But our vision for this digital payment gateway expands beyond that namely consisting of making human body as an agent for the world's most secure payment gateway, to expand from fingerprint scanning to retina scanning and last to make a hybrid security system based on **PCI DSS**, European Standards and use ISO: 27001 (International Standards) as reference.

OBJECTIVE OF PROPOSED PAYMENT SYSTEM

- To make a device-independent payment system.
- To improve the ease of conducting card/digital transactions for an individual.
- To reduce the risks and costs of handling cash at the individual level.
- To reduce costs of managing cash in the economy.
- To build a transactions history to enable improved credit access and financial inclusion.
- To reduce tax avoidance.
- To be more consumer oriented rather than being seller oriented.
- To reduce the impact of counterfeit money.

METHODOLOGY

The proposed method is illustrated through a high-level schematic shown in Figure 8.1. As in Figure 8.1, fingerprint is registered from a user. From the fingerprint, the cloud authentication the user will be done. From the authenticated user, the systems will initiate the transfer of money to another user.

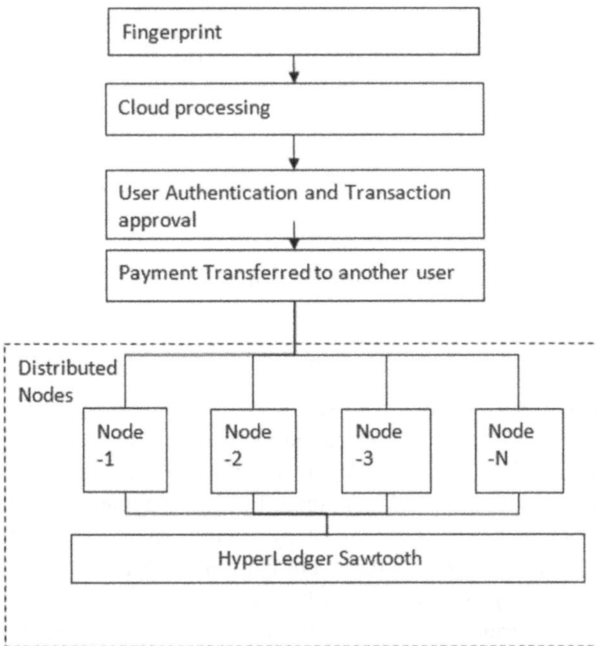

FIGURE 8.1 Higher level conceptual diagram of proposed.

Now this processed transaction with relevant details will be loaded in to a distributed file system such as Hyperledger Sawtooth. After approval of transaction, a suitable algorithm will be chosen which helps in authorization and security of payment process simultaneously in all nodes.

TECHNOLOGY IS THE FUTURE

The advent of technology and the Internet has indubitably favoured the Indian economy to become less cash dependent. As of 2017, approximately 300 million and 480 million people use smartphones and the Internet, respectively. The increased number of affordable smartphones has led to the decreased cost of data plans resulting in an expanded user base for digital payments.

Convenience is the Key

Today's fast-paced generation demands convenience and on-the-go access. This need for speed is seen across various sectors, and digital payments have profited from this drift. Ease of usage in booking tickets, transferring money, paying electricity bills, etc. have become table stakes among young consumers.

E-commerce Boom

Rising internet penetration has boosted the Indian e-commerce industry. Online stores prove to be more efficient, cost-effective and convenient than physical stores, and buyers have increasing purchasing power with incentives and shopping options from overseas merchants. Digital payments are a critical piece of this model.

Demonetization Upshot

There are two sides to an event good and bad. Considering demonetization, as of November 8, 2016, the government demonetized INR 500 and INR 1000 currency notes. The immediate impact of this announcement was a search for alternate modes of payments, leading to a surge in the utilization of the digital payments industry.

Understanding Digital Payment Models

There are a wide range of payment instruments that fall under the digital payments umbrella, including the tried and tested plastic money. The applications for banking transactions initiated by National Payments Corporation of India (NPCI) include *99#, a facility backed by USSD, Aadhaar-Enabled Payment System (AEPS) and United Payments Interface (UPI), used by Bharat Interface for Money (BHIM) application. Consumers can also carry out banking transactions 24×7 online or by using mobile banking provided by their banks.

Currently, the in-trend payment modes are digital wallets and mobile payment technologies wherein users can store debit/credit card or bank information and transact securely. Examples are Paytm, Google Pay, Apple Pay, Samsung Pay, Amex Pay, and SC Pay. These allow for funds transfers, online shopping, bill payments, etc., all via mobile devices.

Mobile payment technologies use mobile phone biometric and encryption technologies for security, and special hardware such as host card emulation (HCE), NFC and magnetic secure transmission (MST) for interacting with a merchant payment machine. With HCE-enabled wallets, consumers can keep a virtual representation of bank cards in their wallets. The application then uses an NFC/MST-based contactless payment system at the point of sale (PoS).

The NFC method permits enabled terminals to process transactions between two devices placed near each other. MST sends a magnetic signal from a compatible device to the payment terminal's card reader and imitates swiping a physical card and does not require the merchant to upgrade the payment terminal. These technologies are revolutionary in PoS terminals and help eliminate the processes through which debit/credit cards are skimmed while swiping to falsify card transactions.

In India, NFC-compliant technologies include Samsung Pay, HDFC PayZapp, ICICI Pockets (Touch and Pay Feature) and Amex Pay. Google Pay in the United States and United Kingdom uses NFC; however, in India it is used as a UPI service provider only. Apple Pay also uses NFC but is not available in India as it is not currently integrated with any bank or NPCI. Apart from wallets, tangible cards like Paytm Tap Card and Visa payWave use the NFC system. MST technology is currently available only in Samsung Pay. Samsung Pay is one of the leading applications in India as it currently has partnered with UPI, all major banks, networks like Visa and Mastercard and wallets like Paytm.

Another emerging, nascent-stage innovation is a smart card which can upload various accounts to one card and displays them on a touchscreen. Users can swipe and tap to use multiple payment methods. Fuze by BrilliantTS is bringing this tech to market, and while it may be useful for ATMs and other scenarios, it will be difficult for them to compete with new mobile payment technologies.

CONCLUSION

Biometric authentication made a way into the payment and identity market through various channels which include KYC (Know Your Customer). This infrastructure is still evolving at a great speed where millions of transactions are taking place right now. Biometric aren't new, when it comes to security. Increasing cyber security attacks, fraudulent transactions and stolen information have compromised current infrastructure where we are still using traditional device-dependent methods. Combining the feature of blockchain and SabPay to create something that provides stability to the current centralized system is thus giving everyone an equal opportunity to pay and authenticate just by their biometrics.

BIBLIOGRAPHY

1. Satoshi Nakamoto. Bitcoin: A Peer-to-Peer Electronic Cash System. 2008.
2. R. Yu et al., "Authentication with Block-Chain Algorithm and Text Encryption Protocol in Calculation of Social Network," IEEE Access, vol. 5, pp. 24944–24951, 2017.

3. J. Kishigami, S. Fujimura, H. Watanabe, A. Nakadaira, and A. Akutsu, "The Blockchain-Based Digital Content Distribution System," Proc. – 2015 IEEE 5th Int. Conf. Big Data Cloud Comput. BDCloud 2015, no. February 2018, pp. 187–190, 2015.
4. L. Zhang, H. Li, L. Sun, Z. Shi, and Y. He, "Poster: Towards Fully Distributed User Authentication with Blockchain," 2017 IEEE Symp. Privacy-Aware Comput., pp. 202–203, 2017.
5. X. Huang, C. Xu, P. Wang, and H. Liu, "LNSC: A Security Model for Electric Vehicle and Charging Pile Management Based on Blockchain Ecosystem," IEEE Access, vol. 6, pp. 13565–13574, 2018.

9 Blockchain IoT Concepts for Smart Cities

Sakshi Jain, Shashank Chauhan and Ishan Adhikari Bairagi

CONTENTS

Introduction 131
Blockchain Technology 132
Internet of Things 133
Use of Blockchain in Different Sectors 134
  Health 134
  Education 134
  Energy 135
  Agriculture 135
  Waste Management 137
Blockchain-Enabled IoT Devices for Smart Cities 137
  Universal ID Cards 137
  Water, Energy, and Pollution Management 138
  Smart Transportation and Mobility 139
  Smart Street Lighting 139
  Autonomous Building 139
  Keyless Signature Interface 140
  Smart Environment 141
  Universal Data Storage Platform 141
  Smart Living 141
Conclusion 143
References 144

INTRODUCTION

In the last few decades, the whole world has experienced unparalleled urban development due to living standards, population growth, resource deficiency, and climate change. The global urban population was 34% of the total in 1960; By 2014, the urban population was estimated to account for 54% of the total, and if it continues similarly, the proportion living in urban regions is expected to reach 66% by 2050 [1]. Honorable Prime Minister Mr. Narendra Modi launched "100 Smart Cities Mission" on 25 June 2015 in India. A total of ₹98,000 crores (US$14 billion) was approved by the Indian Cabinet for the development of 100 smart cities; this is more than the whole budget of

DOI: 10.1201/9781003094210-9

many countries [2, 10]. The Indian government is focusing on advanced solutions to counter this rapid urbanization. They are seeking effective resources to create a reliable urban environment in terms of better usage of waste, water, and energy. Nowadays smart cities are focusing on the latest and upcoming technologies like Internet of Things (IoT), automation, big data, 5G, artificial intelligence, and machine learning. Blockchain is also one of the emerging technologies by which we can achieve more effective, advanced, and secure solutions. In such situations, smart cities require a technology that enables devices to establish large numbers of transactions and rapidly verify their authenticity. Data security, integrity, and confidentiality are essential for devices and services in a metropolitan city [13, 15]. That's where blockchain rises above others as a useful solution for a decentralized platform that ensures public confidence. This chapter outlines the applications of blockchain technology and smart IoT devices, which make smart cities advanced as well as secured.

BLOCKCHAIN TECHNOLOGY

Blockchain is a way of securing information, making it impossible to change, hack, or cheat the system as shown in Figure 9.1 [3]. A blockchain is a digital ledger of transactions that is duplicated and distributed across the entire network of computer systems on the blockchain [13, 15]. Each block in the chain contains a set number of transactions, and each time a new transaction occurs on the blockchain, a record of that transaction is added to each participant's ledger [3]. There are two types of blockchain, one is public and the other is private. The basic difference between a public and private blockchain is that one works in a decentralized environment without any restrictions on the number of people connecting with the network, while the other one operates within the limits set by a controlled entity [12, 14].

Let A and B be two entities in a blockchain-based marketing system and A is paying the product fees to B who is the marketing manager. This transaction is designed

FIGURE 9.1 Blockchain.

as a block online that specifically includes the number, previous block information, and the entire transaction record, and this block propagates to each entity present in the network. The other entities check the block, and if more than 50% of the entities approve the block then the transaction is valid and linked to the chain. After that, the fee is transferred from entity A to the market manager B.

INTERNET OF THINGS

The IoT is a term for the interrelation of things. It connects all technology-based things and creates an advanced environment to communicate between them with the help of the Internet. In this era, IoT is producing a revolution in the advancement of technology to change the way humans live. In the past few years, a lot of research has been going on regarding IoT and also receiving high-quality attention. We cannot consider a future without IoT because it is an integral part of our lives now. IoT is a technology that will not leave any fundamental principle untouched. It works on the communication principle between two network devices. The ambition of the IoT is to connect an object with other objects using an internet network. The IoT is increasingly seen as a stage of success in the development of the Internet. The IoT is looking for linking ordinary objects with the Internet to achieve advanced goals. As the Internet is progressing, it is now not only a common network of computers but also a network of various interconnected IoT devices. Devices such as home appliances, smart lights, smart fans, and other smart gadgets can share their data and information over the Internet.

The IoT is playing an important role to improve the smartness and growth of cities. Figure 9.2 depicts how IoT devices share information among people, other devices and applications. Autonomous buildings, smart street lighting, smart parking, smart transportation, traffic congestion, smart waste management, and city maps are the

FIGURE 9.2 Internet of Things.

main components of a smart city. It can monitor sensitive parts of cities, parking slots available in the city, the range of walkers and vehicles, and equipment for heavy traffic congestion. Besides, IoT offers smart lighting that can work automatically according to weather conditions. IoT-enabled smart highways can provide warning information such as traffic jams and accidents or road diversions.

USE OF BLOCKCHAIN IN DIFFERENT SECTORS

Health

The lack of a central administrator is the one of biggest reasons for the growth of blockchain technology in the healthcare sector as most of the important records are scattered on different systems and sometimes when they are most needed, may not be available. Current healthcare support is typically called complex for managing and transferring information. So, we can generate digital records for patients as well as doctors and staff by applying blockchain technology as shown in Figure 9.3. Healthcare deals with confidential medical records and requires quick access to records; blockchain can efficiently handle these medical records and facilitate their secured transfer [4, 15]. Using blockchain technology, we can also build a supply chain of medicines. And by using smart contracts, the task of approving insurance claims and adjusting payments becomes more convenient [12].

Education

Education technology is advancing rapidly and is meant to go beyond smart boards and remote learning. Future students may use blockchain to keep their records, control the spread of their materials, and use innovative learning platforms [5]. As depicted in Figure 9.4, using blockchain technology, we can safely keep the educational records of the students as well as faculty and staff records. As these records cannot be erased, it helps in data security and confidentiality that it is immutable.

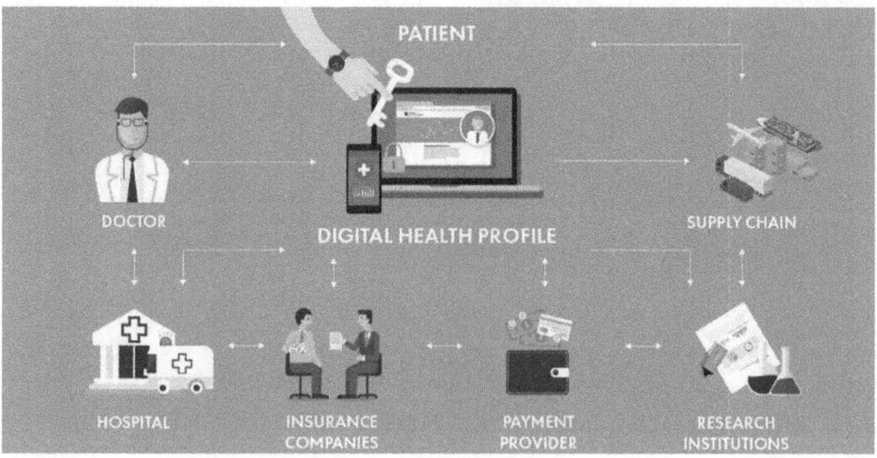

FIGURE 9.3 Blockchain in healthcare system.

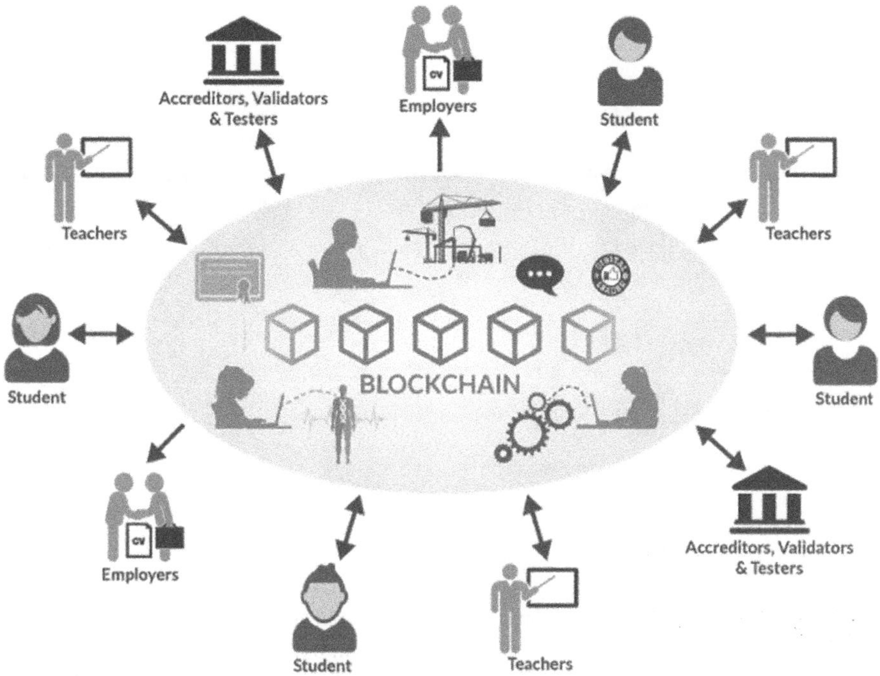

FIGURE 9.4 Blockchain in education system.

Blockchain will contact the student, rather than the institution, and whatever courses a student undertakes, that data will be stored in their account. With blockchain technology, no member can tamper with the records after it has been saved once. Blockchain technology can improve our educational system in many ways. With the help of this advanced technology, many processes can be faster, easier, and safer [5].

Energy

The renewable energy sector has been continuously catalyzed by various effective innovations as solar systems and smart vehicles; that's why energy is one of the most preferred sectors where we can use blockchain technology through the system. Environmental sustainability and reducing the cost are the two main aspects of the use of blockchain in the energy sector (refer Figure 9.5). Especially, oil and gas companies are worried about their record privacy and trade secrets. Blockchain can be used efficiently to provide privacy to their records and deals. Blockchain increases clarity for clients while not compromising with privacy. It has the potential to modify the whole energy sector through its application.

Agriculture

India is the world's second-largest producer of wheat and rice, the world's staple food. India is one of the world's five largest producers of more than 80% agricultural

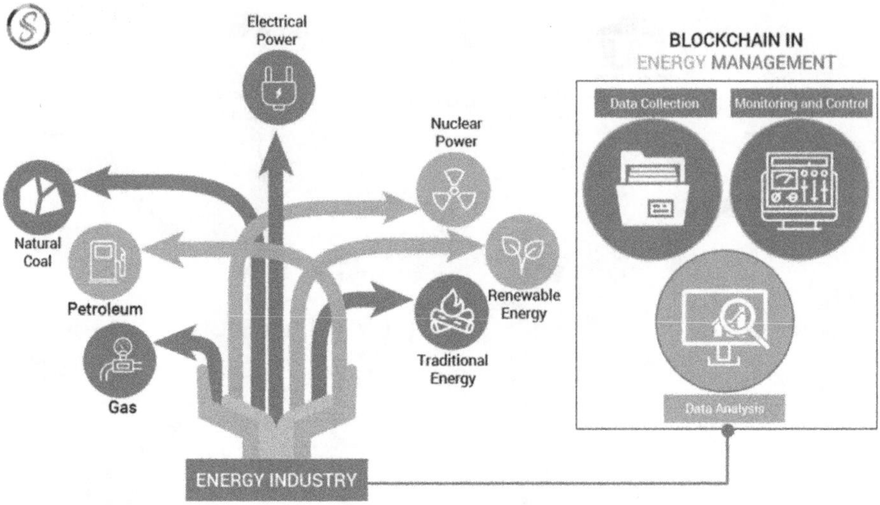

FIGURE 9.5 Blockchain in energy management.

products, including a few cash crops such as coffee and cotton [6, 15]. With the help of blockchain technology as shown in Figure 9.6, we can put all the information about the whole cycle of agricultural constructions on the blockchain so that we can find a clear and reliable source of information for farmers to get instant information related to seed quality, soil moisture, climate, and environmental data, payment, demand, and sales price, etc. on a single platform. Blockchain will help establish direct communication between farmers and retailers. This will give smallholder farmers the right to establish

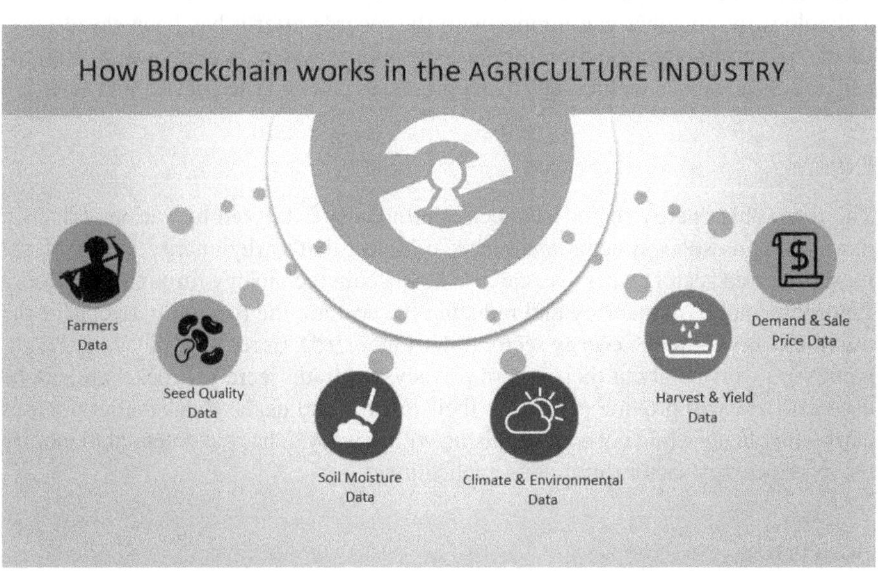

FIGURE 9.6 Blockchain in agriculture field.

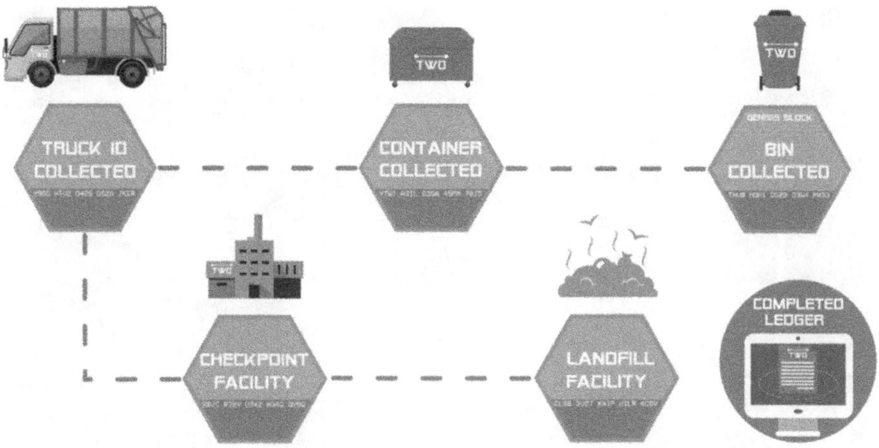

FIGURE 9.7 Blockchain in waste management.

themselves and come together to reach the market without the help of traders [13]. This will alleviate the problems of low income, as the blockchain will provide transparency in the shopping list, which will help farmers to get the true deal about their crops [7].

Waste Management

The world is affected by day-to-day human health, climate, and environment while sinking in an increasing amount of waste. The increasing rate of urbanization and rapid development is responsible for the production of huge amounts of waste. We need adequate waste management strategies to correctly detect waste generation levels. We can easily face this problem with the integration of smart IoT devices and blockchain technology. Plastic Bank, Goodr, and Prism Environment are some of the smart blockchain technology-based solutions used by some countries. These types of smart solutions help fix, reward, and punish waste management companies when they fail to deliver better management. The Figure 9.7 depicts how blockchain technology can be used for waste management.

BLOCKCHAIN-ENABLED IoT DEVICES FOR SMART CITIES

Universal ID Cards

Universal IDs have attracted the attention of many countries over the years. Universal IDs can help in many ways like encounter terrorism, strengthen national security, detect frauds, and make the lives of citizens more peaceful as shown below in Figure 9.8. Infinite times, we need to verify who we are, which in turn means that we waste a lot of time to prove it. The idea of Universal ID is a quickly verifiable method by which we can prove who we are. This idea of Universal IDs is effective, being secure as well as time-saving. Citizens can use these IDs for their identification, digital signatures, banking, and voting purposes. And during these services, all the data of the citizens is protected by blockchain technology.

FIGURE 9.8 Blockchain-enabled IDs.

Water, Energy, and Pollution Management

During the advancement of the smart city, renewable energy, water, and waste management play an essential role. Data about all of these can be stored by the blockchain, regularly updated data that helps a smart city smartly make decisions. These types of strategies should be applied at the individual level so that one can analyze oneself regarding their usage and consumption. There are many smart devices available by which we can measure water quality and detect smoke or pollution and take instructions to rescue accordingly. IoT devices like sensors can be connected to a garbage container that collects the data about the level of waste in the container as shown below in Figure 9.9. This sensor upon a certain level will give a response to the waste management administration and send a notification to the truck driver's mobile application.

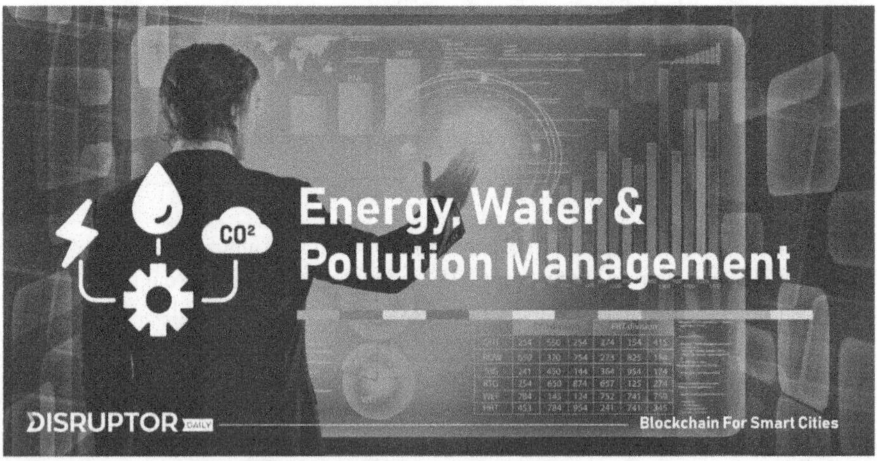

FIGURE 9.9 Water and pollution management.

FIGURE 9.10 Smart transportation.

Smart Transportation and Mobility

Traffic is one of the biggest concerns in cities. Jams on roads and highways cause accidents as well as an excessive number of toxic gases. Congestion sensors to divert city smart cars and drivers use smart parking meters to indicate available parking spaces and reduce driving time. London has upgraded its CO_2 emissions in transit. The city is reducing about 70,000 cars on the road every day by driving away business locations from cars and using cameras to drive drivers to these areas. Copenhagen is another smart city that encourages alternative forms of transportation – they apply GPS-enabled robots that appeal to cyclists, reducing their travel time by 17% [8]. Figure 9.10 depicts how Blockchain play an important role in smart transportation and mobility.

Smart Street Lighting

Figure 9.11 depicts how Blockchain play an important role in smart street lighting. IoT devices can be implemented more cost-effectively for the maintenance and management of street lights. With the help of cloud management solutions, sensors can help operate and schedule switching operations. Smart lighting solutions with smart sensors can be executed to record the movement of citizens and vehicles. With the help of this data, the street lamps can adjust the lights to be either dim, bright, or switch off automatically depending on the circumstances [14, 15].

Autonomous Building

Buildings are the essence of our daily activities, but they also consume a lot of energy. Cities like Singapore want to get it back with powerful IoT cooling systems. These devices optimize heating, cooling, and power consumption depending

FIGURE 9.11 Smart street lighting.

on the function of each room, saving up to 32% on HVAC costs. And these types of machines connect multiple structures simultaneously to enable maintenance. Seattle, a smart city in Washington State, is using smart analytics systems to reduce emissions by 45% of its city buildings [8, 13]. IoT smart devices are making everything more sorted for building structures as shown below in Figure 9.12. The devices can be connected to a smart management system that controls heating, cooling, lighting, and fire safety systems.

Keyless Signature Interface

Keyless Signature Interface is a blockchain technology, which gives a huge range of data evidence without dependence on centralized trust authorities. Keyless Signature Interface is one of the solutions behind the wide functions IDs offer to their holders, Keyless Signature Interface blockchain technology also protects e-services such as the e-Health Record, e-Prescription database, e-Law, e-Court systems, e-Police data,

FIGURE 9.12 Autonomous building.

FIGURE 9.13 Blockchain-enabled signature interface.

e-Banking, e-Business Register, and e-Land Registry [9]. Figure 9.13 shows the role of blockchain technology in keyless signature interface.

Smart Environment

The environment has an important role in all aspects of life. An unhealthy environment can affect all lives such as animals, birds, plants, and humans also. There have been endless efforts to create a healthy environment in terms of reducing pollution and wastage but all went in vain. Now we need advanced solutions to counter this problem. The integration of smart IoT devices and blockchain technology can provide us the smart solution to this problem as shown in Figure 9.14. Smart environment strategies integrated with IoT technology should be implemented for sensing, tracking, and evaluation of environmental objects that provide advantages in attaining a sustainable life in a green world [12, 15].

Universal Data Storage Platform

The average cost of a US enterprise data breach in 2017 was $1.3 million, with $117,000 for small- and medium-sized businesses. Every day, 5 million data records are lost or stolen, making 58 data records every second. Integration of data collected and linked to smart cities – sensor data, intelligent grid data, smart vehicle data, etc. – cannot be compromised by storing them on a centralized, easily accessible data hub. The blockchain serves as the only viable alternative to a universal data storage platform for smart cities that provides both central security and inter-security as shown in Figure 9.15 [11].

Smart Living

By using remote control IoT devices, we can remotely switch appliances on and off so we can save energy. Smart refrigerators also come under IoT devices by which

FIGURE 9.14 Smart environment.

FIGURE 9.15 Data storage.

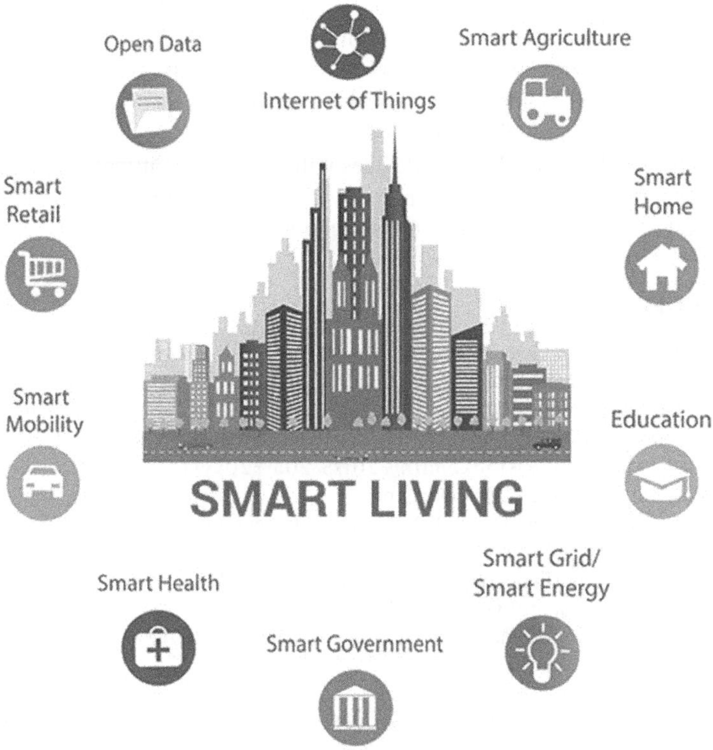

FIGURE 9.16 Smart living.

we can get related data about what is available inside, what is going to expire, or what needs to refill. We can get all this information in our smartphone application so that we can get updates and work accordingly. Besides, a lot of kitchen appliances such as ovens and microwaves can be connected via a smartphone application. In addition, washing machines may allow us to remotely monitor the laundry. IoT can also be used as home security by installing cameras and door detectors as shown in Figure 9.16.

CONCLUSION

The rapid development of urban areas results in better options for citizens. A smart city does not only improve living standards but also makes our daily routines easier and quicker. With the help of blockchain technology and smart IoT devices, we can make our cities and homes more pollution-free, automated, secure, and eco-friendly. We will improve our living standards and increase security, traffic control, efficient use of energy, and lower levels of pollution. Smart IoT devices will revolutionize the way we live through tracing of our daily routines. The possibilities of the IoT are infinite as it produces valuable data for businesses, emergency services, management of various sectors, and more. Blockchain technology has enormous potential when it comes to developing future enhanced smart communities that are more effective and provide a standard life. Blockchain technology can provide solutions to a wide variety of problems that are done on a daily basis by smart cities. This chapter proposes a blockchain technology-based framework to enable the advancement of a smart city. The integration of blockchain technology with IoT devices for smart cities will provide a shared platform where all devices will be able to communicate in a secure environment [1]. Future tasks will aim to review the scalability of various platforms used in a smart city and create a systematic model to act accordingly.

REFERENCES

1. https://www.researchgate.net/publication/311716550_Securing_Smart_Cities_Using_Blockchain_Technology.
2. https://en.wikipedia.org/wiki/Smart_Cities_Mission.
3. https://www.euromoney.com/learning/blockchain-explained/what-is-blockchain#:~:text=Blockchain%20is%20a%20system%20of,computer%20systems%20on%20the%20blockchain.
4. https://hitconsultant.net/2018/01/29/blockchain-technology-in-healthcare-benefits/#.XweNTCgzZPY.
5. https://jaxenter.com/blockchain-education-161738.html.
6. https://en.wikipedia.org/wiki/Agriculture_in_India.
7. https://medium.com/@Zebidata/how-blockchain-can-revolutionize-the-agriculture-industry-691d630dac61.
8. https://www.iotforall.com/what-makes-smart-city-2019/.
9. https://www.e-zigurat.com/innovation-school/blog/blockchain-and-smart-cities/.
10. https://www.disruptordaily.com/blockchain-use-cases-smart-cities/.
11. United Nations. World Urbanization Prospects: The 2014 Revision, Highlights (ST/ESA/SER.A/352), Dept. of Economic and Social Affairs, ISBN: 978-92-1-151517-6, pp. 1–32, 2014.
12. Dutta, S., Saini, K. Securing data: A study on different transform domain techniques. In WSEAS Transactions on Systems and Control, Volume 16, 2021. DOI: 10.37394/23203.2021.16.8
13. Saini, K. Next generation logistics: A novel approach of blockchain technology. In *Essential Enterprise Blockchain Concepts and Applications*. USA: CRC Press, 2020.
14. Dutta, S., Saini, K. Statistical assessment of hybrid blockchain for SME sector. In WSEAS Transactions on Systems and Control, Volume 16, 2021. E-ISSN: 2224-2856 2021, DOI: 10.37394/23203.2021.16.6
15. Saini, K., Agarwal, V., Varshney, A., Gupta, A. E2EE For Data Security For Hybrid Cloud Services: A Novel Approach. In IEEE International Conference on Advances in Computing, Communication Control and Networking (IEEE ICACCCN 2018) organized by Galgotias College of Engineering & Technology Greater Noida, 12–13 October, 2018. DOI:10.1109/ICACCCN.2018.8748782

10 Role of IoT and Blockchain Technology for Enhanced Applications in Different Domains

Ruchi Agarwal and Kalpana Jha

CONTENTS

Introduction 146
Internet of Things (IoT) 147
Advantages of Internet of Things 148
Cost Saving 148
Information 148
Communication 148
Automation and Control 148
Increased Productivity 148
Limitations of Internet of Things 149
Over Dependency on Technology 149
Losing Security on Privacy 149
Lesser Employment Prospects 149
Complexity 149
Introduction to Blockchain 149
Access to Blockchain 150
Security Issue in Blockchain 151
Aim of Blockchain 152
Working 152
Bitcoin Network 152
Effectiveness of Blockchain in the IoT Sector 153
IoT Security 153
Major Components of IoT 154
Security Architecture 154
The Perceptual Layer 154
Network Layer 155
Support Layer 155
Application Layers 155

DOI: 10.1201/9781003094210-10

IoT (Internet of Things) Security: Ways to Protect the IoT Devices ... 155
IoT Cybercrime Now and Tomorrow ... 157
Challenges: Protection and IoT ... 157
AI and Automation ... 157
Home Security ... 157
Insufficient Testing and Updating ... 158
IoT Malware and Ransomware ... 158
Ambiguous Security Standards ... 158
Attack Prediction and Prevention ... 159
Best IoT Security Technologies ... 159
IoT Network Security ... 159
Authentication on IoT Devices ... 159
IoT Encryption ... 159
Security Analysis ... 160
Application of IoT ... 160
Wearables ... 160
Smart Home Applications ... 160
Healthcare ... 160
Smart Cities ... 161
Agriculture ... 161
Conclusion ... 161
Bibliography ... 162

INTRODUCTION

Students who are looking for the institutions having Internet of Things (IoT) programs do not get enough opportunity, as there are no specific institutions that have recognized IoT as a main course. As we know, there is a fixed curriculum in colleges and institutions for a course, such as students who are seeking for business administration, they would find their curriculum obsolete and this is the reason the students are only graduated not business administrative. Nowadays, only theoretical and textbook knowledge get you nowhere in the field of data science, machine learning or IoT and thus theory-based knowledge is not sufficient for it.

By considering the current era, you wouldn't be ready for the market competition, not for jobs, and even you will not be able to face the interview with that much knowledge; only that's why IoT courses need specialized courses. Depending on the results of Google, we found that there are only a few institutions around India that offer IoT courses. Technologies as well as various gadgets are getting developed in the field of IoT, providing the ability and opportunity to develop diverse applications.

In order to develop creative and innovative applications on advanced technologies, you need to be familiar with IoT and understand the concept of IoT; you have to be strong with your basics first, then check yourself that the prerequisites needed for the industry are fulfilled but not just after that you become ready for the course.

After doing all these, the next step is to enroll in any of the program such as IoT analyst and IoT certificate course to initiate your journey. All the courses comprise basics of IoT along with some additional specifications, depending upon your interest field; one should start researching and stay updated. Also gathering information in the field of cloud computing is very significant in the industry.

In order to develop better understanding, having hands-on experience on projects as well as developing miniature programs, robots and devices will add to knowledge and help develop industry-specific technicalities. Furthermore, the job market in the IoT is expanding every day, and newer roles are popping up every other day for you. If you are well skilled, you can fit yourself anywhere in the industry. Depending upon your versatility, you are able to fit in with the industry. Once you are aware of the skills and specialization, human can't be replaced with machines.

INTERNET OF THINGS (IoT)

To set up connection among various day-to-day devices such as electrical appliances, i.e. TV, mobile phones and initiating the communication, we require embedded software and various sensors (Figure 10.1).

Data can be sent and received via the sensors. The next step is the analysis of data; this task is performed by IoT platform. The result of which is the extracted data, that is the information that is required to be shared among various nodes/devices that are connected via IoT.

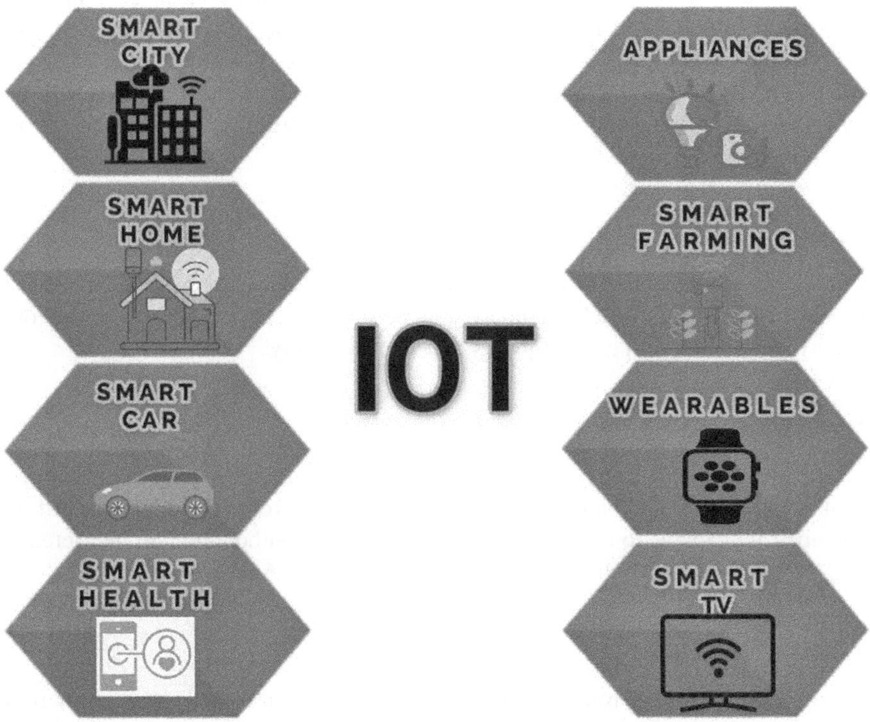

FIGURE 10.1 Devices connected to IoT.

In the diagram, we can see various devices that are connected via IoT from smart city to smart home; these will be intelligent homes connected to an intelligent city. The diagram also shows the smart transport system for better management of the traffic. Smart health services will definitely have a positive impact on people's health as well as smart wearable devices having a variety of features.

ADVANTAGES OF INTERNET OF THINGS

Internet of things has been a boon to the industry. The major advantages of IoT include the following:

Cost Saving

IoT allows user's gadgets to communicate with other gadgets and user in an effective manner, thereby conserving and saving cost and energy; hence, it's helpful to people in their daily routine work problem. By allowing the data to be shared and communicated between electronic gadgets and then render it into our required way, IoT is making our systems well-organized.

Information

It is true that with more information, you can make better conclusions. Whether it is a general settlement as needing to know what to buy at a grocery store or if your company has enough supplies and appliances, knowledge is a great power and more knowledge is always good and we believe on it, so that the gadgets connected to the networks store a large amount of data that gives us required information as per our requirement.

Communication

IoT encourages machine-to-machine (M2M) communication (communication between devices). Owing to this, the somatic gadget is capable to stay connected; hence, total lucidity is available with greater quality and lesser inability.

Automation and Control

Owing to freshly objects getting managed and connected digitally with wireless framework, there is a big amount of technology and control in the workings. All the machines are capable to communicate with each other without human interference, which leads to prompt output.

Increased Productivity

Productivity plays a key role in the advantage of any business. IoT offers just in time training for the employees, better labor efficiency, and also lessened mismatch of skills while expanding organizational productivity.

LIMITATIONS OF INTERNET OF THINGS

Over Dependency on Technology

At present, it is observed that the younger generation is a machinery freak and they depend upon automation and its devices for every little thing. No petition is free from fault and there is some jerk in each technical application. Totally relying on IoT devices may create trouble in the case of a nonworking or crash of an IoT framework.

Losing Security on Privacy

As there is the participation of different technologies and devices, there is a monitoring by more than one company, which directly questions the security and seclusion issues. Data recapture and storage also become the major concern for the companies because all of them are associated at the same time.

Lesser Employment Prospects

With IoT, day-to-day activities getting automated, which will lead to less demand of human assets and less educated staff, which may create employment issues in the society.

Complexity

With all complex systems, there is the possibility of nonfulfillment. Nonsuccess could be skyrocket in the case of the IoT.

INTRODUCTION TO BLOCKCHAIN

"Blockchain" is the technology that keeps the record behind the Bitcoin network and you might be familiar with it. You must have come across a conclusion that "Blockchain is a distributed, decentralized, public ledger" when you were trying to learn about blockchain.

Why this complex technology is called "blockchain?" So most basically, it is a chain of blocks where digital information is stored in the form of a chain inside a database.

There are three components:

1. Information about transactions of your most recent purchase from Amazon and its details like time, date and dollar amount is stored in blocks.
2. Information of participants in transactions is stored in blockchain. Your name along with shopping website will be recorded for your purchase. Your purchase is recorded using a special "digital signature," without any identifying information, instead of using your actual name.

Information stored in blocks is distinguishable from other blocks. A unique code known as "hash" that is stored in each block provides the ability to separate each block. Special algorithms are used in creating hashes that are cryptographic codes. When you make a purchase from shopping website, and again you want to make another purchase, you might see your transaction looks similar, but the blocks can be differentiated on the basis of their unique codes.

The reality is little different from the above example where block stores a transaction from website. Each block contains thousands transactions, depending on the size of transaction.

When new data is stored in a block, it becomes the part of blockchain. Blockchain consists of multiple blocks strung together. To add block to the blockchain, the below mentioned steps need to be taken:

1. A transaction has to occur. In the example of your purchase from a shopping website, after going through multiple checkout prompt, a purchase is made.
2. Now the purchase will be packaged along with other users' transaction details in the form of blocks where a block may contain thousands of transactions, like we discussed earlier.
3. In order to perform critical examination of fresh data entries along with records of public records, proper examination is required.
4. With the help of blockchain technology, the vulnerability of transaction is removed. It is to be checked that the transaction occurs in the form as it is instructed after the transaction from, i.e. then detail is confirmed of the purchase, including the time of transaction, participants and amount.
5. After the verification of the transaction accurately, it is to be stored in a block. The cost of transaction and digital signatures are to be stored in a block.
6. After completing all the verification of a block's transactions, a special code that is a hash must be given. Block may be added to the blockchain once it's hashed.
7. After the addition of new block to the blockchain, it becomes available for access.
8. Analyzing the blockchain of Bitcoin, access to transaction data, together with the details about "time," place and by whom, is now available in the block.

ACCESS TO BLOCKCHAIN

1. Contents of blockchain are available to everyone as well as users can connect various machines as nodes to the network of blockchain.
2. After connecting, the device gets a copy of the blockchain that is updated automatically, which gets updated whenever a new block is added, for example any new feed that provides updates on real time whenever any message is posted.
3. The devices in the blockchain already have their copy of the blockchain, which means that the blockchain has thousands of copies, or in the case of Bitcoin, millions.
4. The copies of the blockchain resemble each other; also the information spread across a computer network makes it harder to control the

information. There are a series of events that can be exploited with a blockchain.

5. Any copy of the blockchain on the network can be exploited by a hacker; blockchain is meant to be a "distributed" ledger. However, if you look over the Bitcoin blockchain, one will find that there is no access to information about the users of transaction. Since the blockchain transactions are not totally anonymous, user's information is restricted to their digital signature.

SECURITY ISSUE IN BLOCKCHAIN

Blockchain technology takes account of security issues in multiple ways. First, new blocks are stored chronologically, which means new blocks are to be the "end" of blockchain. Every block has a "height," which means its corresponding position in the chain. Once a block is added to the blockchain, it becomes difficult to alter the block's contents. That's because each block has its unique hash, and the block hash before it. A math function creates hash codes, which turns digital information into a string of numbers and letters. If that information is edited in any way, the hash code also changes.

Since safety is a major concern, in a case where a hacker tries to perform any change to transaction, so you actually have to pay more than purchase, the transaction amount hash of the block will get modified.

The next block in the chain will possess the previous hash, and that block would need to be updated by the hacker to modify it. This will result in the change of the hash of that block as well as next in the sequence.

Now, hacker has to modify every block on the blockchain, to change a particular block. It would take a huge and unlikely amount of computing power to recalculate all of those hashes. In other words, it becomes very difficult to edit whenever a new block is added to the blockchain, which cannot be deleted.

Tests are conducted for blockchain networks that like to connect and add new blocks to deal with the trust issue. Such tests are called "consensus models" that call for users to authenticate before taking part in a blockchain network.

Devices must "prove" in the work system of the proof and that they have performed "work" by resolving a difficult problem of computation. Once such problem is solved by a computer, new blocks can be added to blockchain. But adding blocks to the blockchain, what the world of cryptocurrency calls "mining," is not an easy process. In January 2020, the problem of solving one of such issues on the Bitcoin network was around 1 in 15.5 trillion. Computers have to run programs that cost huge amounts to deal with complex math problems.

Work proof doesn't make hacker attacks difficult, although it makes them insignificant. When an attack is performed on the blockchain, it would be required to control more than 50 percent of all the blockchain computational power.

Given the Bitcoin blockchain's huge size, a type of attack such as 51 percent attack is not worth the effort.

AIM OF BLOCKCHAIN

Blockchain allows only the recording and distribution of digital information, but no changes. It may be sound complex.

Stuart Haber and W Scott Stornetta first outlined blockchain technology in 1991. The researchers wanted to develop a system in which timestamps could not be changed. But it took decades to develop. After which that blockchain got its real-world application, the result was Bitcoin, in January 2009.

The blockchain builds on the Bitcoin protocol. Introduction to the digital currency, the creator of Bitcoin, Satoshi Nakamoto, developed "a new, fully peer-to-peer, electronic cash system with no trusted third party."

WORKING

Construction of blockchain is as follows:

1. Digital transaction gets transformed into a protected block using cryptography, competing to validate the transaction. Now these are time-stamped.
2. After that, it is added to the series in sequential order.
3. A new block is created in series, using a hash of the previously accepted block.

There are people from around the world, who have Bitcoin. These people have at least a portion of a Bitcoin, who are interested to use the Bitcoin for day-to-day shopping needs. It is here that the blockchain comes in.

In the "decentralized" type of system where for the currency, an authority such as government or bank regulates as well as verifies the utilization of printed currency—but no one controls Bitcoin. Instead, a network of computers verifies transactions done in Bitcoin.

BITCOIN NETWORK

While using Bitcoin, a person can pay for a variety of goods, for which the devices on the Bitcoin network verify the transaction. Following are the steps:

1. Users need to implement a program on their devices and attempt to deal with a complex problem, known as "hash."
2. When a device solves complex problems using "hashing," corresponding algorithmic will also have verified the transactions of the block. Now in the next step, the transaction is recorded and stored as a block on the blockchain at where it becomes fixed.
3. Talking about Bitcoin, and various other blockchain, devices successfully verifies blocks that are rewarded with cryptocurrency. During the public recording of transactions on the blockchain, user data is not kept full.
4. Users have to run a program called a "wallet" to conduct transactions on the Bitcoin network. Two unique and distinct cryptographic keys for each wallet are maintained: public and private keys.

5. The first location is the public key from which transactions are deposited and withdrawn from. It is the key that is used as digital signature of the user on the blockchain ledger.

EFFECTIVENESS OF BLOCKCHAIN IN THE IoT SECTOR

Blockchain is basically a secured, cryptographically distributed ledger, which allows secure transfer of data among the parties.

1. IoT systems having centralized architecture in which information from one device is sent for storage on cloud.
2. After processing, data is sent to the IoT devices.

Since security over the network is the major concern in IoT, one of the common is using "Smart contract" that will not only provide security but also scalability and automation without requiring the third party to oversee the transactions.

Here the information is shared using a cryptographically secured decentralized network. Since decentralized network comes into picture, the risk of single-point failure can also be overcome. In the case of any problem at a particular node, the system can still function properly.

Blockchain technology greatly helps in providing a secure and reliable configuration for IoT machines. Here are the two main approaches:

1. Configuration details and valid final version firmware such as IoT's properties can be hosted on the ledger. The blockchain node is prompted to receive its configuration from the ledge while bootstrap is executed.
2. For the latest configuration file, the hash values for each device can be hosted. To store the latest and reliable configuration, IoT devices need to download the information regularly. After that blockchain is used to receive and match the corresponding hash value, which is to be stored in blockchain. It provides the ability to administrators to regularly remove any undesired configuration in every IoT device in the network with the configurations having latest and reliable information.

IoT SECURITY

Since information is transmitted over the network again and again, security becomes a matter of concern. Privacy and security of data is very important since the data may be of the interest of the hacker.

For example, the attack that affected the Internet known as DDoS (distributed denial of service) attack. Another example is hacking of vehicle to expose vulnerabilities in IoT devices.

IoT security is the technology area concerned with guarding various connected devices and networks in the IoT. It includes connectivity of interrelated computing devices, people, machines and gadgets. Each device is uniquely identified and they have the ability to transfer data automatically over the cloud. It is expected that devices that allow connecting with a network have serious vulnerabilities if they are not protected.

Major Components of IoT

- Devices
- Sensors
- Data processing
- Control and feedback
- Cloud-server

IoT security has been implemented in various ways:

- Machine-to-machine(M2M) interaction
- Cyber-physical systems(CPS)
- Cyber transportation systems(CTS)

Security Architecture

There are four fundamental layers of security architectures as shown in Figure 10.2:

The Perceptual Layer

It works in the similar fashion as people's sense organs such as eyes and nose work. This layer is responsible for identifying things and collecting information from them. The sensors that are used to collect information are 2-D barcode, RFID and sensors that are connected to the device.

In accordance to the application, necessities of sensors are chosen. The information that is gathered by this sensor can be about your contact details, location, motion etc. The target of attackers is that they want to utilize them to perform some changes in the sensor with different ways. The perceptual layer is also called sensor layer.

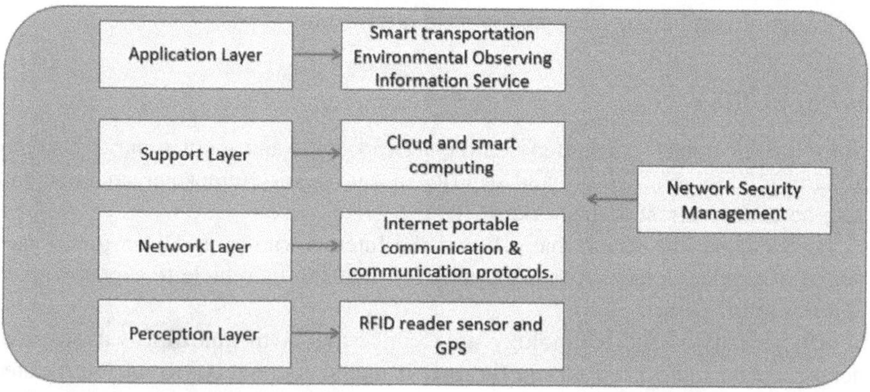

FIGURE 10.2 Security architecture.

Network Layer

The information collected by the physical sensor is carried by the network layer. The transmission can be possible by wireless or wired-based network, which is sensitive to attacks from attackers' side. This layer is also called as transmission layer, which forms a connection between application layer and perceptual layer.

Support Layer

The information is sent only by the users who have successfully obtained authentication. Information is verified by many ways. In order to send information to the third layer, there is a potential risk of threats over the network.

Because of the imperfection that was available in the three-layer architecture, a new layer is proposed. The information from the perception layer is sent to the support layer, in layered architecture. Security is the key concern to make a layer of protection in architecture of IoT. The key responsibilities of support layer are as follows:

- Verify the user's information and confirms that the information is being sent by authentic user.
- The second function of the support layer is to send information to the network layer. The transmission of the information from the support layer to network layer can be wireless and wire based. Different types of attacks can affect the functions at this layer.

Application Layers

Application layer has several issues having security as the major concern. It has several applications using the IoT technology or in which IoT is implemented.

The applications include smart health, smart cities, smart homes and tracking systems. The application layer is responsible for services to the applications. Sensors are used for collecting information.

IoT is also implemented to make a home smart; it introduces many threats and vulnerabilities from both inside and outside.

The smart devices used at home uses low power requirement and generally have low amount of storage. The key concern is related to security as attacker can easily hack and change the coding/script of application as per his requirement. Thus, to have a strong security in IoT-based smart homes, data has to be securely collected by sensor. Figure 10.3 shows the typical diagram for security of devices.

IoT (Internet of Things) Security: Ways to Protect the IoT Devices

So, this is the reason to protect your life by using secured IoT-enabled devices. These are the several methods to secure IoT centralized over the protection of your Internet-enabled devices that are connected wirelessly. IoT security safety component is tied up with IoT and strives for the protection of IoT devices and networks against cybercrime. IoT technologies create potential threats to your Internet security.

FIGURE 10.3 Diagram for security of devices.

1. Do research before you buy any device because digital devices are smarter as they collect information and your personal data.
2. You must keep an eye on the data that are stored and gathered by devices. Be assured of the protection of data collection while the data is shared.
3. Secure your devices' accounts, Wi-Fi networks and connected devices with strong and unique passwords. Don't use those common words such as "12345," your phone number or DOB that is easy to guess.
4. Verify the apps first before use. Check and study the privacy policy of various apps of various IoT devices, and also check the plan before using your information over that application.
5. Install Internet security software on various devices such as laptops and smartphone. Different software provide real-time protection against various types of attacks.
6. Before accessing the devices' application, check the permissions regarding that application of whether it is necessary, and if not then deny permission of that application to make safe measures.
7. Devices having Bluetooth should be turned off, when not in use. Because automatic sharing with other users in close accessibility is a feature in some devices.
8. Regularly check the firmware updates of the IoT devices with the help of manufacturers' websites.
9. While using the social sharing feature, use caution, because social sharing feature may lead the cyber criminals to track your daily movement that may cause cyberstalking or any real-life danger.
10. For providing security in the transmission of data, Wi-Fi must use a VPN which helps to secure the transmitted data.
11. Never keep your smartphone unguarded in a congested or public place. In that places, do not forget to turn off the Wi-Fi.

IoT Cybercrime Now and Tomorrow

Nowadays, the IoT is getting more popular, with so many different types of products and devices in this digital era. But there is a risk of stealing your personal data and making profit with that when your information is on the cloud with help of your accessed IoT devices.

Devices connected wirelessly especially with your smartphone can be more secured by changing your own privacy concern settings.

As per the current scenario, IoT security is the great concern nowadays. Because of the following reasons:

1. Your devices that are connected wirelessly are data collector. Here personal information is obtained.
2. Stored on these devices—such as your personal data, images and contact details—all your personal information that attracts hackers and the data is on the cloud so it can help criminals to steal your identity.

To see how it works, whenever you accessed your IoT devices remotely for your basic needs such as to lock or unlock your doors and turn on or off your light or fans, they need few taps to do the same, but by adding more functions to your smartphone, you need to store more. This can make anything connected to such devices permeable to various types of attacks that can be really very dangerous.

CHALLENGES: PROTECTION AND IoT

AI and Automation

If you're hearing anything about tech, you've also heard about AI and automation. They're already helping experts in a multitude of industries to sort through huge quantities of data and make critical decisions.

Eventually, automation and AI could be used to benefit IoT administrators and network security officers. Tools like these would allow those parties to detect potentially problematic traffic and data patterns.

AI might even be used to help enforce data-specific rules. But there's a problem: when people use autonomous systems to make choices that impact lots of real people, it becomes really obvious that one awkward nonhuman decision could cause a lot of damage. So, if someone wants to build an IoT-based app soon, they should consider security challenges like this. For solving the security challenges, AI and automation pose in IoT settings that require the following:

1. Protecting IoT from attacks
2. Protecting user data from theft

Home Security

A growing number of people are integrating IoT connectivity into their homes and offices. Huge, innovative names in the building industry even develop entire residential and commercial buildings with IoT built into their fabric.

It's almost too easy for something to go wrong. All it takes is an IP address exposure to start a downward spiral: residential addresses and other consumer contact information can be exposed afterward. Then, it's easy for a malicious party to use the information.

Insufficient Testing and Updating

IoT devices are becoming increasingly popular; when we trust normal tech companies to produce those devices, we have to accept some risk. Tech companies don't always do their due diligence when it comes to IoT device handling and mitigating security risks.

1. Lots of IoT devices are under-updated
2. Secure devices become insecure over time

When our early computer systems faced the same problem, we (somewhat) fixed it through automatic software updates.

When it comes to IoT devices, longevity isn't always a priority for manufacturers. There's no easy way to update IoT devices as you go. Manufacturers just make something to capture their audience's attention and then work on the next gadget that fits that bill. IoT devices need adequate testing before they're launched to the public. The current insufficient efforts to do so do not protect consumers or hardware.

IoT Malware and Ransomware

IoT products have become popular and commonplace very quickly. This makes it difficult to predict cyberattack permutations. We can't always protect those products against attacks like these anyway, but in a lot of settings (like with normal computers).

We have enough experience to sort things out eventually. If an IoT-enabled camera (for example) captured private, confidential information, the information could be compromised during a system hack. Traditional ransomware uses encryption to protect data. It locks out users from platforms and devices they shouldn't access. Cybercriminals are now merging malware and ransomware strains to try to create a new type of attack.

Ambiguous Security Standards

We rely on clear security standards to keep us safe every day—at school, at work, on the web, in vehicles, standing in front of refrigerators. The security standards that govern IoT devices are not clear. They're ambiguous at their best.

Most IoT devices are made up of lots of components manufactured all throughout the world. It's because the parts that make up these devices are very specialized—only some entities can make them. That creates a problem: when all the parts are created separately, they all rely on their own sets of security standards. Different security standards leave IoT devices vulnerable. It's a big issue when it comes to protecting user privacy.

Attack Prediction and Prevention

It's not just the attacks themselves that are risky in IoT settings—it's predicting and preventing those attacks that pose the greatest challenge. IoT cyberattacks are tremendously unpredictable; most hackers use new, modern methods to breach security and evade detection as long as possible.

IoT device security leaves a lot of questions for anybody who's interested in the subject for the long term. IoT devices need to be able to process data instantly, which makes implementing security processes difficult.

Those security processes slow down an IoT device's ability to perform functions. AI-powered monitoring could help with attack prediction and prevention in the future. Experts need to locate vulnerabilities and fix them as they occur.

Modern cloud services already use threat intelligence to predict security problems. We're inching toward some security solutions for IoT, but it will take time (and work) to get there.

BEST IOT SECURITY TECHNOLOGIES

IoT security technologies are as follows:

IoT Network Security

IoT involves connectivity of internet and all peripherals' devices be it digital or mechanical devices. IoT network security is important as connecting devices to internet open the possibilities of hacking if they are not protected properly. This kind of connection that connects the IoT devices with the back-end systems communication on the Internet can be made secure by providing traditional security at various end point features using antivirus and firewalls.

Authentication on IoT Devices

In order to verify users of IoT devices, multiple users are managed for using the same device, different passwords and different techniques like digital certificates and two-step authentication. Networks involving authentication processes consist of human interaction, authentication scenarios involving IoT.

IoT Encryption

In order to perform secured communication of data traveling between devices and back-end systems, using cryptographic technique, preventing attack from hackers and maintaining integrity of data encryption are performed. IoT devices and other hardware restrict the use to have standard encryption processes and protocols. IoT encryption must be accompanied by full encryption key administration processes, because use of poor key to conduct such operation will not help the security concern.

Security Analysis

It includes various processes such as:

- Collection
- Observation
- Normalization

Data from IoT devices have the ability to provide reporting facility and alert on certain activities, for example activities that do not follow traditional policies.

Providing solutions such as machine learning, big data technique and AI further provide predictive cast and detection of anomaly.

APPLICATION OF IoT

Wearables

The basis of IoT applications is wearable technology in which industries deployed the IoT as their significant technology. For example, devices such as health monitoring equipment that are developed to help people having diabetes. A small sensor called glucose sensor that detects the glucose level in the body. Radio frequency is used to relay the information to a monitoring device.

Fitness, health and entertainment requirements are covered in wearable IoT. The most personable item that person can own are wearable and they offer high functionalities that can help someone perfectly to analyze his or her activities. It becomes easier for enterprisers, manufacturers, retailers, automotive companies and hospitals to build collaboration between employees and devices with the help of IoT.

Smart Home Applications

Smart home is the best thing ever happened in IoT. If we talk about "JARVIS," the AI automation stated by the CEO of Facebook, it is the best example of a smart home. Another example is Allen Pan's Home Automation System. Smart home system increases the comfort and quality of life, and because of this, they achieved great popularity in the last decades.

We can control smart homes with smart phones and microcontrollers and we will be able to monitor home functions.. The concept of smart home shows the integration of cloud computing and IoT.

Healthcare

IoT also take part in a medical-based system. Research in the field of medical has the shortage of critical information that is required for different purposes. They use data that is examined in controlled environments and for other examination purposes.

But with the help of IoT, we see important data analysis such as:

1. Real-time field data and testing
2. The current devices in power having significant precision

3. Improvement in the availability of devices
4. Easier in terms of pocket and also accessibility
5. Use of technology for diagnosis
6. Comfort for the patient

Application of this technology in the healthcare sector provides medical centers to function more perfectly and improving the quality and efficiency of treatment.

Smart Cities

Smart city is a term heard by everyone. But it differs from one city to another. For example, people living in Rohtak have different problems than those who live in Noida. The problems of other cities are different from Hong Kong. All the problems affect each city differently. To analyze these often-complex factors, government and engineers can use IoT. Certain emergencies can be aided in areas with the use of IoT applications.

The first city that had a completely new approach toward monitoring of traffic is Palo Alto, San Francisco. They analyzed that the main cause for traffic in the city is that the vehicles on the streets move around the same block, in search of parking space. To overcome this situation, sensor was installed at all different spots in the city. The drivers can easily get the shortest route to a free parking space.

Agriculture

It is estimated that the world population will reach approximately 10 billion by the year 2050. In order to provide food to the population, it is required to get the best result in agriculture. There are many ways to obtain good results in agriculture but one of them is smart greenhouse.

We can control environmental parameters by using the greenhouse farming technique. However, the results of manual handling are production loss, energy loss, and labor cost and many more. We can control the climate inside it and also it becomes easy to monitor with the help of devices embedded in greenhouse. Different parameters can be measured with the help of sensors that are needed by plant.

Following are the applications in the field of agriculture:

1. Monitoring using sensor-based systems
2. Connected to agriculture spaces
3. Analytics of required data
4. Data visualization techniques
5. Using smart agriculture vehicles
6. Identifying various factors for better production
7. Management systems for different purposes

CONCLUSION

After the detailed study of IoT, we can conclude that using the latest automation enabling IoT has various benefits. At the same time, it is also very important to analyze and consider the negative aspects. This is an area of important research. This chapter talks about both positive and negative aspects. One should make the best use of the positive aspects as well as great work is still required on the challenging aspects. The future is all about IoT.

BIBLIOGRAPHY

1. Y. Zhang and J. Wen, "An IoT electric business model based on the protocol of bitcoin," in *Proceedings of the 2015 18th International Conference on Intelligence in Next Generation Networks, ICIN 2015*, pp. 184–191, IEEE, France, February 2015.
2. M. Pilkington, Blockchain technology: Principles and applications. *Research handbook on digital transformations*, F. X. Olleros and M. Zhegu, Eds. Edward Elgar Publishing, 2016.
3. M. Díaz, C. Martín, B Rubio, "State-of-the-art, challenges, and open issues in the integration of internet of things and cloud computing", *Journal of Network and Computer Application*, 67 (2016), pp. 99–117.
4. J. Rivera, R. van der Meulen, Forecast alert: Internet of things—Endpoints and associated services, worldwide, 2016 (accessed 20 June 2020).
5. World Health Organization, Food safety fact sheet, 2017. Available online: http://www.who.int/mediacentre/factsheets/fs399/en/ (accessed 1 February 2020).
6. Blockchain disruptive use cases, 2016. Available online: https://everisnext.com/2016/05/31/blockchain-disruptive-use-cases/ (accessed 2 June 2020).
7. The best way to learn IoT, 2018. Available online: https://www.jigsawacademy.com/best-way-learn-iot/ (accessed 2 June 2020).
8. S. Nakamoto, Bitcoin: A peer-to-peer electronic cash system, 2008. Available online: https://bitcoin.org/bitcoin.pdf (accessed 1 July 2020).

11 IoT for Smart Healthcare Monitoring System

Supriya Khaitan, Priyanka Shukla, Rashi Agarwal and Supriya Raheja

CONTENTS

Internet of Things: Introduction ... 164
Key Qualities of Internet of Things ... 164
Benefits of IoT ... 165
Limitations of IoT ... 165
IoT in Healthcare ... 166
Role of Internet of Things in Healthcare ... 168
  Use of Smart and Wearable ... 168
  Need for Workforce Optimization by Utilizing Electronic Health Records ... 168
  Increasing Interest in Self-Health Measurement ... 168
  Need for Healthcare in Remote Locations ... 168
Challenges of IoT in Healthcare ... 169
  Infrastructure ... 169
  Underdeveloped Initiatives ... 169
  Possible Lack of Available Resources ... 169
  Difficulties with Regular Updates ... 169
  Personal Sensitive Data Security ... 169
  Global Healthcare Regulations ... 169
  Integration ... 170
Advantages of IoT in Healthcare ... 170
  Disadvantages ... 170
Application of IoT in Healthcare ... 171
  Application Based on IoT Technology ... 172
  Apple Watch ... 172
  Asthma Monitor System ... 172
  Ingestible Sensors ... 173
  Smart Contact Lenses ... 173
  Smart Continuous Glucose Monitoring (CGM) and Insulin Pens ... 173
  Coagulation Testing Device ... 175
  Smart Hearing Aid ... 175
  SmartSole ... 175
IoT Architecture ... 177
  Sensors/Actuators ... 177

DOI: 10.1201/9781003094210-11

Data Acquisition ... 178
Cloud Storage ... 178
Analysis of Data ... 178
IoT Platform ... 178
IoT Project Initiation ... 179
Conclusion and Future of IoT ... 180
References ... 180

INTERNET OF THINGS: INTRODUCTION

Technology throughout the years has consistently achieved a progressive change throughout the entire existence of humankind. Be it fortunate or unfortunate, it has consistently affected us in an enormous manner and has moulded the advanced 21st-century world. In spite of the fact that it has prompted war and annihilation, it has additionally helped keep world harmony and solidarity. Throughout, humanity saw many fascinating and stunning revelations which have reformed various parts of regular day-to-day existence. The Internet of Things (IoT) is one such point which has advanced or rather run over far since its revelation during the 1990s. It has spearheaded the route for progress and improvement. It has associated different individuals over the globe and has prompted way-breaking revelations and endless innovations which expect to give a superior future to us all. It has vanquished numerous fields including science and medication. Brilliant items propelled by IoT are found in every single different background, for example, smart parking system, smart homes and smart agriculture. The IoT is a perfect innovation which has assumed a key job in correspondence. We have seen that during that time how the web turned into the base for different projects. In this universe of IoT, each item which has been associated, be it a telephone or a room and so forth, is viewed as shrewd. It has been modified so that it very well may be utilized to its most extreme capacities with the assistance of existing advancements, for example, RFID and so forth.

IoT is a network of objects embedded with the latest technology so that the objects can communicate and interact among themselves and with the objects that reside in the outside environment. This is to increase the ease of life and make it more comfortable and friendly. Objects are converted into robots with well-equipped knowledge and intelligence, with expertise and experience. Different technologies are integrated and used together to convert objects into intelligent objects [1].

KEY QUALITIES OF INTERNET OF THINGS

Users can achieve deeper automation analysis in IoT-embedded technology systems. Modern attitude towards technology, price fall in hardware devices and advances in software brought major changes in the services, development and delivery of products. The major contribution of technology in IoT-embedded systems is towards artificial intelligence (AI), connectivity and enhances every aspect of life to be "smart," e.g. if your refrigerators can know about the quantity of milk in it sensors, active engagement and use of smart devices.

- *Artificial Intelligence*: IoT or if your cabinets can give you the information about the quantity of your cereal and can place an order for you.
- *Connectivity*: Connectivity not only refers to create a connection within a major network but also create small and cheaper networks in-between the systems.
- *Sensors*: Sensors are the devices which are able to convert passive objects in an IoT-integrated system into active objects to achieve real-world integration within the system.
- *Active Engagement*: Introduction of IoT in Technology enables the users to interact with active objects like content, product and service engagement.
- *Small Devices*: Sizes of the devices become small over time. Also, cheaper devices are specially designed for the specific purpose of delivering services to the user.

BENEFITS OF IoT

Now, every part of life and business is blessed with the benefits of IoT. The technology is used to create smart society and smart homes. Focussed area to work in the field of IoT are smart environment, smart society, smart traffic monitoring, smart water supply management, agricultural products and food sustainability [2, 5, 6]. Smart device is shown in figure 11.1.

Some of the advantages of IoT are:

- Reduced waste
- Technology optimization
- Improved customer engagement
- Enhanced data collection

LIMITATIONS OF IoT

Although IoT devices have a wide variety of applications, there are a lot of challenges also [4].

- *Security*: IoT is a network of connected devices that communicate over the network. The system requires some security measures otherwise it is exposed to various kinds of attackers.
- *Privacy*: IoT systems provide extreme detail of personal data without any participation of user.
- *Complexity*: To achieve integration of multiple technologies and adaptation of new technologies in the system, IoT systems are complicated from design, deployment and maintenance point of view.
- *Flexibility*: To achieve the integration of multiple technologies under one system, IoT systems should be flexible.
- *Compliance*: People who create and use IoT devices have to go through some rules and regulations.

FIGURE 11.1 Smart devices.

IoT IN HEALTHCARE

Healthcare systems are extended to some limits only in terms of providing services to their patients. Capabilities of hospitals, equipment and facilities are not enough to improve patient's health because of rise in chronic diseases. Patients require their care during day and night, but medical practitioners are not able to fulfil their need. These challenges promote the healthcare department to adapt new technologies [8]. Nowadays, artificial intelligence and IoT are achieving the solutions of all such type of problems. Revolutionary technologies are filling these gaps in the healthcare industry [9].

Nowadays, the medicinal services sensors are expecting a basic part in our regular day-to-day existence. Human services checking systems is one of the genuine overhauls taking into account its propelled advancement. At the point when patient goes for a clinical test, the specialist has not only general clinical/lab testing dependent on static elements of patients organic and metabolic, but also in addition plentiful better information from sensors. Utilizing introduced information, and helped by decision, bolster plots additionally will have permission to a lot of observational information that others have; your nervous system specialist can make a much unrivalled guess of your well-being and be prompt on treatment. Such a problematic skill with a ground-breaking effect could have overall wellness plans and an extreme reduction in human services costs and recuperate the flurry and exactness of investigation. In everyday life, where everybody is occupied, where no one has a lot of range to check on one's well-being, sensors with the right and appropriate yield are a greatly improved choice than old clinical instruments [1].

For perpetually sending a message from the individual's area to clinical, enlightening GSM electronic gear is utilized. Presently days, heart maladies are surpassing up to a risky level which brings about the death of such a lot of people. Recognition of patient condition whenever it is intense and specialists additionally can't watch unequivocal patient for complete working hours. In a few significant conditions like patient is discovered far off from the emergency clinic or conjointly if there should be an occurrence of an old patient who is enduring with a heart condition and physical issues, constant recognition of the patient isn't possible. The challenges are to keep devices up to date, calibration of devices and maintenance. Most of the IoT providers are working towards the maintenance of devices.

To provide the services to patients during 24 hours, sensors enabled the medical devices to collect the data remotely and provide that to medical supervisors. Medical supervisors are able to take the actions accordingly as shown in Figure 11.2.

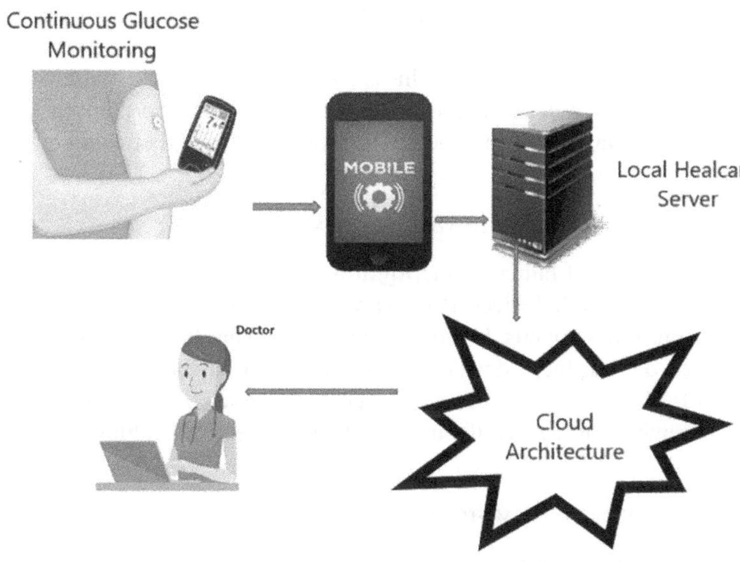

FIGURE 11.2 IoT in healthcare systems.

ROLE OF INTERNET OF THINGS IN HEALTHCARE

All over the world, healthcare industries are transforming themselves into patient's-centric industry. Because of digital evolution of the healthcare industry, devices are more integrated and interoperable. The healthcare of the patients becomes more effective because of centralized access of health records and information. Patient's emergent requirements have created a lot of challenges. Technologies advanced themselves to achieve success in this field also. Real-time monitoring and tracking of patient's activity have created the new requirements. But the use of advanced technology in intelligently connected devices, systems and things operated by users helps the healthcare industry to make timely, specific and useful decisions. The following factors have increased the adoption rate of IoT in the healthcare industry.

Use of smart and Wearable

The use of smart devices and wearable increased because of their capabilities. These devices like smart bands, smart watches and sleep headphones can collect the data, transfer the data and also analyse the data. Patients with chronic illnesses are getting a number of benefits using these devices. Also, some of the devices have features to help the patients in an emergency like push buttons. Blood pressure and heart rate monitors helped the patients in reducing their medical expenses and hospitals visit. They are connected with their doctor online. Also, these devices are able to transfer data to computers, tablets and smart phone etc. for further storage [2].

Need for Workforce Optimization by Utilizing Electronic Health Records

IoT in healthcare industry creates a network of connected devices. This network is expanded to create a connection with workers and has promoted to create a stronger network with other departments also. This is another critical task to optimize the productivity of workers as well as equipment. Certain scheduling algorithms and applications are used to ensure that staff allocated to patient is right and is at proper time.

Increasing Interest in Self-Health Measurement

The increasing desire of human being towards their health is another factor for the usage of innovated health devices. People are able to keep track of their fitness measurements using fitness bands, blood-pressure-monitoring instruments and glucose meters. Stored data in these devices can be further used for the analysis of their health records. These devices reduced the cost of regular health check-ups. These human requirements influenced the use of IoT in the medical health industry.

Need for Healthcare in Remote Locations

Medical health facilities are very limited in areas, especially in developing and underdeveloping regions. The patients from these areas have to be travelled for their routine check-ups and for the diagnosis of the problem. IoT-enabled health equipment can help these patients online. As a possible result, health issues can be resolved up to some extent.

CHALLENGES OF IoT IN HEALTHCARE

The main issue that must be taken care for the success and implementation of IoT in healthcare are [4]:

Infrastructure

Infrastructure is the basic challenge in the implementation of IoT in health department. Hospitals have lack of resources to use it. Healthcare providers are not interested to invest because they are not confident about the success of implementation of IoT applications.

Underdeveloped Initiatives

A lot of hard work is required to use the technology for finding the solution of many chronic diseases or the initiative to use IoT in medical problems. Many issues are there that must be focussed. Technology still must grow to provide regular enhancement and positive results in this direction.

Possible Lack of Available Resources

A large amount of data is important and must be analysed for possible solutions. This leads to a question of how to store and create a data repository that can hold data for an indefinite amount of time.

Difficulties with Regular Updates

To use technology for finding the solution of any problem, it occurs in the form of hardware and software. These solutions must be updated timely for smooth functioning. To make available the updated version of software, constant and regular efforts are required to update and solve technical issues.

Personal Sensitive Data Security

An IoT-enabled object functions through the Internet. This creates a problem of private data to be hacked.

Global Healthcare Regulations

Any medical solution must be approved by global healthcare bodies worldwide. This requires some time formalities to make the solution available for the patient.

Integration

During the implementation of IoT applications, it is also a critical task to integrate multiple devices. Differences in the communication protocols of different devices reduce the scope of applicability of IoT applications.

ADVANTAGES OF IoT IN HEALTHCARE

Some advantages of IoT in healthcare are given below [18].

- *Cost Saving*: Patients have to pay a lot for real-time monitoring in frequent visits to hospitals, hospital stays and fast-relieved treatment. It will be beneficial for the patients to pay less for independent IoT-enabled systems in the long run.
- *All-around technology enhancement*: It was a time-taken process to stand in long queues and waiting for a doctor call. Now, well equipped and smart hospitals, using advance technology, prevent unnecessary visits to the hospitals. The IoT in healthcare are producing tech applications for online monitoring of the patients.
- *Accessibility:* The interconnection between all the devices through the Internet can easily transfer the data to other devices, so real-time conditions of doctors and patients are accessible to each other online.
- *Improved and Faster Diagnosis*: Continuous real-time and on-time monitoring helps the physicians to diagnose the problem at an early stage and plan their proactive evidence-based medical treatment and make it absolutely transparent to the patient.
- *Drugs and Equipment Management:* Maintaining the information about the equipment and the drugs is the most challenging job in the health history. Intercommunication between the different departments made it possible to manage and utilize all the resources efficiently with reduced efforts, errors and waste.

Disadvantages

Massive implementation of IoT in healthcare industry also comes with some downsides like:

- *Privacy can be potentially undermined*: All the devices used in IoT-enabled healthcare systems can communicate with each other through the Internet only. As per the security issue concerned, devices can be hacked. So, a lot of security measures and attention is required in the usages of such systems.
- *Unauthorized access to centralization:* There can be a problem within the system that some of dishonest interlopers access the data with some cruel intentions and harm the humanity.
- *Global healthcare regulations:* Some guidelines that are already issued by International health administration regarding the working principle of IoT-integrated devices. These restrictions may put some restrictions on the capabilities of new technologies to some extent.

APPLICATION OF IoT IN HEALTHCARE

IoT for patient: These devices are wearable, which is may be like a wrist band that monitors the different measures like heart rate, calories and blood pressure; life for people has changed because of these types of IoT devices, specially people living alone can take care of their health; if there is any change in the daily routine which effects health, this reflects changes in the measures so that a one can take the precautionary health advice from doctor. And can send the signals to the family members [3].

IoT for hospitals: IoT devices also help in hospitals as well. IoT devices embedded in the hospital may help in searching the actual location of medical equipment like nebulizer, wheelchair and other equipment's used in healthcare. This can also help in finding the location of medical staff deputed at different locations. And another use of IoT devices in medical care is to maintain the hygiene as well so that persona does not get infected and monitors the environmental observation humidity and temperature control.

IoT for physicians: These devices can be embedded in homes so that this can monitor the patient health helpfully. Healthcare experts need to be more attentive while using IoT device while for their patients the data that is received from the IoT device may help to detect the treatment process of the patient [19].

According to Gartner report of August 2019, the segment with the largest growth is automation of connected lighting devices followed by automotive and healthcare. Chronic condition monitoring healthcare industry in 2020 may grow up to 29%. The healthcare industry has been increased from 0.21 billion to 0.36 billon in year 2020. The embedded IoT devices will be upcoming market force. Figure 11.3 shows the market analysis of various IoT devices for years 2018, 2019 and 2020.

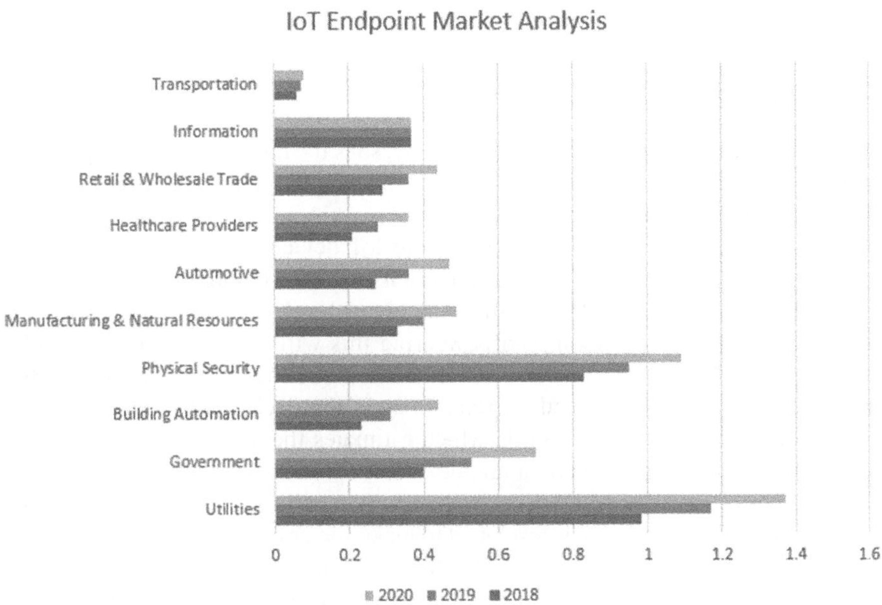

FIGURE 11.3 IoT endpoint market analysis.

Application Based on IoT Technology

There are so many examples that are based on technology implemented on IoT in healthcare. There is a chatbot Tess that works as a psychological coach. Symptoms can be sent through text messages on the instant app. AI technology has inbuilt it to make it coach for people. This app is created by Babylon health. This app works on mental health of a person whereas Wyse is also similar to Tess. In this, digital impression will be the input to detect the mood and facial expression, emotions while doing conversation. ArogyaSetu is one of the apps in this pandemic situation to help people to not go into infected areas. One important thing is Bluetooth should be always enabled to get the correct information. If a person visited an infected area, they will get the notification, and then they can take precautionary measures.

Apple Watch

Apple launched the Care Kit in 2017, an open-source framework intended to help the developers to implement an app for handling medical conditions. Apple introduces so many apps to monitor health like depression, cardiac problems. Apple has appended a novel "movement Disorder API" to its open-source research kit that is monitored by apple watches.

Apple disbursed $4.2 billion on development and research in the quarter ending in June. Apple's research and development bill is out to 7.9% of its total revenue, the highest percentage since 2003, when Apple was still focusing on iPods and Macs. Apple is on step to spend over $16 billion on R&D in 2019. Apple research is ongoing with regards to hearing, women health, heart and movement studies. This is done in conjunction with phone and watch. Watches have sensors that monitor the heath measure and record in the app in mobile phone.

Asthma Monitor System

Air pollution is increasing globally day by day, so is the number of asthma patients. Millions of people are getting asthma due to the increase in air pollution and drastically changing climate. In Saudi Arabia, the severity of asthma is because of the hot climate and quick sandstorms. There are IoT devices which can monitor the symptoms of an asthma attack. A wearable sensor device to monitor the symptoms of asthma is called ADAMM. In this, the algorithm has been implemented for the normal conditions. Person who is wearing this will get some vibration to be notified of the forthcoming asthma attack and will get the message as well to the device to which it is connected. A sensor-based approach is developed which is connected with the patient's mobile which estimates the asthma pointer and collects the data that supports patient and healthcare professional.

This project is called MyAirCoach project. A mobile app is developed in this project called CNet. The app is developed to make life easier for asthmatics patients. In the connected inhaler, a sensor or Bluetooth spirometer is present to monitor the cause and symptoms of asthma. That inhaler is connected with the app in the mobile device, which keeps all information like causes and what could be the medication. Figure 11.4 shows smart inhalers.

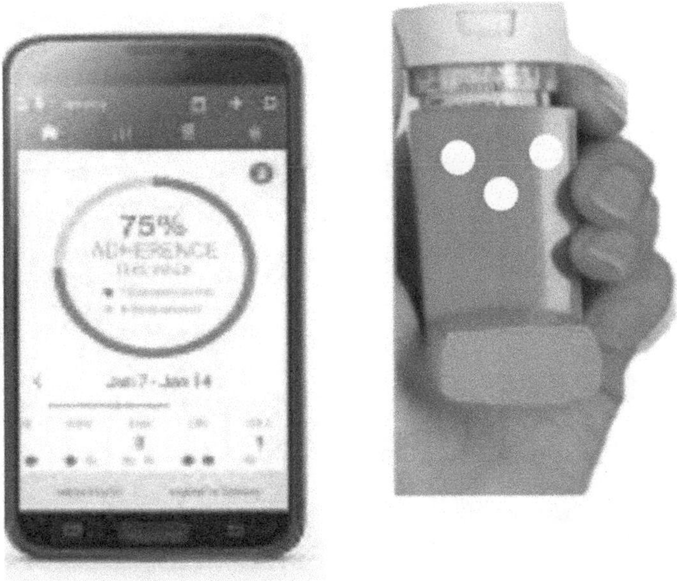

FIGURE 11.4 Smart inhaler.

Ingestible Sensors

Ingestible sensors are used in healthcare by ingesting it along with capsules. A smart pill concept is developed by Proteus Digital Health along with that of a smart phone with pitch. A 1 square mm sensor is coated in digestible metals and is ingested in a pill shown in Figure 11.5. Metal which is in pill is not harmful rather some multivitamin tablets also consist of it and we take it in our diet too. The sensor gets activated after swallowing a pill by electrolytes in the body. Digital records will be sent to the mobile and the activity and rest will also be sent by patch. With the help of these pills, the temperature, PH level and medicine, whether taken or not, are monitored [11].

Smart Contact Lenses

Google Life Science has announced in 2014 that they are going to introduce smart contact lens (as shown in figure 11.6) to measure glucose in tears and can give an alert when blood glucose level increases or decreases. And the other work which is going on by Verily in 2018 is that smart contact lens will monitor the loss of elasticity because of long sightedness [10].

Smart Continuous Glucose Monitoring (CGM) and Insulin Pens

Diabetes is a common disease nowadays; imbalance in diabetes may cause major health issues and needs to be monitored timely. Every day visiting the doctor to monitor it is not possible. So, a device is introduced called a continuous glucose

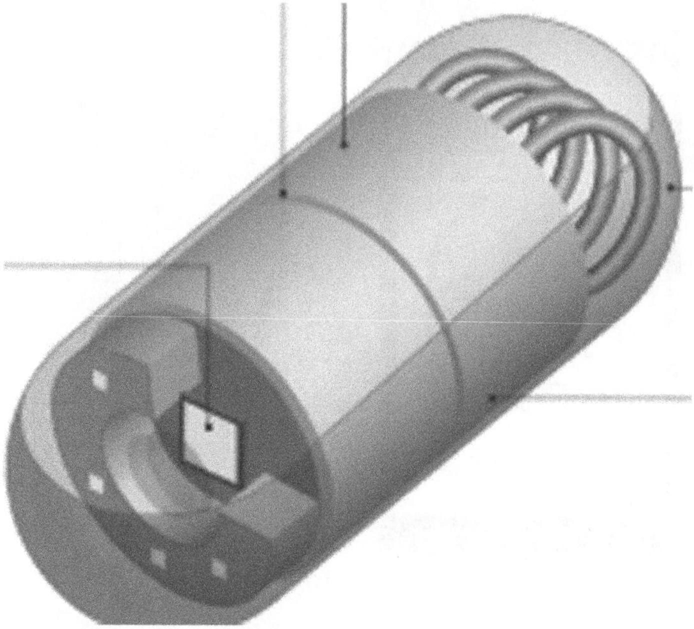

FIGURE 11.5 Smart pill.

monitoring (CGM) machine as shown in figure 11.7. This makes life easy, according to doctors' suggestion, one can monitor it every day or a number of times in a day. And the smart CGM is connected with the android phone, iPhone or can watch through an app [13]. With the help of it, one can check the details, maintain record of it and notice the trend. Another IoT device to measure the diabetes is an insulin pen as shown in figure 11.8. This works together with a smart phone that stores data for long time. Diabetes patients can get help from this pen for calculating the insulin dose and can observe the record of food and insulin intake which is affecting their blood sugar [12].

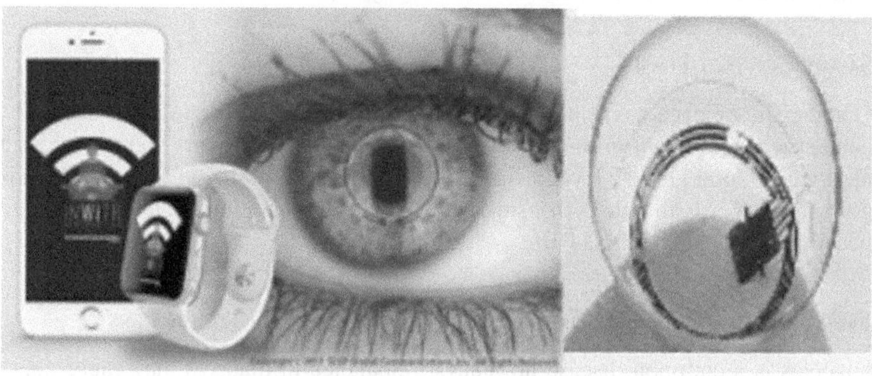

FIGURE 11.6 Connected contact lens.

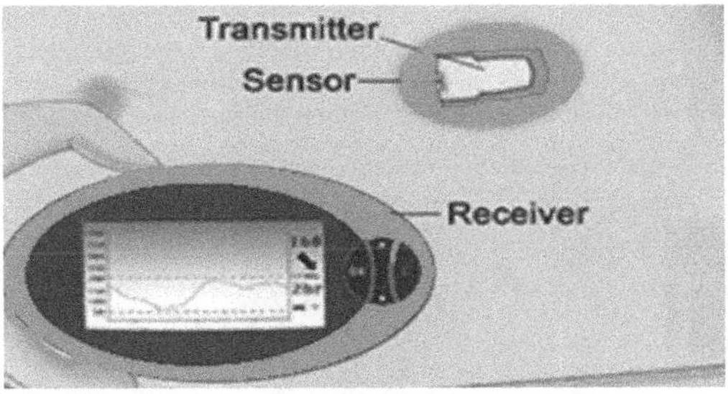

FIGURE 11.7 Continuous glucose-monitoring device.

Coagulation Testing Device

Coagulation System as displayed in figure 11.9 is the first device for self-test and was launched in 2016. It has Bluetooth feature, and with that, patient can check their blood clots rapidly. Patient can do self-tests that reduce the risk of stroke or bleeding. This device allows patient to add comment on their result. Coagulation monitoring system is important, especially to those who have cardiovascular disease. QCM is one of the sensors that is widely used. QCM is an acoustic wave sensor that was also used to monitor the PH level and electric field [14].

Smart Hearing Aid

It is an electroacoustic device that fits in or behind the wearer's ear. It is intended to amplify and modulate sound for the wearer. Previously devices were called as ear trumpets or ear horns. Many of the people are facing hearing issues [15]. Internet and IoT wearable devices are playing an important role in that also. These internet-enabled devices made people's life easy. These devices may help to listen to music, helpful to listen to environmental noise and can listen to conversations among people [16]. Smart Hearing Aid is shown in figure 11.10.

SmartSole

An Alzheimer's patient is not easy to handle. These people forget their daily routine task and are found to be lost. SmartSole is the device in which cellular and satellite

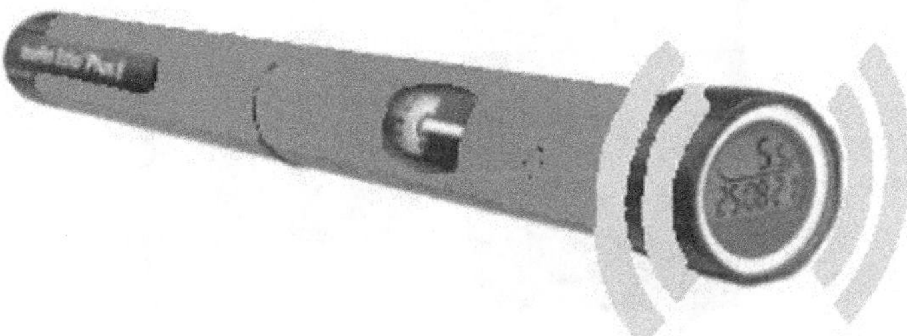

FIGURE 11.8 Smart insulin pen.

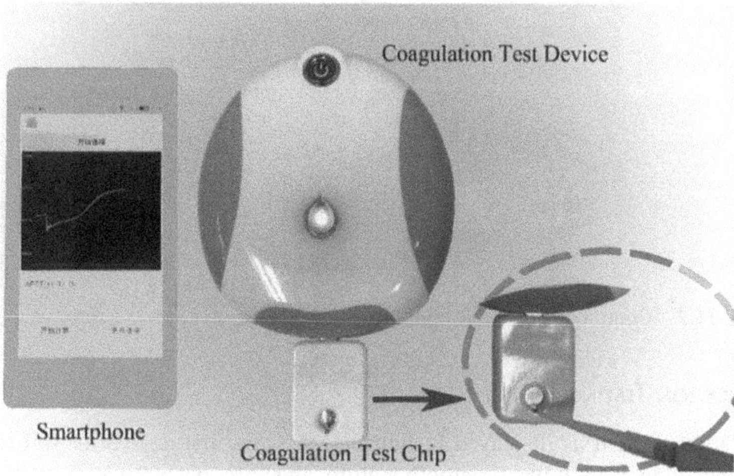

FIGURE 11.9 Coagulation testing device.

technology is used in GPS. This insole fits into footwears of elders easily and is also comfortable. It has a wireless charger. If the patient is in doubt, then it sends the notification. This is a rainproof sole. It is an unseen device implanted in the sole of the shoes as shown in figure 11.11 [17].

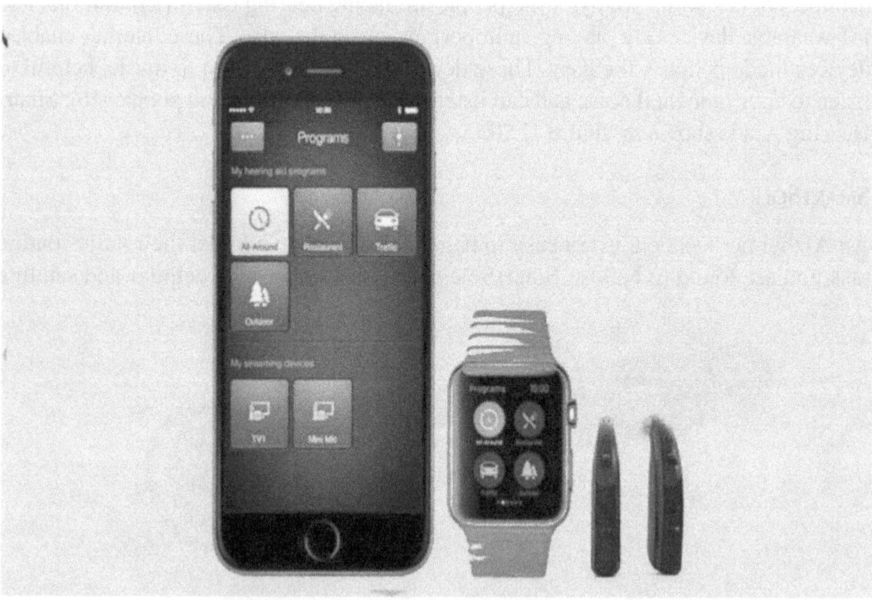

FIGURE 11.10 Smart hearing aid.

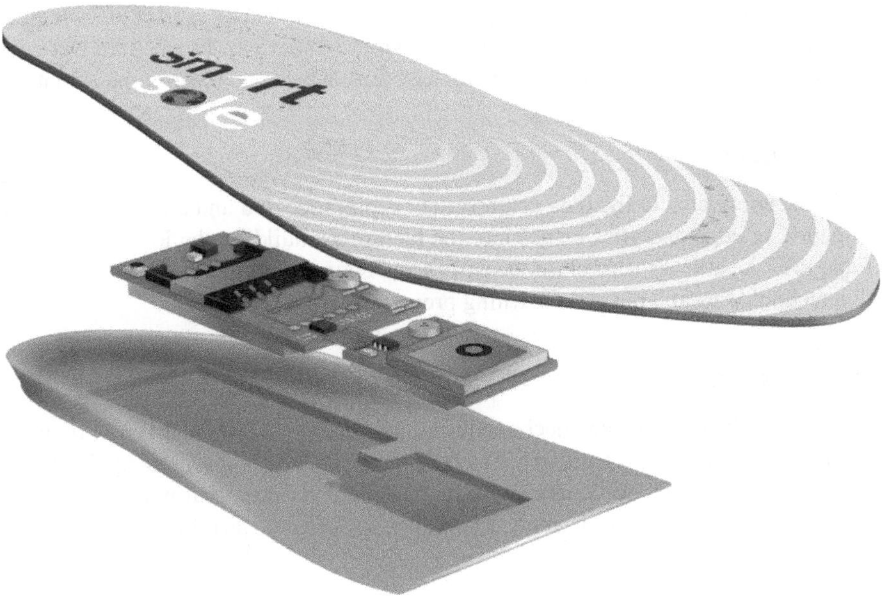

FIGURE 11.11 SmartSole.

IoT ARCHITECTURE

Many organizations seek the inclusion of IoT products as the ideal solution in their business processes because of outstanding opportunities of IoT-based applications. However, for the implementation of IoT products as solutions in real problems, the reliable architecture of IoT inevitably enters the stage. To create an IoT architecture as shown in figure 11.12, various elements like sensors, protocols, actuators, cloud services and layers are required. IoT engineering is a crucial method to structure various components of IoT. For IoT engineering, following are the required stages (layers) [7].

Sensors/Actuators

The outstanding characteristic of sensors and actuators is their ability to transform outer world information into data for analysis. Actuators or sensors can transmit,

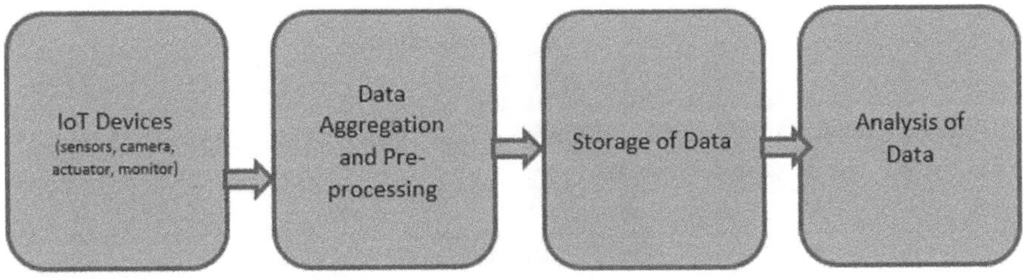

FIGURE 11.12 IoT architecture.

process information and acknowledge over the system. These sensors or actuators are present in the sensing layer that may be wired or wireless. Local Area Network or Personal Area Network can be used for association between sensors and actuators.

Data Acquisition

Before sending data to the data centres, data is preprocessed and analysed. So, here Edge IoT or edge analytics comes into the picture. In building the IoT architecture, Edge IoT's location is very close to sensors and actuators. It adopts many visualization technologies and machine learning preprocesses for the data.

Cloud Storage

After going through all the checks required to meet quality standards and requirements, the information is transferred back to the physical world for real applications. The data centre or cloud comes under management services that manage the data where it is used by end-user applications like agriculture, farming, defence, aerospace and healthcare.

Analysis of Data

Analysing the data on healthcare and sensors is done to monitor health of patients.

IoT PLATFORM

All the IoT gadgets are associated with other IoT gadgets and applications to send and get data utilizing conventions. There is a void between the IoT gadget and IoT application. An IoT platform depicted in figure 11.13, fills the void between the gadgets (sensors) and application. In this way, we can say that an IoT stage is an incorporated help that satisfies the void between the IoT gadget and application and offers to bring a physical item on the web.

Following are some uses of IoT:

- IoT platform connects sensors and devices.
- IoT platform handles different software communication protocol and hardware.

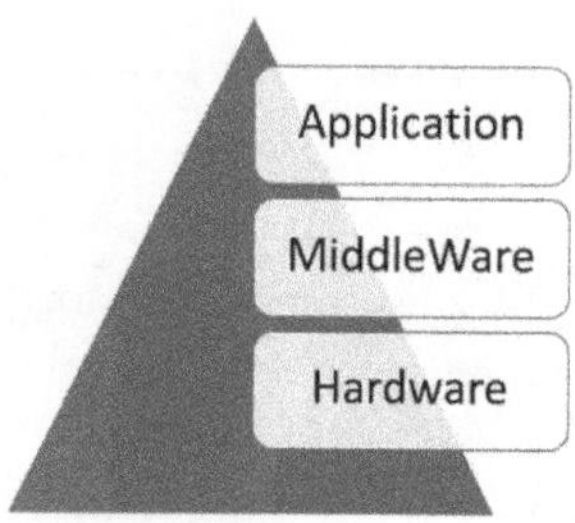

FIGURE 11.13 IoT platform.

- IoT platform provides security and authentication for sensors and users.
- It collects, visualizes and analyses the data gathered by the sensor and device.

Some of the platforms are:

- AWS Web Services IoT Platform
- Google Cloud
- Microsoft Azure
- IBM Watson

IoT PROJECT INITIATION

"We regularly observe that IoT ventures are trying for undertakings and that they accept some unforeseen turns as they experience the design and usage process. This is because of an assortment of reasons, including unforeseen unpredictability in arrangement plan or incorporation, unexpected deterrents that should be worked around, unexpected execution issues in the field and arrangements with greater expenses than arranged," says Nathan Nuttall, research chief. "The majority of these difficulties are feasible, yet they can result in IoT executions that stray from the unique arrangement. It is basic to reconsider IoT extends occasionally during usage to approve that the undertaking will in any case convey the business objectives, targets, results and business esteem initially anticipated. Something else, accomplishment of this IoT undertaking and future tasks in your guide might be imperiled." Outlining the prescribed procedures for getting an IoT activity off the ground, including forthright understanding and planning of the IoT to business targets, improvement of utilization cases and making of a vision and guide, can assist you with remaining on target to convey on the expressed business goals as your IoT venture advances. Business process map is depicted in figure 11.14.

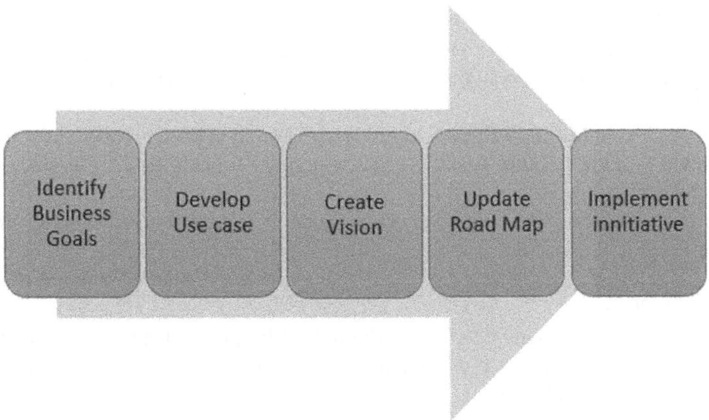

FIGURE 11.14 Business process map.

CONCLUSION AND FUTURE OF IoT

An energizing flood of future IoT applications will develop, rejuvenated through instinctive human-to-machine intelligence. Human 4.0 will permit people to collaborate progressively over huge spans – both with one another and with machines – and have comparative tactile encounters to those that they experience locally. This will empower new open doors inside distant learning, medical procedure and fix. Vividly blended reality applications can possibly turn into the following stage after portable – acknowledged through 3D sound and haptic sensations and turning into our primary interface to this present reality [20]. Rejuvenating future IoT will require close cooperative energy between the IoT and system stages. This keeps on being a key centre territory of Ericsson research.

REFERENCES

1. Ahmadi, Hossein, Goli Arji, Leila Shahmoradi, Reza Safdari, Mehrbakhsh Nilashi, and Mojtaba Alizadeh. "The application of internet of things in healthcare: A systematic literature review and classification." *Universal Access in the Information Society* pp. 1–33, Volume: 18, 2019.
2. Abdul Ghaffar, Abdul Aziz, Saud Mohammad Mostafa, Ammar Alsaleh, Tarek Sheltami, and Elhadi M. Shakshuki. "Internet of things based multiple disease monitoring and health improvement system." *Journal of Ambient Intelligence and Humanized Computing* 11, no. 3, pp. 1021–1029, 2020.
3. Abdulwahid, Ali Hadi. "Modern application of Internet of things in healthcare system." *International Journal of Engineering Research & Technology* 12, no. 4, pp. 494–499, 2019.
4. Selvaraj, Sureshkumar, and Suresh Sundaravaradhan. "Challenges and opportunities in IoT healthcare systems: A systematic review." *SN Applied Sciences* 2, no. 1, Pages 1–8, 2020.
5. Hameed, Ali, and Alauddin Alomary. "Security issues in IoT: A survey." In *2019 International Conference on Innovation and Intelligence for Informatics, Computing, and Technologies (3ICT)*, pp. 1–5. IEEE, 2019.
6. Charulatha, A. R., and R. Sujatha. "Smart Healthcare Use Cases and Applications." In *Internet of Things Use Cases for the Healthcare Industry*, pp. 185–203. Springer, Cham, 2020.
7. Maktoubian, Jamal, and Keyvan Ansari. "An IoT architecture for preventive maintenance of medical devices in healthcare organizations." *Health and Technology* 9, no. 3, pp. 233–243, 2019.
8. Dang, L. Minh, Md. Jalil Piran, Dongil Han, Kyungbok Min, and Hyeonjoon Moon. "A survey on internet of things and cloud computing for healthcare." *Electronics* 8, no. 7, pp. 768, 2019.
9. Marques, Gonçalo, Rui Pitarma, Nuno M. Garcia, and Nuno Pombo. "Internet of things architectures, technologies, applications, challenges, and future directions for enhanced living environments and healthcare systems: A review." *Electronics* 8, no. 10, pp. 1081, 2019.
10. Hahn, Sei Kwang, Young Chul Sung, Beom Ho Mun, Keon Jae Lee, K. E. U. M. Dohee, and Su Jin Kim. "Smart contact lenses and smart glasses." U.S. Patent 10,399,291, issued September 3, 2019.
11. Klugman, Craig M., Laura B. Dunn, Jack Schwartz, and I. Glenn Cohen. "The ethics of smart pills and self-acting devices: Autonomy, truth-telling, and trust at the dawn of digital medicine." *The American Journal of Bioethics* 18, no. 9, pp. 38–47, 2018.

12. Klonoff, David C., Victoria Hsiao, Hope Warshaw, and David Kerr. "Smart Insulin Pens and Devices to Track Insulin Doses." In *Diabetes Digital Health*, pp. 195–204. Elsevier, The Netherlands, 2020.
13. Reutrakul, Sirimon, Matthew Genco, Harley Salinas, Robert M. Sargis, Carlie Paul, Yuval Eisenberg, Jiali Fang et al. "Feasibility of inpatient continuous glucose monitoring during the COVID-19 pandemic: Early experience." *Diabetes Care*, 2020.
14. Gorin, Michael, Robert S. Hillman, Cory Lee McCluskey, and Hubert Martin Schwaiger. "Blood testing system and method." U.S. Patent 10,288,630, issued May 14, 2019.
15. Bentler, Ruth A., Monica R., Duve. "Comparison of hearing aids over the 20th century." *Ear and Hearing* 21, no. 6, pp. 625–639, 2000.
16. Krystek, Paul N., Mark B. Stevens, and John D. Wilson. "Smart hearing aid." U.S. Patent 9,374,649, issued June 21, 2016.
17. http://www.mli.gmu.edu/papers/2018/p18-1.pdf.
18. Formisano, Ciro, Daniele Pavia, Levent Gurgen, Takuro Yonezawa, Josè Antonio Galache, Keiko Doguchi, and Isabel Matranga. "The advantages of IoT and cloud applied to smart cities." In *2015 3rd International Conference on Future Internet of Things and Cloud*, pp. 325–332. IEEE, 2015.
19. Alansari, Zainab, Nor Badrul Anuar, Amirrudin Kamsin, Safeeullah Soomro, and Mohammad Riyaz Belgaum. "The Internet of things adoption in healthcare applications." In *IEEE 3rd International Conference on Engineering Technologies and Social Sciences (ICETSS)*, pp. 1–5. IEEE, 2017.
20. Rehman, Habib Ur, Muhammad Asif, and Mudassar Ahmad. "Future applications and research challenges of IoT." In *2017 International Conference on Information and Communication Technologies (ICICT)*, pp. 68–74. IEEE, 2017.

Index

Note: Locators in *italics* represent figures in the text.

A

Aadhaar-Enabled Payment System (AEPS), 128
Active engagement, 165
ADAMM device, 172
Advantages of IoT, 170
AES-256 algorithm, 69, 71
Agriculture, 161
Ambiguous security standards, 158
Android app module, 98, 99
Apple Pay, 129
Apple Watch, 172
Application Binary Interface (ABI), 24
Application layers, 155
Applications of IoT
  agriculture, 46–47, 161
  AI, 47
  endpoint market analysis, *171*
  healthcare, 160–161
  smart cities, 46, 161
  smart home, 46, 160
  smart metering, 47
  smart supply chain, 46
  wearables, 160
Artificial intelligence (AI), 2, 20, 165
Asymmetric encryption, 9
Asymmetric key encryption, 54, *55*
Attack prediction and prevention, 159
Autonomous building, 139–140, *140*

B

Benefits of IoT, 165, *166*
BigchainDB, 23
Biometric authentication, 129
Bitcoin
  BCT, working, 27, *28*
  block size, 33
  cryptographic verification, 27
  decentralized, centralized and distributed database, 27, *29*
  miners, 12
  network, 152–153
  public and private keys, 52–53
  robust and secure, 52
  transaction details, 52
Bit-wise mixing algorithm, 7
Blockchain as a service (BaaS), 20
Blockchain-based smart cities, 114–115
Blockchain-integrated IoT model, 96, *96*
Blockchain ledger, 2, 14
Blockchains; *see also* First generations; Reference architecture; Second generations
  characteristics, 30
  consortium, 17
  definition, 2
  private, 17
  public, 17
Blockchain technology (BCT), 132, *132*; *see also* Smart cities
  agriculture, 135, 137, *137*
  components, 149
  decentralization, 93
  hash, unique code, 149–150
  health-care system, 134, *134*
  immutability, 93
  multiple blocks, 150
  renewable energy sector, 135, *136*
  transparency, 93
  waste management, 137, *137*
Blockchain with IoT (BIoT), 61–62, *62*
Blocks, 3, *4*, 5, *5*, 81, *81*, 91
Block size, 117
Bolster plots, 167
Business process map, 179, *179*
Byzantine Fault Tolerant (BFT) method, 10

C

Centralized architecture, 94
Centralized model, 5, *6*
Certificate Authority (CA), 22
Ciphertext, 48
Client-server architecture, 51
Cloud architecture, 51
Cloud computing concept, 94
Cloud integration, 20–21
Cloud storage, 178
Command line interface (CLI) method, 19
Communities and smart cities, 114
Connectivity, 165
Consensus algorithms, 55, 81
  BFT, 10
  DPoS, 13
  PBFT, 10, 13
  PoET, 13
  PoS, 12–13
  PoW, 11–12

Consortium blockchain, 17, 83
Constrained straightforwardness, 79–80
Continuous glucose monitoring (CGM), 173, *175*
Conventional television (CCTV) systems, 113
Counterfeiters
associations, 83
FDA, 78
medical supply chain hierarchical storage flow, 83, *84*
Cryptography technique, *54*, 54–55, *55*, 91, 92
Cyberattacks, 65
Cybercrime, 157
Cyber networking structures, 106
Cyber-physical systems (CPS), 154
Cyberthreats, payment ecosystem, 125
Cyber transportation systems (CTS), 154

D

Data acquisition, 178
Database *vs.* blockchain, 17–18
Data ownership and privacy, 117
Data transparency, 54, 100
Decentralization, 53
Decentralized applications (DApps)
back-end functionality, 15
Bitcoin and Ethereum, 15
"blocks," 15
validators, 15
Decentralized consensus, 100
Decentralized control, 6, 100
Decision support systems (DSS), 94
Delegated Proof of Stake (DPoS), 13
Demand response (DR) systems, 109
Demand-side energy management (DSM), 111
Deterministic, 57–58, *58*
Digital instruments, 104
Digital ledger, app end-only, 13–14
Digital payments, 123, 125
Digital signatures, 9–10
Digital transaction, 152
Disadvantages of IoT, 170
Distributed blocks, 92
Distributed database, 27, *29*
Distributed denial of service (DDoS), 94, 153
Distributed energy sources, 111
Distributed ledger, 21, 80–81, 90
Distributed system, 6–7, 53
Distribute information, 101
Drugs and equipment management, 170
Drug supply chain
absence of detectability, 79
blockchain-enabled, *84*, 84–85
consistence challenges, 80
constrained straightforwardness, 79–80
Hyperledger venture plans, 86
MedicalChain issues prescription tokens, 85
MedicoHealth, blockchain-based venture, 85–86
MedRec, bitcoin-based arrangement, 86
obsolete methods, information sharing, 79
partner doubt, 79

E

e-Banking, 140–141
e-Business Register, 140–141
E-commerce Boom, 128
e-Court systems, 140–141
EdgeChain, 100
E-governance smart services, 106
e-Health Record, 140–141
e-Land Registry, 140–141
e-Law, 140–141
Electric vehicles (EVs), 112
Electronic health records (EHRs), 65, 66, 168
Elliptic Curve Digital Signature Algorithm (ECDSA), 3, *4*
Encryption attacks, 50
Encryption process, 48
e-Police data, 140–141
e-Prescription database, 140–141
Ethereum, 22–23, 29, 66, 70
Ethereum virtual machine (EVM), 24
European Union's General Data Protection Regulation, 125

F

Features, blockchain
fast exchange settlement, 82
low expense, 82
reliable, 82
transparent and auditable, 82–83
Field Area Networks, 107
Firewall gateway, 96
First generations, 28
Fog architecture, 51
Fog computing, 61
Food and Drug Administration (FDA), 77–78
Full node, 93

G

General Data Protection Regulation (GDPR), 73
Genesis block, 32, 58–59, *59*, 66
Global healthcare regulations, 169, 170
Google Pay, 129
Google Wallet, 124
Gross Domestic Products (GDPs), 65

H

Hackers, 124
Hardware wallets, 67

Hashing technique, 7–8, 52, 56–58, *58*
HDFC PayZapp, 129
Healthcare, 112
care applications, 34
difficulties with regular updates, 169
global healthcare regulations, 169
infrastructure, 169
integration, 170
management, 72, **73**
personal sensitive data security, 169
possible solutions, 169
systems, 166, *167*
underdeveloped initiatives, 169
Healthchain, 67
Health Insurance Portability and Accountability Act of 1996, 34
Hierarchy of related blocks, 97, *97*
Home Area Networks (HAN), 107
Home security, 157–158
Human services checking systems, 166
HydraChain (HC), 23–24
Hyperledger Sawtooth, 128
Hyperledger venture plans, 86

I

Industry-specific technicalities, 147
Inefficient threat detection methods, 48
Ingestible sensors, 173, *174*
Insulin pens, 173, *175*
Integrated blocks, 16, *16*
Internet-enabled devices, 155–156
Internet of Things (IoT); *see also* Limitations of IoT
architecture of, 89, *90*
authentication, 159
automation and control, 148
BCT, 90
central coordinator devices, 89–90
cost saving, 148
decision-making, 90
devices connected to, 147, *147*
encryption, 159
offline data storage, 90
productivity, 148
security analysis, 160
share information among people, 133, *133*
smart health services, 148
iOBridge, computer hardware modules, 107
IoT-embedded systems, 164
IoT index framework (IoT-DS), 40
IoT platform, *178*, 178–179

K

Keyless Signature Interface, 140–141, *141*
Key performance indicators (KPI), 100
Know Your Customer (KYC), 129

L

Language-specific software development kit, 19
Ledger, digital, 13–14
Light Chain, 100
Limitations of IoT
complexity, 149, 165
compliance, 165
flexibility, 165
lesser employment prospects, 149
over dependency on technology, 149
privacy, 165
security, 165
security and seclusion issues, 149

M

Machine learning (ML) algorithms, 20, 98
Machine-to-machine (M2M) communication, 44, 60, 148, 154
Magnetic secure transmission (MST), 129
Malware, 158
Management hub, 100
MedBlock, 67
MedChain, EHR management system, 67
Merkle Tree, 8–9, *9*, *58*, 58, 82
Message blocks, 7
Metamask, 68, *69*, *72*
Micro transaction, 54
Miners, 28, 56
Mining, 33, 93
MIStore, 67
Mobile/digital/e-wallets, 124
Mobile payment technologies, 129
MQTT software, 100

N

Near-field communication (NFC), 125
Network attacks, 49–50
Networked nodes, 92
Network layer, 155
Network security, 159
NFC method, 129
Nodes, 28, *29*, 66
Nonpublic blockchain, 83

O

On-demand manufacturing, 31
One way function, 57
Online monitoring, power lines, 110
Ontology IoHT concept, *39*, 39–41

Open information admittance, 104
Open-source blockchain platforms
BigchainDB, 23
cloud service providers, 22
ethereum, 22–23
Output hash, 8

P

Password hacking, 50
Patient records (PRs), 66
Payment Card Industry Data Security Standard (PCI DSS) compliances, 126
Payment system, 53
Paytm Tap Card, 129
Peer-to-Peer (P2P) network, 53, 80
Personal Identifiable Information (PII), 73
Personal sensitive data security, 169
Phishing attacks, 48
Physical device attacks, 49
Plain text, 48
Plastic Bank, 137
Point of Sale (PoS), 129
Pool miners/solo miners, 33
PoW *vs.* PoS, difference between, **59**
Practical Byzantine Fault Tolerance (PBFT) algorithm, 10, 13
Prism Environment, 137
Private blockchain, 83
Proof of Elapsed Time (PoET), 13
Proof of Stake (PoS), 12–13, 59; *see also* PoW *vs.* PoS, difference between
Proof of Work (PoW), 11–12, 59, 91; *see also* PoW *vs.* PoS, difference between
Protection and IOT
AI and automation, 157
ambiguous security standards, 158
attack prediction and prevention, 159
home security, 157–158
insufficient testing and updating, 158
malware and ransomware, 158
Pseudo random, 57
Public blockchain, 17, 83
Public Key Infrastructure (PKI) platform, 22

Q

QCM sensors, 175

R

Radio frequency identification (RFID), 106
Ransomware, 158
Reference architecture
AI, 20
applications, 18, *19*
cloud integration, 20–21
distributed ledger, 21
implementation, 19
integrated applications, 20
IoT integration, 21
ledger conduits, 21
logical layers, 19
security, 21–22
Remote patient-monitoring (RPM) system
blockchain structure, 36, **36**
data security, 37
internet access and RPM framework, 35, *35*
Machine Learning (ML) model, 38
medical patients, 34
mHealth program, *36*, 36–38, *38*
sectors, 35
sensors and vital signs, 37
wearable devices for patient, 35, *35*
Root hash, 52

S

SabPay (Sab meaning everyone can pay)
convenience and on-the-go access, 128
demonetization upshot, 128
digital payment models, 128–129
E-commerce Boom, 128
higher level conceptual diagram, 127, *127*
objectives, 127
personalized digital wallet, 126
Second generations, 29–30
Secure communication, 95
Security, 21–22, 117
Security attacks
encryption, 50
network, 49–50
physical device, 49
software, 49
Security awareness, 50–51
Security challenges
botnets, 48
encryption process, 48
increase in number of IoT devices, 47
inefficient threat detection methods, 48
infrequent updates, 47
IoT financial-related breaches, 49
phishing attacks, 48
small-scale attacks, 48
user privacy, 49
weak default passwords, 47–48
Security issues, BCT, 151
Security of IoT
application layers, 155
architecture, 154, *154*
components, 154
connectivity of interrelated computing devices, 153
diagram for, 155, *156*

network layer, 155
perceptual layer, 154, *154*
support layer, 155
Self-health measurement, 168
Semantic Data Platforms (SDP), 40
Semantic Information Broker (SIB), 40
Sensor layer, 154, *154*
Sensors, 165
Sensors/actuators, 177–178
Sensors module, 98
Service-oriented architecture (SoA), 100
SHA256, hashing algorithm, 52
Shared distributed ledger, 92
Shipment tracking, 31
Small devices, 165
Small-scale attacks, 48
Smart card, 129
Smart cities, 161
autonomous building, 139–140, *140*
Keyless Signature Interface, 140–141, *141*
smart environment, 141, *142*
smart street lighting, 139, *140*
transportation and mobility, 139, *139*
universal ID cards, 137, *138*
water and pollution management, 138, *139*
Smart city model
controller unit, 105
and digital towns, 105–106
electrical manufacturing, 105
micro- or macrocells, 105
theoretical and experimental consequences, 105
Smart contracts, 14–15, 29–30, 67, *70*, 81, 91, 115–116
Smart diagnostics, 31
Smart farming, *98*, 98–99, *99*
Smart grid (SG), 104, 116–117
Smart hearing aid, 175, *176*
Smart homes, 110
Smart inhalers, 172, *173*
Smart living, 141, 143, *143*
Smart metering, 47
Smart parking lot, 110–111
SmartSole, 175–176
Smart street lighting, 139, *140*
Social issues, 118
Software attacks, 49
Speakthing platform, 107
Supply chain tracking, 31
Support layer, 155
Surveillance systems, 113–114
Symmetric key encryption, 9, 54, *54*
System resiliency, 7

T

Technology innovations, 31–34, *32*
Temporary hash, 7
Transaction log of contracts, 71, *71*
Transaction Merkel root hash, 98
Transactions, 3, *4*, 91
Transmission layer, 155
Transparency, 10
Trust, 117–118
Trustable IoT nodes, 96
Twofish algorithm, 97

U

Underdeveloped initiatives, 169
United Payments Interface (UPI), 128
Universal data storage platform, 141, *142*
Universal ID cards, 137, *138*
User authentication, 67, 95–96
User privacy, 49

V

Vehicle traffic information, 108
Virtual reality, 106
Visa payWave, 129

W

Walmart, 14
Water and pollution management, 138, *139*
Weak default passwords, 47–48
Wearable and Implanted Body Sensor Network (WIBSN), 45
Wearable IoT (WIoT), 45
Wearables, 160, 168
Weather and water systems, 108, 112–113
Wide Area Networks (WAN), 107
Working principle of blockchain
hashing SHA256 algorithm, 55–56
public key, 55
transaction process, 55, *56*

Z

ZigBee, 107